The Narration of William J. Moore

One Man's Memoirs

Omar R. Canty, Jr.

Aria M. Antyc-Arolf Publishers
Centreville, Virginia

The Narration of William J. Moore
by Omar R. Canty

Published by :
Antyc-Arolf Publishers
Post Office Box 1237
Centreville, VA 20122

Printed in the United States of America
Publication Date - February 2006

Contents

FOREWORD

There is a joy and warmth in all recollections of slaves' efforts to deal with the day to day living hell of slavery. Their struggle was twofold. First they had to learn to live in the present, to understand that no matter how dreadful life for them was, theirs was a need to endure, to survive, and look ahead. It has been said that unlike Leroy Satchel Paige, they could look back. Nobody was gaining on them. How then, could they look ahead? That was the second part of the struggle. Slaves accomplished this by protesting the most degrading of all institutions and they did so through disobedience. It was slaves who created the political awareness that caused the War Between the States. The slaves had one, and only one tool to call upon in their struggle. It was their own humanity.

This is just one of the many accounts of creativity, perseverance, determination, and love for their fellow African sisters and brothers that speak of and to our struggle. That struggle continues today. It can only be updated by a return to the values and commitment of people like Aunt Sapphire, Ole Fedderson, Cassie, Fredericka, Esau and Isaac, of slaves and former slaves who fought for freedom. Many, the real heroes among our forebears, displayed their disobedience to the extent that they gave their own lives to free others.

Above all else, slaves maintained their sense of dignity and self worth, no matter how hard that was. The moral of the Narration is this: That sense is necessary today if our race is to regain focus, and reach the promised land that Martin Luther King foresaw. As a youngster, I recall the conversations that Omar Canty had with my mother about the need to regain that focus, to fight with our last ounce of strength, to reach our own singular manifest destiny, to become the best teacher, the best athlete, the best factory worker, the best secretary, the best plumber, the best electrician, and so on that each of us could become. I admire all African Americans who hold true to that credo. In my personal life as an educator, and Christian missionary, I strive to help anyone who so agrees, to gain that focus. I am inspired by the lessons of the Narration

Slaves learned never to glorify their masters. They learned to hate slavery as doggedly as their owners misinterpreted scripture to enforce it. They learned that it was necessary to call upon Almighty God in times of extreme crisis. As such, slaves learned that their owners, and the puppets of their owners (preachers, clergy and politicians) could not be trusted to provide the truth, the truth that would set them free. Not until African men and women learned to read, and explain the meaning of the Holy Bible did real progress occur. Today, no matter what the cost, we cannot allow that ability to learn, to know, to stay the course of the truth, to be trampled. The Narration speaks to that.

Omar Canty has always been motivated by the lessons in keeping with the Narration. As his forebears were, so has he sought to address a need in our never ending struggle to reach the promised land. The lectures from his grandfather, and the influence of his family , particularly his parents, Omar Sr. and Dorothy, are stridently manifest.

Jack Liotta

Preface — Note to the Reader

Though the attempt to retell this story was sincerely based on a desire to relate only the message as my grandfather delivered, it was impossible for me to truncate. The times, the effect of the times on our generation, and the effect of my reactions to those times could not be dismissed. In penning this narrative a few names, places and name places have been changed. They have not altered the message.

These accounts are not dissimilar from many others. Indeed, a number of black people seem to understand the relationships, conditions and attitudes created from slave-life, and the perplexing social milieu of slave life-extended for the freedmen in the North. How could they not? Whether we want to admit it or not, conditions that still exist in this country continue to remind us of the past. On the one hand, the sons and daughters of our oppressors admonish, 'You people have to let go '. But the reality is that they continue to demand that we accept their leftovers, the housing they used, then vacated, only to accuse us of destroying; the jobs that they have devalued, and ridicule us for forced acceptance; the education that is still based on glorification of their misguided historical account; and allegiance which denies our own value, contributions, and worth to the shaping of this nation.

Even before your reading begins in earnest, you should stand forewarned that there are already many critics of, and detractors from this work. Just as the race of our oppressors used Scripture, and quotes from learned men and women to support the subjugation of Africans, now I have cited Scripture and quotes from learned men and women to depict a point of view that first found meaning when black men and women learned to read the 'Americanized' concepts of English. My cites are not new. Neither are the words of the critics.

Many of you will be shocked by some references in this book. The intent is neither to be shocking, nor to create controversy. The purpose is simply to relate a story of true incidents that occurred over an all too brief period in the lives of slaves from plantations in Collinsville, Mississippi. That you have decided to read this book demonstrates one fact. It was time to tell this story. Two individuals encouraged me to attempt this writing. They were Carl Berry (when we were in 7th grade at Hughes-Quinn Junior High School) Naomi LeB. Naylor (supervisor/mentor at the University), and Ruth Berger (when we were co-workers at the Labor Department). Their importance cannot be overlooked.

Omar Canty

About the Author

Omar Canty has been a writer all of his life. Until now his market (in writing) has consisted of professional/government manuals in vocational rehabilitation; preparation of correspondence for members of Congress; members of the Executive Branch in the Federal Government , and the development, design, and the production of training materials in human services.

Prior to his career in vocational rehabilitation with the Federal Civil Service in Boston, Massachusetts and the District of Columbia, and the State of Illinois in East St. Louis, and Chicago, Illinois, Omar was a faculty/staff member at Southern Illinois University, and a research associate for Project Head Start. During these periods, he served as President of the Youth Council for the National Association for the Advancement of Colored People and as Chairman for the Congress on Racial Equality, and as the first executive director of The Mary Brown Community Center.

In addition to his writing, Omar is developing a human services agency specializing in providing job placement services for persons who have disabilities. In this regard, the first book he wrote, '**Hey Buddy, Can You Help Me Get a Job?**' is due for publication later this year. It is also included in the Truncated Trilogy. He announces and explains the concept of the *New Key in Vocational Rehabilitation* in this book.

Omar credits influences from key individuals, from whom he learned dedication and commitment to those factors in life that uplift and define. These factors were awareness of oneself; improvement of oneself; and the value of oneself and of others. These beautiful people were Lucille Reed Lusk (his grandmother) good friends Helen Gillespie, Teretha Washington, Earl Jimison, Carolyn McGillberry, Doris Burnett, Johnny Campbell, Elijah Owens, Frank Bender, Charles Harris, Marlene Neely, Warren Reliford, James Cowan, Will McGaughey, Willie Walker, Ronald McClelland, Freddie Murdock, Earline Cotton, Gladys Murray, Robert Perkins, Michael Ward, Florrine Norris, Darlene Faulkner, Lorrine Norris, Paul Malone, Ladell Olion, Karen Morris, Marlena Gregory, Danny Mosley, Clifton Neely, Charlotte Haymore, Linda Green, Jewel Cole, Mary Granger, Eugene Harvey, Carlos Grimmett, Roosevelt Harvey, Minnie Bacon, Arnold Sampson, B.J. Shanklin, Sherman Brewer, Adrian Stone, Betty Carter, James Long, Bruce King, Johnnie Brooks, John Black, Willard Fulton, Billy Lathan, Curtis Thomas, Walter Haire, Harold Mullins, Frederick Armstrong, Betty Carter, Maxine Knight and Sondra Davis; his Aunts, Marvine, Doris, Essie, Mary, Illa, Mildred, 'Dot', Jane, and Ruby; Uncles John, Henry, Howard, Hugh, and Eugene, and great aunts, O'Vell and Eddie. Omar attributes special significance to his parents, and his brothers and sisters, Raymond, Mallory, Jeanne, Diane, and 'Janet' and cousins Juanita,

Donna Kaye, Bernie, Geneva, Valerie, Deborah, Milton, John Moore, Evelyn, Tawana, Marva, Dexter, John Smith, Lisa, Kearney, Nathaniel, Charles and Lena, Charlotte, Mary (Birdie), Joan Marie, Lillian, Crystal, Frank, Eva, Delores, Lillian, Marvin, Quincy and most especially, Corliss. And, of course, great thanks to his very good friends, Marilyn, Mark and Donna.

Omar also especially recognizes and pays tribute to his teachers (in Sunday School and in public schools) and sisters and brothers in the movement, most notably Roberta Lewis and Ora B. Bennett-Hoard (Sunday School teachers and his aunts), Ethel Scott, Homer G. Randolph, Jean Allen Faulkner, Douglas Clark, Lillian Adams Parks, Russell Scott, Blanche Wright Dotson, Katie Wright, Ellis T. Moore, Augusta Branch, Willie Mae Gardner, Clyde Jordan, Elijah Langford, Clarence Goldsmith, T.C. Glenn, Ramon Hill, Kermit Jeffers, Malvin Jones, Alfred and Mary Gregory, Curtiss Paradise, George Holliday, Bettie Skaggs, Ruby Stovall, and LeRay King. Indeed, not a day passes that Omar does not remember the positive effects of education in East St. Louis, Illinois. Every teacher, every lesson, and every red mark on his work are fondly remembered. Not a day passes that life changing events from the civil rights movement are not remembered.

Omar was enthusiastic about the marriage of the Narration to print by heartfelt encouragement from many family and friends. His purpose is to provide expression for a story that should be told, and provide a tribute to the man who told it, his grandfather. Brother Moore lived by the Word of The Bible, as exemplified very much in one, among his favorite Scriptures. It comes from the Book of St. Matthew, Chapter 20, vv. 26 - 27. It was also often quoted and paraphrased by The Reverend Doctor Martin Luther King, Jr. 'He who is greatest among men is he who serves the greatest number'.

Still very much the activist, Omar is working as a volunteer in the gubernatorial campaign in the Commonwealth of Virginia as this book goes to press. His life finds expression as much in the printed word as it does in purposeful action. Omar hopes that this book will inspire you to get out there, get involved and stay involved. As always, 'Do the Right Thing'.

More than any other person, Omar is appreciative of the patience, understanding, guidance, and wit of his wife, Flora Newell. She is one, among so many beautiful black people, daughters and sons of the forced African transgration, born and reared in Mississippi, who like so many others survived slavery's aftermath, emerging with dignity, self-respect, and most importantly, first hand awareness of the historical perspective that slaves and the sons and daughters of slaves had to bear. Without this awareness and perspective, beautifully articulated by Flora and given meaning by her, this book would not have been completed.

Introduction

My grandfather was a big man. By that I mean he had a commanding presence, one respected simply by his demeanor, and the manner he carried himself. Ever since I was very young, I held the fondest of remembrances of this man. I loved him as much as a young boy could love a grandfather. He never told me that he loved me. He never hugged me, and even considering the many favors I used to do for him, the help I gave him, and there were many favors and lots of help, he never once said "thank you". I suppose that in his way he simply decided that people ought to think how fortunate they were to have him as a friend, an uncle, a brother, a co-worker, a cousin, a husband - he was married a number of times - a father, a grandfather, and a great grandfather. At times, due to his method of discipline, his children would fear him. Yet they shared a genuine love that my mother and her sisters and brothers would describe with real affection. As he was with us, his many grandchildren, as far as I could see and as far back as I can remember, I never saw him hug or kiss his children either. Of the former, there are forty one of us, and of the latter there were fourteen.

In addition, not too many can recall kind words from him. In retrospect, I think that with those closest to him, it was his way of motivating us to do well. Even so, the big question is why did we, his children and his grandchildren, have such unconditional love for this man. That feeling did not exist simply in the confines of the family. All his grandchildren, his nephews and nieces and even my friends, and second and third cousins remembered him fondly. Why did they share the same feelings about my grandfather as we? He was even less involved with them. Looking back, and assessing what was really going on, it became clearer and clearer as I grew older. My grandfather, this sly, slick old man, who lead a relatively simple life, living alone during the last third of his life, in spite of the marriages, children from three unions, step children and roomers, had something that I have come to realize occurs all too seldom in this life. He had a good heart. He had a very good heart. That was the singular trait that set him aside from many.

In my life, I feel so fortunate because I have been blessed with other relatives and friends whose hearts were as big, as brave, and as good as my grandfather's. These were my own father Omar Sr., his mother Lucille, my brother Raymond, my wife Flora, her sister Rosetta, my cousin Janet, my mother in law Cindy, Flora's grandmother Carrie, my aunt O'Vell, my daughter Rakiyah, my uncle Henry, my aunt Ila (Mike), Uncle Howard and his wife 'Dot', my friends and co-workers like Marlena, Michelle, Juanita, Freddie, Olvester, Kathy, Brenda, Will, Mr. and Mrs. Gregory, my aunt Marvine, my aunt Eddie, my aunt Doris Jean, my sisters Jean and Diane, Harvey and Mescal Thompson, Norma Jordan, Melvin and Ara Goodwin, Calvin and Kathleen Bradford, Marty Grossack, Viola and Chester Carruthers, My cousins Mary and Charles and Lena Brown just to name a few, and most of all my mother. I never knew Carrie, who reared my wife, but through association I feel that I knew her very well. Indeed hers was the kindest heart of all. My cup doth runneth over because their entry into my life has revealed a singular blessing.

What made these people so unusual, so outstanding, so unique, even though some have had a difficult time expressing true regard for others with words? One quality, and only one quality of my grandfather's, is singularly responsible for the esteem in which his children, his relatives, his friends, and his grandchildren have held him. That quality was his, and their ability to share, and that is the attribute of a good heart.

My paternal grandmother used to say that often a person with a good heart would marry a person with an evil one. She also told me that evil doers often gravitated toward intrinsically good people because they could be exploited very easily. In my later years I have found that to be so true. It was as if the Golden Rule, the credo by which she lived, was extended as if inseparable to its own quotient - 'Goodness is its own reward '.

When an entire family living a block from my grandfather's home was burned out of their home, he took in one and of all from that family. He offered them food, clothing, the comfort of a roof over their heads and freedom from fear, while their house was rebuilt. When neighbors were unable to get their children to the local hospitals in times of medical crises, he drove them to the nearest available medical facility, often a distance of a number of miles because the 'white only' hospitals in our town did not care whether black folk lived or died. No favor was too big to provide and he never accepted cash or any kind of remuneration. These things he would do out of the goodness of his heart.

What about my brothers, sisters, cousins, and friends whose needs could not be met in those ways? For those who appeared to need nothing, what did he do for them? He did something far more worthwhile. He listened. He paid attention. He made us feel important, worthy. He gave us advice, good advice, when it was needed. He told us what we needed to hear, not what we wanted to hear. That man was never, ever wrong. He gave us the greatest gift of all. He gave us his time. How strange that at various times he was harsh to his own children when they ran afoul of his rigidity. In a way though, turning them away was a reaction to their actions, for they never wanted for anything.

Looking back, the best memory I have of his is telling us his stories, histories that had passed down in our family from one generation to the next. He had anecdotes of the fear among blacks and whites during the Race Riot in East St. Louis in 1917, when black citizens were slaughtered, lynched with no provocation. He told us about the great blues wars in the Honkytonks, about gifted musicians (many who inspired his guitar picking, blues singing style) competing just to see who was best. (My grandfather preferred the title 'Gospel Music' to his style but it was really the blues.) We now refer to it as the blues because the only difference then was the words.

He told us about his brothers in law, Tom and Joe Lewis, who were great civic and political leaders in a city that strove to maintain its black population under poverty living conditions. He told us they fought against these conditions by demanding jobs, education and respect. This was in an era when black folk could not make demands. In fact, this was during a time when black folk could not even meekly ask for such dignity. These two brothers were despised so strongly by white leaders that their homes were set afire and their businesses were bombed with dynamite. Yet, in spite of this terrorism, they never gave up the fight for justice for themselves and their people. They vowed to fight on until their death. My grandfather even had stories that began during the time of slavery and they were remembered by many others, even people who never knew him or heard of him. To a person, however, they all swore to his truthfulness and some knew others who could, and did, verify his recollections. This is a story he told to my friends, my brothers, and me, during the course of a number of visits to his home.

With me during those visits were Raymond, Harold, Bernie, Billy, Mike, Mallory, Milton, John, and Eugene, just to name a few, all at varying times. Also paying rapt attention was my grandfather's step son, whose name the visages of time have worn from my memory. Yet, I remember that boy's kind smile, and his keen intellect so assuredly that were I to see him today, a full forty-five years hence, I would instantly recognize him. His mother, my grandfather's fourth (or was it fifth?) wife, I remember as the most beautiful of all his wives. She had the full lips of Billie Holliday, the smooth dark skin of Juliet Pace, the sparkling eyes of Lena Horne, and the cantilevered torso of Josephine Baker, only with fuller legs. (Yes, I am not ashamed to admit that I noticed.) This man had an eye for the most beautiful and the prettiest and they all seemed to be attracted to him. My maternal grandmother, his second wife (or was she his third) was known most of her young life, and even into her late middle age as 'the pretty one'.

Therefore all things whatsoever ye would that men should do to you, do ye even so to them: for this is the law and the prophets. St. Matthew 7-12

Chapter I - Power in Slavery

And he that stealeth a man, and selleth him, or if he be found in his hand, he shall surely be put to death. Exodus 21:16

And he who profiteth from a man who has been kidnapped, shall be put to death. Exodus 21:16 New American Bible

As far as the eye could see there was whiteness. The sun beamed down shining on the fields as if to bless the crop, the king, the beauty of the fields, the meaning to our existence. There was where most of us worked and toiled, from sun up to sun down, performing the back breaking work of picking cotton, loading it into baskets at our side. It was the only work we knew.

It was miserable work, hard work, back breaking work. But, it was all we knew. From it, there was no escape. What else for us was there? Over the boundary from the master's plantation was another plantation and they planted cotton. No matter where you looked, no matter where you might be able to go, for those lucky enough to reach the ends of the plantation, they could only see another plantation, with its landscape dotted with hundreds of slaves, just like us, picking, ginning, baling and processing cotton.

If you didn't work the cotton fields, a few worked the corn, wheat and other vegetable crops. If you didn't do that, you worked the animals, birthing sows, mares, cows, and getting eggs from the chickens. On a large plantation there were few 'easy' jobs. Well, anyway, they were considered easy if you can call that kind of existence easy. Man, that was a stretch. Actually, the 'easy' were the favored jobs. These tasks involved tending the master's fighting cocks; tending the master's race horses; tending the master's prized bull and prized boar; and the most favored of all, tending to the 'needs' of the master's young slaves girls when they first entered their womanhood. All these choice jobs, except for the last, were maintained by cousins, my cousins, some barely three, some even two generations removed. The last job, the one for which many a young black man still lays claim to today, was performed by none other than the father of generations. In his lifetime, every day of which he lived on that plantation in rural Mississippi (even after such was ended) one man was documented to have fathered 157 children. Rumor had it that he fathered at least 43 more for whom no birth records were maintained. The master often 'sold' his services out to neighboring plantations in Mississippi and Alabama.

[It gives me pause to reflect, and wonder,
to this very day, when I see young women
and young men, children and toddlers, moving
to or visiting this area from down home,

because they bear such a strong resemblance
to me. Some have my nose, my big beautiful
broad ridged nose that God gave me. Others
have my hair, my straight, coarse strands
that so many people refer to as good hair,
simply because it has the same appearance
as that of the white race. Other people
of color have my deep inset eyes, so cold,
so dark, steeled like two black diamonds,
gifts from God. Still others share my high
cheekbones. When I see them I quietly utter
to myself, there goes a cousin and he or she
knows not the hatred, the unfair hatred I feel
against my forebears for letting the slave
master thrust that upon us. Then later, just
as was done then, I feel hatred toward my family,
my brothers, my friends and all my relatives for
this existence as living reminders of how we
continue to be ruled, controlled, and manipulated
by white people. The sorrowful base to this self
loathing is that we are encouraged, forced and
misguidedly directed to love this enemy of ours
as much as we hate our own people. Then I start hating
myself. This is the true legacy of slavery.
We must overcome this legacy. And the only way is to
learn to love oneself, and then each other. William J. Moore]

Will had a choice, preferred task. His primary job was to fulfill birthrights of young slave women. He met many a young slave woman in the slaves' quarters, where the master gave him an hour alone, each day for a week, exactly thirteen days after every girl's first menstrual period. Master had it worked out quite scientifically. On his plantation, the first born of every woman or girl had to be fathered by Will. Will was big, standing well over six feet tall. Will was strong, often performing the tasks around the plantation that required great exertion. He never was given any work that would occupy him for long periods of time. After performing one such chore to help construct a new barn, Will had to meet a young slave girl who was just one week or more past her first menstrual period. Her name was Cassie. Just barely more than twelve years of age, the rule of the master required her to begin the production of new slaves. Still yet a child, she had to meet Will, after he had worked to lift the felled lumber which buttressed the new barn. She had been in the fields that morning working to pick cotton with the other field slaves. Since he had a number more of young slaves to attend that day, he was quick, extremely quick with Cassie. No matter her pain, no matter her embarrassment, the master forced her to return to the field to continue where she had left off, picking cotton. Some of the men and women had quietly stuffed some of their work into her sack. They knew that the overseer would not have let her leave the field until it was filled.

Although everyone knew what she had just been through, nobody uttered a single word. It had to have been a horrible enough ordeal as it was, so she was better left alone. Although slave girls didn't talk to each other very much, the few times they were permitted to discourse, they could not, no they had better not speak of sexual activity. The topics of discussion sure to get a slave girl ten lashes with a whip on her back were freedom, escape, talking back to the overseer or one of the master's children or the master, and sex. There also lay a sure curse from the devil for discussing sex, or so every slave had been led to believe.

Frightened, in pain and fearful that she was about to die, this mere girl, only weeks beyond her twelfth year, had to undergo a veritable raping, all for the purpose of becoming pregnant, to create another slave for the master's fields. Barely five feet tall, and all of ninety pounds, she smelled of Will's musk and of the horses which he had ridden that morning. The return to the fields after that ordeal, where she could be among friends, brothers, sisters, aunts and uncles was a welcome relief from what had just been stolen from her. She was in serious pain, heavy pain because Will was a big man in every way. Added to that was the fear, uncertainty and ignorance of what was going on with her body.

Having just encountered her first menstruation barely a fortnight earlier, undergoing examinations by older slave women for the immediate days following, and not being told anything, she was yet very fearful as any child would be. There followed more examinations, day by day, week by week, until the older slave women were sure that now, she was pregnant. Based strictly on the timing of her cycle, and the timing of her pregnancy, and based on the master's calculations of her date of fertility, they concluded that the baby would be a male. After hearing what for him was good news, the master didn't care whether Cassie would continue to have sexual intercourse or not. He believed that a ready number of available female slaves was a good way to keep his male slaves content with their lot. When some of the other slave women encouraged Cassie to make herself available, Cassie refrained. After a few weeks, they discontinued this encouragement. More than a few of the men, including Will, was after her. But she just said no. And she meant it too.

She was inherently bright, pretty, and at times mischievous at play. Her teeth were perfect, and her thick lips formed the lovely shape of a dark valentine, framed by a chin that was pointed. Her cheekbones were high and regal. They disguised cutting eyes which took in all that surrounded her.

As time passed, Cassie grew to understand the changes underway in her body. Work, the slave's lot, was more demanding. It required her to be out of bed and in the field just before dawn, and they toiled even later than dusk. There was too much cotton to be picked, it seemed, and too much of the crops to be tended. Worse yet, there was too much cleaning to be done of the quarters where the master kept his livestock. Even the pigs had better digs than the slaves. In Cassie, the puffiness about her face developed; then it extended to her fingers and toes. Yet, these changes never interfered with her readiness to spend the extra time with the animals. She appeared very comfortable, at ease, and accepting of them all.

When the cotton yield slowed due to cooler weather, fewer slaves were needed in the fields. Cassie was assigned winter crop duty. She had to pick gourds, greens and apples. She also had to plant cabbage, spinach, potatoes, and lettuce and transplant bulbs. Her late evening chores included animal husbandry. Mares in foal, and sows in litter had to be attended. She appeared to take well to that work and her smile and kindly manner generally attested to her love for everything that was alive. Everyone recalled how, after this assignment, she discontinued eating meat. The critters, as she called them, were like her pets. She could never eat a pet. As she interacted with the young children about the plantation, she began to refer to them as her gentle critters. The women about the slave quarters often admonished her to revert back to the dietary habits necessary for slave labor and most assuredly for a woman with child. In addition, they feared her dietary habits may have rubbed off on the young ones. But that Cassie, that young slave girl had a stubborn streak in her that was as strong as a slave's day was long. Her love for her critters was as strong, deep and abiding as the faith of Job from the Good Book. Soon, even the smell of cooking flesh became repulsive to her. One day, they assigned her to bug killing detail. Back then, they had no effective pesticides or pesticides that didn't taint the foods. The master didn't approve of their use, even where vendors extolled their worth. The slaves were required to inspect every plant and flower among the various crops and flowers for insects. Once found, they had to be crushed by hand. This usually involved squeezing between one's hands or fingers. Cassie would just swoop up a bug in one motion and then coax it from her grasp. Next she would gently release it into the air while feigning to kill it. She would have none of such killing.

That winter, the weather was so mild, it seemed, that cotton was ready to be picked before it was planted. The slaves were back in the cotton fields in late January. The land seemed plumper and whiter than anyone could ever remember so early in the year. Of course that meant more work for all hands.

The master was excessively proud of that winter because he had more young slave girls expecting. Most of these, easily 48% were Will's progeny. When born, these would increase the number of slaves on his property by fifty-eight. This was remarkable because before the slave trade was 'outlawed' by the United States Congress, Master Brookshire's grandfather had run the most prolific slave trade business in the entire South, having surpassed Virginia fourteen years earlier. For those slaves who were unable to conceive through the master's careful and precise calculations of their dates of fertility, he permitted extra duty by Will. He wanted to be sure that every fecund, young slave woman would manifest her duty, as he saw it. For Master Brookshire, the reproductive process among his slaves was a business process; the more slaves he had, without resorting to the trade, the better his business dealings were. There was 'runoff' in which he benefited in other areas. The ratio of five to three meant that the politicians found great favor in Master Brookshire. This translated into procurement deals with the manufacturing houses to the North and meat processors nationwide. Legislation favorable to his concerns was enacted in the state legislature, thus insuring prosperity, power and influence.

Hardly a matter of political or economic significance was discussed without his consultation. His influence was so strong that the original copy of every bill from his county had to be delivered to him before it reached the statehouse floor. As his power grew, this requirement extended to every bill of economic and educational bearing, and it had to be reviewed by him first.

All his slaves, and white employees from the town had at least one change of clothes and a pair of second hand shoes. It could never be said that his slaves and field hands were not well treated and well clothed. One year, word even got out that in two of Master Brookshire's slaves' quarters, slaves had been permitted to use as floor boards, the rotting wood taken from a barn that had to be destroyed. As a rule, newborn babies and their nursing maids were assigned these quarters. This was to ensure a certain degree of cleanliness. As such, he enjoyed a reputation as a plantation owner whose slaves had it quite a bit better than any slaves elsewhere in the country. This included what memory served of George the Great, as how the first president was referred to back then in Mississippi and other states, North and South. This reference, for the slaves and for many people (white men and women) who really knew him, had more to do with the size of the man than greatness as a man. The other reference, of course, had to do with his leadership and statesmanship, qualities for which most whites loved and revered the man. Master Brookshire wanted to enjoy the same kind of favor and esteem from his slaves. His eventual goal was to see to it that their shoes were in good repair and that some day soon, every slave hut on his estate would have floor boards and real beds. Up to that point, the only thing that prevented him from moving forward with these revolutionary ideas was that he needed reassurance that after providing such niceties, his kindness would not be reciprocated with laziness. After all, if you treat a slave too well, prevailing wisdom dictated, then they just might become lazy. Worse yet, they could entertain fanciful ideas of longer breaks, real food at lunch, and these notions might just get out of control, to the point that they might get ideas of freedom. The master decided, therefore, that any ideas of better treatment must be tabled until he could be better satisfied that his slaves would work harder than they did now. The strangest aspect of all his suppositions was that he knew there was no way he or anyone else could draw more than another ounce of work from them. But, that didn't prevent him from trying.

On that plantation, the worse thing that could happen to one of the slaves was serious illness. They did fall prey to any illnesses and sicknesses that befell others. After all, slaves were human beings too. However, slaves learned the hard way that the most effective means to deal with serious illness was to deny that they were sick. There were many reasons for this. The overseer of the plantation always believed that slaves faked injury and illness to avoid work. Therefore, the treatment for anyone who claimed to be injured or ill was ill treatment. When one slave saw that another was truly sick, seriously sick, he or she would double up on their work to ensure that the sick slave could preserve his or her strength to fight the sickness. This system worked well among the slaves who toiled in the fields. Their buddy system was key to their day to day survival. The problem is that it also could be a detriment. The life span for a slave was not very long. This was due directly to the stress of slavery. Since slaves also covered for each other, it appeared that slaves, who really were sick or injured, simply worked through these problems. It was not unusual, as a result, for one slave to have a massive heart attack, or die from 'consumption', as slaves referred to cancer.

Other diseases also exacted a heavy toll. These included tuberculosis, grand mal epilepsy, and a host of other infirmities. The overseer, who drove the slaves harshly, had no awareness of the extent of their illnesses. A prevailing joke among whites in the South was that slaves would rather die than work. The truth was that most slaves would rather kill the master and the overseer. As far as work was concerned, slaves wanted to be paid a wage for their work. They wanted to live among their own people, and were willing to pay for their freedom to accomplish this goal.

Those in the big house, where the master's wife and children were tended, fared worse, because they were not even supposed to get sick. They couldn't catch a cold, have a headache, and didn't dare complain of back pain. After all, it was reasoned, they didn't have hard work to do when compared with the field slaves. Since the field hands don't get sick, how could house slaves fall ill, or get hurt? For them there was no escape. Sick or well, there was no change from their routine. They had to do their work, and though they tried to cover for each other, there were too many eyes in the house to get away with it.

The babies started popping out just after the first Wednesday before Palm Sunday that year of 1848 on Master Brookshire's plantation. Cassie was two months from her due date, but she was well nigh larger around the middle than all the women who delivered in late March and early April.

The most important person on the plantation then was Aunt Sapphire. She was known as a zovan, skilled in the art of midwifery. Nobody knew exactly how or when she became so skilled and knowledgeable in this field. It seemed to begin many years previous when Doc' Pritchard was unable to reach the plantation during the peak birthing period because of a late winter's-early spring's snow. Aunt Sapphire seemed to take to this naturally. It was all the more unusual because she was never able to have a child of her own. She had even taken to examining the young girls, who were with child, to make sure they would remain well during the pregnancy.

Master Brookshire had planned the majority of the pregnancies so that slaves would give birth during the late winter, when there would be less of the most grueling work to be done. Of course, when the winters had been exceptionally mild, like this one, with child or not, all the slaves had a great deal of work to do. Aunt Sapphire, who usually worked in the fields, had to cook dessert also. This requirement was a daily duty as she had to scurry from the field to the baking chamber, just off the kitchen. However, her role as zovan had become so important that she was excused from her baking duties during peak childbirth periods. It was important to Master Brookshire that he never lost an infant, or mother during childbirth. He entrusted Aunt Sapphire with this responsibility. To her credit, even Doc' Pritchard envied her skills and her record. She never lost a patient, a boast he could not make.

A big, broad faced, broad shouldered stout woman, Aunt Sapphire had an abiding love for all about her. A woman of remarkable creativity, there was nothing she couldn't do when she put her mind to it. There was one time that the overseer, ailing with a toothache, asked her to get him something to ease the pain. For her ability to concoct a cure from herbs, and roots she used from the fields, she was rewarded with the task of beating the slaves who were accused of slacking off at work. Even here she showed her true mettle.

Having created a fabric made from animal hide, mud and dung, she simply attached this to the back side of the slaves and then applied the corporal punishment ordered by the overseer. Word got around the plantation that when the overseer or one of his assistants asked a slave who he wanted to beat him, the answer, every time, without fail, became "anybody cept' Aunt Sapphire".

One year she was so busy cooking desserts, working in the fields, birthing babies, and administering these beatings, that Master Brookshire ordered that she discontinue her work in the fields. The beatings had to continue because there were reasons, other than slacking off, that slaves had to be horse-whipped. Talking back to any white person demanded ten lashes. Looking at a white person eye-to-eye, or making any kind of eye contact unless so ordered, required twelve lashes. Using a drum carried a penalty of fifteen lashes and speaking in an African tongue would get the offender twenty. Every offense, real, contrived or imagined carried its own penalty. Often, when no infraction had been committed, a slave incurred a beating simply because he had to be controlled. The strap on one's backside was a most effective means to keep the slaves from getting into trouble. The whip

Aunt Sapphire had fashioned really caused no pain. It just looked as though it did. Each slave had been instructed to yell and scream more loudly than a beating administered by the overseer caused. The other aspect of her beating whip that seemed so terrible was that, due to the mud and dung, it made it look like the bleeding was much worse than actual. In reality, she caused no wounds or bleeding.

Having heard of it from Doc' Pritchard, Aunt Sapphire liked to refer to herself as a parturient. Once, even the master himself was about to take the lash to her backside, because he thought it was a word from an African tongue. Only the good doctor himself was able to save her, taking great liberty to explain to Master Brookshire that it indeed was a term from the English language. When he heard the other slaves use of the term zovan, he simply assumed that it too was English, never realizing that its roots were from Africa. At other times the whites in the Brookshire family, and the townsfolk who worked the plantation came to believe that the reference was a medical term with English derivation or a diminution of Aunt Sapphire's name. They felt that slaves were wont to create rather odd enunciation of common words, names and phrases.

[I wonder how many times she spat into the
desserts she prepared, or much worse.
It's a mean thought, but I just wonder.
William J. Moore]

Aunt Sapphire was a God fearing woman, she explained, and she knew that God didn't want her to hate. Hating was ugly, slaves believed. She would tell those slaves that she realized she could trust, to refrain from hatred, because their death might come on a day that they had a lot of hatred in their hearts. On that day, if they should die, God could show no mercy on their souls. She would tell them, most importantly, however, that she was ready to die, and that when she saw that her time was nigh, she would not go by herself. By taking from this world, at that point, just one who harmed her people, she would be of service to her race. She believed that some of her generation had to sacrifice their spot in heaven to ease the suffering of her people here on earth, as a slave in America. She truly believed that hell could be no worse than slavery for a black slave. She believed more strongly than anything, except her belief in God, that the deaths of those like the master, his wife, the overseer, and the children of the master would go a long way toward ending the suffering and the brutality of her people.

[These simple truths were manifest not
only by my forebears. These simple
truths were all too prevalent in all
areas where slavery existed as the law
of the land. William J. Moore]

That last winter found Aunt Sapphire as busy as she had ever been. Babies needed to come forth, and misbehaving slaves needed to be beaten. When an expectant mother's labor was delayed, she even had to return to the fields for hard labor of the other kind.

[When you see someone named Sapphire, don't
make fun of the name, or the person. It is a
name from the book of Genesis in The Bible.
Honor the one who bears that name, so that she
will wear it proudly. Also, bless all our
brothers and sisters whose names come from the Bible.
They have a difficult, but honorable legacy
of namesakes to uphold. William J. Moore.]

Aunt Sapphire never seemed to object. She was physically strong. Perhaps, she was as strong as any man on the plantation with the exception of Will. There might have been one or two others, but they were unwilling to arm wrestle her, or engage in a weight lifting contest. Though her work was far more demanding and strenuous than that of any others, she never complained. She just smiled, and carried on. Quietly, she just seemed to be waiting until she could exact a measure of revenge.

Nobody ever knew who Aunt Sapphire's father was. It could have been any of the three men who master's grandfather used for this function in that day. She recalled that she had been born in the summer of 1808, and she barely was five years older than the master, for whom she sat as a child, and with whom, and his sisters, she played. All that changed abruptly when she turned seven. Suddenly she was assigned to work in the laundry on the plantation. There were times, she recalled, when she had to continue to play with the master and his sisters and brothers after she completed her chores. On those rare occasions when she still had work to complete, and because they wanted her as a playmate, her chores had to wait until the children of the master were done with their games. Not until they were tired could she return to her work, no matter how late, and no matter that she had not eaten dinner, such as it was. Even as a child of eight and nine years old, life had taken a regretful turn, and play was no longer fun anymore.

Aunt Sapphire was a natural when it came to assisting the women through childbirth. She knew exactly which herbs and roots to use to ease the pain and cause no harm to the mother or child. She knew what other concoctions would be necessary to strengthen them against loss of blood, fatigue, and fainting because they had to go right back to the fields immediately after giving birth. Even the house slaves had to work in the fields immediately after delivery because the master's wife believed them to be unclean, not worthy of working in the dwelling of a white woman, so quickly after bringing forth a new life. It was during these times that Cassie learned who was in the house and who was assigned to the fields. Although field slaves would then be given household duty to cover for these new mothers, Cassie never wanted to work there, even late in her last trimester.

The few times that Aunt Sapphire would chance to see Cassie, she would sit her down for just a few minutes. She wanted to teach her about the symptoms as she neared her delivery date. She also just wanted the child to stop, relax, and take a few deep breaths. It was important that she made no mistake about the frequency and intervals of the pains, exactly where they were, and whether they moved lower into her pelvic area. This was more important than what might have been related simply to delivery, in itself. Whenever the pains were false labor, and not the real thing, slave girls were accused of faking for the sole purpose of avoiding work. The penalty for this was that they had to run, full speed back to the field, with the overseer's first assistant directly behind them beating on their backs, their legs, and anywhere else as they ran. He was on a horse. These administrations of beatings stopped only when the running slave reached her work station and actually commenced work. At that point, the beaten, pregnant woman was ordered to smile, and sometimes even laugh in glee for the opportunity to return to work. She also was required to thank the overseer and show, and admit that she was happy to have been found out as a lazy, unhappy worker. How well did all the slaves remember the many times the overseer beat one of them, witness to the joy that was in his face, the elation those beatings brought him. How even better yet, slaves remembered when one of the overseer's assistants administered the beating. They seemed to relish it more than the overseer, more than any joy, that a person could imagine. The slaves just wondered, 'What kind of people were they?'.

Looking back, the worse purveyors of these beatings (other than Aunt Sapphire, who thoroughly had them all fooled) was the beatings that came from a fellow slave, when so ordered by the overseer, or the master. After a few years of service as the chief impregnator (for want of a more appropriate word), Will was given this job, and he would take to it as earnestly as he did his former task. Eventually, he would even betray Aunt Sapphire because he wanted to administer each and every beating.

Aunt Sapphire had figured accurately to within two days, when Cassie should be due. Everyday for the two weeks prior to her anticipated due date, she had stopped in the field when she had a break. If time was scarce, Aunt Sapphire would make time. She would also visit the slave house where Cassie slept to examine her each night.

[It gives me pause to reflect nowadays because I see where the idea cropped into our minds that parents of our children need not be there to care for them. Somehow, all we need do is continue as we have, forsaking the babies we have created, then wondering why, after they have done so well in the white man's competitive world, they want nothing to do with us? After all, didn't we bring them into this world? That is a remnant of slavery that continues to this day and it was then, and still is now a harsh lesson. Then we had no choice. If the master sold us away, or took us away from our children, we were powerless to change that. Unfortunately, we have not learned that we don't have to do that today. Will it ever be unlearned? I don't think even the half has ever yet been told. William J. Moore.]

"Hand me my guitar, I feel a song comin' on", Big Daddy, as we called my grandfather, asked. Harold turned, removed it from the corner and handed it to him. He strummed a few chords, then sang in his hillbilly twang a song about slave boys running away from the plantation, only to be captured the following morning by pursuers, including slaves owned by Master Brookshire, county sheriff's deputies, and bounty hunters.

Deuteronomy 23:16 You shall not hand over to his master a slave who has taken refuge from him. Let him live with you, wherever he chooses in any of your communities that pleases him. Do not molest him.

[After that song, he sang a very moving version of Steal Away, our first introduction to the true meaning of Negro Spirituals. Those songs were written for a reason. But now we have to turn to God. Big Daddy had become a Bible toting, born again Christian and it shone through, in all he did at that point in his life.]

Think not that I am come to send peace on earth: I come not to send peace but a sword. St. Matthew 10:34

Chapter II - Death Begets Life

And Jesus said unto them: Suffer the little children to come unto me and forbid them not; for of such is the Kingdom of God. Verily I say unto you, Whosoever shall not receive the Kingdom of God as a little child shall not enter therein. St. Mark 10:14-15

Cassie's labor began as soon as she bended over to pick her first ball of cotton to add to, and spin into a roll. She let out the most awful, high pitched wail ever heard anywhere near that plantation. As best anybody within hearing distance could describe, it was worse than the gelding process for yearling ponies back behind the barns and worse even than the two teenagers apprehended the morning after their second attempt at escape. Their punishment, and they knew it when they were caught, castration - in full view of all the slaves and workers on the Brookshire plantation.

After letting loose those uncontrollable symptoms of her pain, Cassie displayed a perfect smile, a contentment about herself belying the understanding of what was soon to happen.

Within seconds Aunt Sapphire was summoned. She had supervised hundreds of births, and always displayed a concerned, though assured, countenance about herself. She checked Cassie's pulse, then listened closely to her heart. Turning her over onto her side, she listened at her back, and the concerned look about her face changed. For the first time in her work as a zovan, her face displayed a disturbed mood. It showed fear, the worse kind of fear that could come upon a person. It showed uncertainty. As best anyone could tell, these signs were never like the fear and uncertainty they had seen before and the others too became distressed. Aunt Sapphire knew that Cassie was sick, but that her offspring would be strong. As the young men lifted Cassie onto the makeshift stretcher and carried her to the birthing room, Aunt Sapphire turned to the field hands and told them all to pray. More than anybody else, if a child needed God's help, it was Cassie. She then summoned Little Nebednego, a son of Will's, and therefore, a half brother to Cassie. She told him to go fetch Old Fedderson. Fedderson, the only slave permitted to read The Bible, had become what could best be described as a minister of the Gospel to slaves. Aunt Sapphire, like the other slaves, was undergoing an understanding of the nature of God, and the role that religion could play in their lives. They had come to hope that upon death, a slave would ascend directly to heaven.

For his part, Fedderson never took it all too seriously. He had led Sunday service for slaves. They had learned that going to his service meant a day off from their dreadful lives of heavy physical toil. He had seriously tried to find meaning in the Scriptures he had taught himself to read, but could not find that meaning. He resolved to play it out for those who wanted to believe, often praying for the sick, and offering prayers for runaways. He had been summoned many a time by Aunt Sapphire, and since she never had lost a patient, expectant mother or infant, even when death seemed imminent for some, Fedderson's prayers were thought to have made the difference.

His prayers had been extended for many and he had taken to laying his hands on those who ailed. He would command the illnesses to be gone; there was not one slave on that plantation who didn't believe that The Almighty didn't work through him.

His prominence had become so appreciated that Master Brookshire would have him summoned when one of his children was ailing. He would always seem to wait until they were very low. Fedderson, for his part, realized that the master's children usually ailed from a local virus and by the time he was called, they would surely be up and about soon, because the virus would soon run its course. As time went by, he gained an understanding, from his observance of the various vegetation, of the influence that oils and plants could have. He would boil down many substances, extract the oils and secretions, and tell people it was miracle juice. Much of this he had learned from Aunt Sapphire. Truth be known, it was primarily juices from the vegetables and fruits, skins, peels and all, from the garbage tossed away at the Brookshire dinner table and conscripted for garden roughage.

One look into Cassie's eyes and the color on her face was all Fedderson needed to reach one unmistakable conclusion. No amount of miracle substances, and no amount of praying could make a difference. The young slave girl, Cassie, so big with child, so small of frame, so intelligent of mind, was about to die.

"Can you hear me, Baby-Girl?" he asked, bending over her as she lay on the cot. There was noise all about from babies wailing, new mothers in labor, and new mother's delivering. "I say, Baby Girl, can you hear Old Fedderson's voice. He be tryin' to talk to you."

She lay there silently, blinked her big, dark eyes, and just smiled. Everyone seemed to either smile at him, or turn their heads away in fear, the first time they saw him. Cassie was assured by his demeanor and the softness in his voice. She had no fear of this kind man. "Sure, Old Fedderson. Ah hears you."

He took her hands and held them tight, struggling for the right words to say. Aunt Sapphire came over and checked her body temperature and pulse, urging him to hurry.

"Cassie, Baby-Girl, God is talking to you. God, he want you to know everything go be all right. You believe in God?"

"Yes, Old Fedderson. Ah does believe."

"Baby-Girl, I wants to baptize you. It ain't go hurt, you hear?" He was very patient, yet intense of his purpose. He turned and asked for some lukewarm water. He then raised her up to a seated position, and doused her head, the water running through each nostril, her mouth, eyes and ears. Then he washed her feet and hands with the small amount of water left, using a clean handkerchief from his pocket. "Baby-Girl, I done Baptized you in the name of God, his Holy Son, and the Holy Ghost, and I throws in the names of a few prophets. Cain't nothing hurt you now, Baby-Girl."

To that point, her pain had been excruciating. Remembering the pain she had first felt in the fields, she never winced again, quietly putting all her faith for deliverance and well being into Aunt Sapphire. Understanding what she was going through, Aunt Sapphire administered a topical pain killer through her rectum, and forced whiskey down her throat; slaves provided whiskey from a secret steel, in the wooded area beyond the slaughter house.

Cassie trusted Aunt Sapphire, and Old Fedderson. She pushed when they ordered. She pushed again, then again, then one final time. With all the force she could muster in her frail, tiny body, with all her might, she forced out the baby she had nurtured for the nine preceding months. Aunt Sapphire then delivered the after birth, and cut the umbilical cord. She applied another topical solution to Cassie and had Old Fedderson apply a hot towel to her head. The baby boy was turned over to another elderly slave who assisted Aunt Sapphire. She washed the baby and handed him to yet another slave to feed the baby with the milk from her own breasts.

While Sapphire turned to assist other mothers, Old Fedderson helped Cassie to her feet. Supporting her, with her one arm over his shoulder, and his arm around her waist he walked her back to the cotton field.

In about ten minutes Aunt Sapphire had delivered another baby. As soon as she was done, she returned to where she had left Cassie. "Where Cassie?" she demanded, her voice betraying a sense of alarm no one had ever heard. "Where that chile' done gone?" If ya'll let that chile back in them fields in her condition, ya'll bet not be done done that. They's go be hell to pay. Ya'll best be believe in that!"

Fedderson knew that the dear girl was near death. He also knew that if she were not back in the field, at her work station picking cotton, the overseer's assistant would be there to beat her. If nothing else, her death would not come from a beating as far as Fedderson was concerned.

"Git that thar Niggah bitch up so she can do her work", the assistant ordered as Cassie fainted under the hot afternoon sun, a cotton ball with burrs still attached in her palm. "Ah'm go beat this here bitch to death if you all don't git this black heifer bitch up." Nobody moved. It wouldn't have done any good either way anyhow.

And he said unto them, if ye had not plowed with my heifer, ye had not found out my riddle. Judges 14:18

Just as he readied his bullwhip, raising it to deliver the first strike across her face, Aunt Sapphire burst onto the scene and lay herself prone over Cassie. It all happened so fast. It was like a flash. One second she was standing there looking at the white man, and the next she was arching her back, all fours to the ground, looking up to the sun from the East. Then she turned her head, and looked to the assistant, her eyes transfixed squarely on his. A black person, slave or free, had never looked at him like that before. As far back as he could remember he had never seen any black person look at a white person, man, woman or child, eye to eye. He was determined to beat Cassie and then beat Aunt Sapphire too.

But, something strange took over, and grabbed hold of that man. It was as if that look in her eye possessed him and he seemed to fear that if he lay a hand on either of them at that point, something bad might have happened to him.

Ever the opportunist, Fedderson knew what was going on with the young man. He decided to play it up. "Ah can tells you, Suh, she done gone put something on you. Now your soul ain't got no chance to even so much as think about heaven, let alone go there."

"What that old bitch done done?" he asked, fearful of the worse.

"Why, suh, she done put a haint on you." Fedderson continued to milk it. The other slaves knew he was making a fool out of the man, but they weren't about to give it away. Though they said not a word, they looked as serious, and as frightened as Fedderson.

"Is that like a hex?" the young man asked, now shivering, and quivering in fear. He constrained himself to force back the tears.

"Zactly, suh."

"What can ah do? Ah sho don't wanna perish in no goddam hell."

"Well suh, Old Fedderson, he do know a little bit about these here thangs. But he gots to study up on all this here. Old Fedderson, he be workin' with you after he study up."

The assistant was becoming more disturbed now, than perturbed. The poor fellow had always believed that a slave's looking a white person eye to eye had as much to do with never letting them put themselves onto the white man's level as anything. To that point, he never understood the 'paranormal' qualities of this act. The feeling that overcame him was the most uncomfortable, most uneasy, feeling of dysphoria he had ever experienced. It was as if he had become tainted with a dreaded disease, like leprosy, and would never overcome the squalor which had befallen him. "What can ah do?" he pleaded, taking care not to look upon Fedderson while tugging at his shirt, rumpled out from his bib-overall. "Please help me out. Ah don't wanna go to hell on account of no hex put on me by no niggah bitch heifer." He pleaded, even begged as if more than his life was at stake. To him it was. He had been taught that above all else, don't let your soul perish in hell.

"Old Fedderson, he go study up on the matter, boy. In the meantime, you has to git yo'self away from black folks", Fedderson now ridiculed him. No black man could refer to a white person as boy. Clearly he had the upper hand now. "Now you listens good to Old Fedderson, boy. You goes back home and stays put among your own white folks. You stays put, ah says, till ah calls you to come nigh. No matter what you is doing, boy, when you hears Old Fedderson, he calls to you, you comes directly. You drops what some ever you be doing at the time."

"Ah unnerstands, Old Niggah."

"Now you cain't eyeball nobody else, and most specially don't you be eyeballin' no slave. Do and this here haint, it go become a curse and ain't nothin', even Old Fedderson can do to save yo soul from the gates of hell."

"Ah unnerstands, Old Niggah. Ah do exactly as you say so." He walked away promising to obey the instructions, never looking at a soul as he staggered down the path to the main road leading from the Brookshire Plantation. He headed for town and the shanty village on the outskirts where he lived. Fedderson and the other slaves had quite a laugh over that, and they needed one to break the mood as Sapphire attended Cassie.

They crowded around her, removing their shirts to fan the air toward her and Cassie. Other slaves removed their shirts, and some even their cotton underslips for Cassie to lie on. They did provide some comfort in the opening in the field. Otherwise, cotton plants bordered them on every side. Suddenly there was another wail like the one Cassie had made earlier that day. This time it was not so loud but it seemed eerie. Yet, the noise was joyous, for it was the celebration of another newborn, just delivered there by Cassie. Aunt Sapphire shouted praises to God, even uttering words and phrases that she could not recall having known. The truth is that they harkened to a distant past in Africa. Old Fedderson seemed to understand, and knowingly responded also using the same, strange sounding foreign language. He knew the words were the very same often spoken by their forebears.

This young mother, giving life, looked up and smiled, her eyes opening wide as a wise countenance upon her and within her seemed to tell all about that all was well. Then, sadly, she breathed her last breath of air, her life ending in the field.

Some among the slaves around her said they saw a misty shroud around her head as she died. Others described what they saw as a halo. Some said it was her very soul departing her body, heading directly to the heavens above. The final description was that of mere heat, which they could feel as they steadied her still warm, lifeless body on the ground. Soul or heat, nobody could deny that they had witnessed a remarkable death, a death that would prove victorious over slavery for Cassie was a girl, they all knew, who went directly to heaven. This woman, yet a child, certainly had outdone any birth that had ever been recorded anywhere. Barely an hour earlier she had given birth to one child, only to be returned to the fields of hard labor, to give birth to another with her last breath of life.

Fedderson moved to the center, lifted her frail, lifeless body and carried her to the slaves' quarters. There, he and a few others washed her clean and placed clean clothing about her. That afternoon, they had a short viewing ceremony, placed her into a pine box, sealed it with tar, and lowered her into the common burial area. The slaves' burial area was just beyond the primary burial area, for white members of the master's family, extended. It was at the Southern end of the plantation. As far as anyone could remember, this marked the very first time that a deceased black person was not simply dropped into a hollow pit for burial. Cassie had clean clothes, and a box, sealed with tar.

The women who are pregnant or nursing at the breast will fare badly in those days. The distress in the land and the wrath against the people will be great. Luke 21:23

The slaves sang; a few, including Aunt Sapphire, offered comments. Fedderson prayed. They ate a light meal together, and for once, the house slaves joined the field hands in common sorrow. Even they realized that no braver person had ever felt the harsh cracks of her flesh peeling from the overseer's bullwhip, or had seen a woman so bravely nurture and deliver two such beautiful baby boys and in so doing, give her own life. This was the harsh reality of slavery at its worse. They all felt a sense of relief that for the price Cassie had paid she had reaped her reward, a good reward in heaven. Even Old Fedderson believed that too.

That night more slaves sang. Others danced. Still others lamented. A few sang spirituals and finally, Old Fedderson told them all that they had witnessed a triumph of good over evil, the evil of slavery, because Cassie was surely in heaven. For Fedderson the thought, the idea, the essence was no longer a concept. It was real. "Ah cain't rightly say how ah knows it, chillen, but ah knows it. That baby-girl be with her maker right now. If ah don't do nothin' else as long as ah lives, ah be workin' to make sure that all o' us gits there. And ah be workin' just as hard as Old Fedderson be able, to see that all white folks goes to hell."

On the one hand, slaves wanted to believe Fedderson, but they could not understand how he could take the lessons from the Good Book and on the other hand, express such hatred for white people. Due to their plight, slaves could not understand how all whites derived substantial rewards from the institution of slavery. It wasn't just the overseer and his assistants that administered slavery, but the slave should not help but love the free whites on the plantation and in town. Through systematized development and mind control, slaves had become conditioned, really programmed to accept as a blessing in a sense of mixed bewilderment the harshest treatment by the masters.

[What happened to slaves on the
Brookshire estate was no different

than the treatment of slaves
throughout the South, and in the
North before slavery was abolished.

The events rendered above occurred in
18 hundred and 48. I know, because my father
was Cassie's brother. William J. Moore]

Will somebody hand me my guitar?

[The musical instrument rested near the feet of my youngest brother, Mallory. He had started reaching for it before my grandfather asked for it. I had often heard the Negro Spiritual **'Swing Low, Sweet Chariot'**. Now, all of a sudden, I realized why our music teachers in the black schools, with teachers like David Brown, Jane Moore Walton (my aunt), Jacqueline Hatter, and Miss Westbrook wanted us to learn and understand what those songs stood for. I had never before been so proud of my grandfather, his children, my father, and the teachers in our public schools. We had learned so much. Compared with what we would have to learn, we didn't know anything. We had so much more to learn.]

And if a kingdom be divided against itself, that kingdom cannot stand. And if a house be divided against itself, that house cannot stand. St. Mark 4 - 24,25

Chapter III - Esau and Isaac

People who provoke me continually to my face, Crying out, "Hold back, do not touch me; I am too sacred for you!"

These things enkindle my wrath, a fire that burns all the day. Lo, before me it stands written; I will not be quiet until I have paid in full. Your crimes and the crimes of your fathers as well. Isaiah 65: 3,5,6,7.

[We had decided to return to my grandfather's house that next week, but on the Thursday, rather than the Wednesday. He said it was okay. He used the extra time to prepare for us a special treat. This time he had made fresh lemonade, and bought longhorn cheddar cheese and crackers. I could see where my mother and her sisters Jane, Ruby, Doris Jean, Mildred and Marvine gained their skills with the lemon. Gifted and creative cooks, they excelled in lemon pound cakes from scratch. My grandfather's two sons, Henry and Howard, each of whom married two most beautiful young ladies, demonstrated traits they inherited from their father. They had proudly courted these two charming young ladies who were just as creative and gifted as their sisters. No one will ever know the numerous times I stuck out my chest proudly when my friends talked about how fantastic my uncles were. We put them all onto a pedestal. In addition, we had the men, who married my aunts up there too. They were Kirk, Hughie, Eugene, James and Jesse. They rightly belonged there too.

We called my grandfather Big Daddy, as noted. His children, they all called him Papa. We took seats on Big Daddy's porch. Before he could continue with the narration, Mallory ran inside to get his guitar. Some of us preferred his singing to his narration. Others liked both. As time went by, we picked up new members, lost a few, but he always had an audience. If someone missed a week, we had to bring him up to date.

He started strumming that guitar, singing folk songs from an era too far back for any of us, except my cousin, Bernie, to understand. However, we could all tap our feet and hum along when he refrained into the music of the "Balm in Gilead". He always used a Negro Spiritual like that to move into his lecture. Everybody was all ears.]

[Just yestiddy I was reading in the newspaper
about a boy who was lynched down in Mississippi.
This boy was from Chicago, but he had relatives
there. Here we are now, about one hundred years
from the time this story unfolded, and a black
boy, girl, man or woman can be lynched down
there now just as quick as when this country
held your forebears and my parents as slaves.

If any of you should happen to go there, you had better remember that. Don't let it happen to you, not that Emmett Till tried to get lynched. Here is some advice. Don't ever go back there to live unless our numbers have increased so large that we can take over the whole state, or unless you are involved in a Southern strategy to become the majority race there. That means we elect all state office holders. This includes the Senators, every Congressman, and I do mean every state office holder: the governor, every sheriff, and take control of over half the city and county offices in that state. I give you fair warning. It's time we all commence to taking notice.
William J. Moore]

[From our group back then, Bernie was the bravest. A naturally gifted musician, and one who understood all types of music, he made a promise to himself at that time. He told us that he intended to write a symphony that would epitomize these stories from my grandfather, and he would live to see the day that his symphonies about the race riot in East St. Louis, and slavery of our forebears in Mississippi would be presented respectively, and respectfully in each locality. We all knew that if anybody were to accomplish these two great feats, it would have to be Bernie. He suggested that he would relate the full and complete narrative, as best he could remember, to a writer. Bernie had dreams and could see himself in the future meeting gifted people - some writers, some musicians, some poets, some actors - who would have a role in helping to portray the story narrated by my grandfather. We all suggested that no greater story from the modern era could be written, and no greater movie could be presented on the screen. With Bernie writing the musical score, what more could anyone ask?]

[At first they couldn't agree on what names to give the two baby boys. There was so much disagreement, my father used to tell me, that there were only two things that slaves would agree on back then. The first was that survival was the only real thing that mattered and the second was that only a fool would ever let the master, or the master's favorite slave know what you are thinking. Other than those, they could never agree on anything. Before I get more into this story there is another point that I have to tell you. It is this. No matter what the master let on of how he felt about the slaves, the truth

> is they all hated him. Oh yes, the house slaves didn't too much care for the field slaves, but the field slaves didn't really care about them either. This, in turn, eventually led to the erosion of love and true regard from one group to the other. However that might have been, they all, deep down in their souls, hated all white people, to a slave. William J. Moore]

The slaves argued and argued about what two names to give the twins. They asked Will, but he really didn't care. One thing about Will, he stayed out of arguments, and refrained from most discussions. Old Fedderson was asked, and he said he would only give an opinion if they would stop bickering. Within a few minutes, they agreed, provided there was some basis to the names. Owing to how their mother had died, they felt the boys' names should be of importance. Since Cassie's death, Old Fedderson seemed to be looked at in a different light. Due to her death, he began to take the Scriptures more seriously and her death convinced him that people who behave themselves, and do the right thing, will go to heaven when they die. He had begun to quote scripture more authoritatively. When he preached on Sundays, he spoke with an earnestness about him that they had not seen before. He was helping the slaves to see more things in a renewed, and religious manner.

"Ah knows it would come to this, and ah knows you chillen wouldn't agree", he explained, calmly but assertively, pulling the Bible from his side pocket in his overalls. "You chillen ain't been listnin' to the lessons I been teachin' on Sunday mahnin'."

There was silence, dead silence, and he looked about the dirt floor in the big barn, the older barn. Since the horses were moved to the new barn, this now became the quarters for the men. For Sunday morning sermons, the female slaves were allowed. The tub was squarely in the middle of the barn. Then someone finally spoke up. "We's sorry, Old Fedderson. We's powerful sorry. We ain't go forget them lessons no more. Please be patient with us, Old Fedderson. Lawd knows we tries. We tries mighty hard to remember."

"Ah been studying more bout' this here Book, and the Spirit, he commence to lead me to the names of them two boys. They comes out of what we calls the Old Testament." He raised the Bible and waived it in a sweeping motion, as if fanning the entire room. "It be like this. It go back to Abraham. Now somthin' I believes it to be the Spirit, the Ole Spirit commence tellin' me that Abraham be the father to all o' us. He be done had two twins, at a old age. So he commence to callin' that twin by the name o' Esau. Then the other twin boy, he commence to callin' that boy Isaac, cause he like the outdoors. That be why one baby be born inside, and the other baby be born outside. Blessed be the names of The Lord." Old Fedderson didn't have it exactly right, but even for the times, he was close enough.

At that, the matter was settled. All the slaves, young and old alike struck the 'AMEN' chord in unison, a number of times and they all repeated the phrase, blessed be the names of The Lord. Then as Fedderson cued them in again, in unison, they struck the phrase 'Blessed be the Word of The Lord'.

After that Old Fedderson said a few more words. They wanted to hear more, and indeed, at that point, every slave within earshot wanted to learn more about the significance of the lives of the twins and why their mother had to die as she did. Death, and an afterlife in heaven seemed the only real way out of the misery of slavery. Since the life of the slave was exactly like the living hell, each slave believed that he or she had already punched a ticket to heaven. They believed that the only way to lose that ticket was to have strong feelings of hatred for the master, manifest in their heart at death.

As Old Fedderson preached more about the Old Testament, the slaves believed that the similarities between their lives and the lives of the Israelites were not mere coincidence. Old Fedderson disliked the names Old and New; he preferred the First and the Second as names more befitting. The slaves had grown to believe that one of their own fellow slaves would emerge. This black leader would confront the president, who the slaves saw as the living embodiment of the Pharaoh of Egypt. To that extent the new leader would be just like Moses. Just as all the subsequent leaders of the Israelites, the leaders of the black race of America would fall, one by one to the evils of the world. At first they would be victorious; eventually, however, they would fall, just as Israel did in the First Book. As a nation, black people in America were never stronger than immediately after the War Between the States. They just never knew it, or understood how to use their power.

Old Fedderson used the First Book to predict this coming success and the Second Book to predict the aftermath. He cautioned that the only way the race could overcome the similarities between the Israelites and the black race of America was for the slaves, once free, to remove themselves from the white man and his society. To move to a land that could be claimed as their own was the answer, based on the Book. And that answer came from the First Book.

[This interpretation was news to us. Of course my grandfather did point out that this reasoning was not his own. It was simply the way slaves looked at their existence. It was due to their sordid conditions. It made a lot of sense to them. We discussed this with him. Even though the comparisons between 1954 and 1854 were vivid and the lessons were also very real, we all agreed that we were far removed from those conditions. After all, it was the 1950s in East St. Louis, Illinois. That was a century ago, and white people, we were convinced, could not be held responsible for the sins of the past.

The lynching of Emmett Till was anecdotal, we believed, or

happened to believe. Notwithstanding that, we just couldn't relate to the hatred that our white brothers might have had for us in the North and the South. After all, everyone of us attended Sunday School, and often had Bible lessons during the week. So, there we were, to a person impressed that in today's world, white people meant us no harm. In our weak, feeble minds, the 1950s were a total difference from the 1850s. We simply could not accept the truth when intelligent people like my grandfather pointed it out to us. Our brains weren't simply washed. They had been removed, sanitized, and rinsed with gallons of stupid water.

My grandfather was an avid reader of the daily newspapers. He read every column, every article from beginning to end and he had an opinion about everything in the printed word. I remember that one evening we came to his house and he had his car jacked up, and positioned on cinder blocks. We could see the expression on his face and it was one of a high degree of anger. One might have used the adjective 'extreme' to describe his anger. The set of tires was practically new, but he had removed each one, and the spare tire and piled them in the middle of his back yard. There he applied coal oil and set them ablaze. We said nary a word, but watched him methodically go about his business. When I was a child there was always something mystic about the smell of burning tire rubber. It was quite unmistakably different from the smell of any other substance, except, of course, human flesh. The smoke seemed to emit fumes and these fumes, I thought, were quite pleasant. Clearly these fumes served as our introduction to sniffing substances which could provide a pleasant, though harmful effect - a high. I am sure that had he understood how we achieved a modest 'high' from the smell of new rubber burning, he would not have allowed us within two full city blocks of his backyard that day.

In Natchez, Mississippi, the newspapers reported, a black man had been lynched because he accepted a promotion to a position that would have earned him supervisory duties over other black men, and, white men too. The company for which he worked, and down the street from where the lynching was done was the Armstrong Tire and Rubber Company. My grandfather was not the type who would verbally communicate his outrage about that lynching to anyone. Nor would he have engaged in direct action or picketing against the company. We believed that the company should have promoted the man. We also held that Armstrong Tire and Rubber Company owed protection to this employee. When there was talk of a boycott, and a mass meeting to initiate the boycott, Big Daddy would not attend the meeting. He simply decided on a course of action, and keeping the reasons to himself, executed his plan. Now when community folk saw him burning five perfectly good tires rumors spread about his mental condition. For me, I hated folk who spread rumors. Among many people discussing my grandfather's state of mind were some of the very same people for whom he had provided countless favors and for whom he would continue to provide many more. I don't know how many customers Armstrong Tire and Rubber lost in East St. Louis. I do remember that my father attended a meeting of the National Association for the Advancement of Colored People (NAACP). NAACP sought to raise interest in picketing the local company of Armstrong Tire. Even though it was on the corner of Tenth Street at Broadway, within the very block of Hughes-Quinn Junior High School, firmly situated in the black community, the prevailing wisdom was that to demonstrate against the company was not in the best interest of black citizens. How odd, this all seemed to us. We discussed the matter with my father, but we didn't get the point. And during the whole while, we prided ourselves on our greater enlightenment and sophistication than our poor brothers and sisters in the South, especially in Mississippi. I am sure that my grandfather hoped we would learn the truth about all that, as he took us back to life on the Brookshire plantation, a mere century earlier in Mississippi. What made the whole incident so sordid and kept us well behind the progress our brothers and sisters in Mississippi were making is that Armstrong Tire and Rubber Company in East St. Louis, Illinois never had a black person in its employ.]

Esau and Isaac, as twins everywhere, were the centers of attention around the Brookshire plantation during their formative years. Will, their father, enjoyed an extension of his duties, just based on their remarkable births, as if he was responsible for Cassie's conceptions. The truth was that Master Brookshire hoped Will could duplicate the feat, producing sperm sufficient to create multiple births again. The master, bating enthusiasm, read as many books on the subject as he could and finally came to the conclusion that Will really had little to do with it. The multiparous trait occurred only in the female, not the male. That was the singular time that Master Brookshire lamented the death of Cassie. Had she remained alive, he reasoned, she could have produced far more slaves than any other female slave on his plantation, and perhaps for all the plantations around. He decided to maintain a keener interest in the conditions of his female slaves during their pregnancies and to ensure that any who were likely to conceive more than one through the production of multiple eggs or might have the capacity to split an egg, would not be returned to the field immediately. He provided additional counseling, tutoring and advice to Aunt Sapphire about what he had learned. At length, he even had Doc' Pritchard give her a few extra hints on what to look for and expect in her examinations. It never occurred to them that she knew Cassie was having twins.

Looking back, it was probably that research that caused Master Brookshire to reevaluate Will's role. He learned that it was always good to expand the gene pool. That meant that he needed to move another slave into that role for a period not so long as had been enjoyed by Will, or consider other methods. He could permit assigning his slaves for marriages based on what he deemed as necessary expansion of the gene pool. On the other hand, he could simply bring in another slave from another plantation, nearby for breeding purposes. He considered even using a newly arrived young 'buck' from Africa, or even purchasing one from a distant plantation. Eventually he decided to do all of these, thereby creating the greatest variation and success of the race as could be afforded, and accorded.

For many slaves, this meant simply that their lives would be altered very little. Only a few were permitted to elect life long mates. These few did build familial relationships, but they were often shattered when their children were removed for work on other sections of the large plantation. In some instances, this meant that a mother and father could be separated by merely a score or two of acreage. The upshot was that this separation, almost always within shouting distance, was so far away because they were not permitted to travel from one section of the plantation to another. In truth, they could go no further than their assigned working area. Children at an early age were forced to associate with their parents only on Sunday morning on a regular basis. Such association was also permitted at a funeral, on an irregular basis.

Amidst it all, Esau and Isaac were developing and showing physical strength beyond their years. Not yet having to work as slaves because of their ages, they seemed to share a strong interest in horses. Master Brookshire had permitted them to tag along when his youngest son, John William, whom the children called Massa' John Bill, when he went for his daily equestrian lessons. They seemed to notice every detail about the ways the handlers managed the horses. They saw how to put the bit, bridle and reins into perfect position. They observed with keen interest how the blanket was selected, fitted loosely, and then the saddle was positioned and cinched, just so, underneath. Then a slave brought up the ladder, and Massa' John Bill was helped onto the horse, firmly into the saddle, reins in his hands. He seemed, to them, to be afraid of the horses the master used back then. However, he learned to mask his fear, and after the first year, never showed any fear for a long time. Horseback riding and lessons about controlling the animals were the routine for the boy from that day at three years old and would continue for a few more years. The twins trailed along, keeping quiet, but were never permitted to ride. The master envisioned using them in the stables and maybe even at the races eventually. They only had to maintain their interest in equines, and of course, be good slaves when it was time for them to take on work.

The rest of their time in those early years was spent playing with the other children, white and black, slave and free as if they had no responsibilities whatsoever. Yet they learned how to address whites, no matter what their positions on the plantation. Moreover they learned on those few visits to the city and downtown with Massa' John Bill and his governess how to always defer to whites.

The real change for the twins, about three months into their fifth year, was abrupt. Southerners prided themselves on their way of life and always objected to abrupt changes, especially in matters of politics, race relations, social custom, and education. Their watchword, or slogan was always, 'keep it slow'. That followed every application except to slaves. It just didn't apply.

The slave who aroused them from their slumber, at four o'clock that summer morn was a tall, dark muscular fellow they had vaguely recalled about the plantation. His name was Absalom. How sad. No one had prepared them for this day. Very few slave children were ever prepared for this day. Their lives changed from carefree play, into forced labor, literally overnight. They had drawn, as their first full day of work duty, hog care. Of all the requirements of a young person on a plantation, no job lacked danger. Even a young girl who had to remove eggs from the laying hens' nests endured many a hard peck on her hands and wrists. They also encountered a hungry fox, or a coyote, and rarely a cougar. They had to do all that could to run these wild animals from the coop. If a hen was lost, they had to pay by being beaten. There was no such solution as to run for help. For the hen, they had to learn to hit the hen just hard enough to dislodge her from her nest, then swoop up the egg. Then they had to run quickly. Compared to hog care, that was easy. In the hog pen, or sty, the slave had to be quick and he had to understand one thing. Pigs are dangerous. They could, and would kill when protecting a piglet. They also would kill when a sow was in heat.

Piglets were permitted to nurse for exactly one hour, at four intervals during the day. In the pig pens on the Brookshire plantation, there were exactly fifty nine nursing sows at any one time. They were big, ornery, and they stank. The boys had never smelled anything so bad as these pig sties. They were located at the Southeast end, down from the main house. Their spot was situated where they would always be downwind from the mansion, no matter which way the winds blew. The trees - elms, hickories, magnolias, and pecans, created the perfect blockage and redirection of the wind to ensure that the odors from those sties would never come within a couple hundred feet of the Brookshire mansion.

The boys were quick learners. Absalom told them to watch another boy, barely two years older than they. He would show them how he managed the sty. His name was Joshua. He waited for just the right second for the sow to position herself on her side, and the piglets were gathered at her teats. In one quick motion he jumped into the mud and filth, snatched a piglet and deposited him on the other side of the fence, in the same sty. The sow sprang to her feet, some of the other piglets still attached to her teats, some falling, and some barely hanging on. In a flash the boy was safely atop the fence, just beyond her reach. She grunted, snorted and breathed very heavily, but finally lay back down in the mud, filth, and mess that were that sty. This went on all day long until at day's end the pigs were forced out of the sties by Absalom. Then the sty boy raked the dung into a pile just beyond the entrance to the sties. From there, other slaves, some from the fields, some from blacksmithing, some from boat making, some from fishing, all, in fact, who performed heavy labor of some kind, came and bagged up the dung to take to the fields where it would be mixed with cow and horse manure. They had just bagged the latter at the barns prior to coming to the sties. These were mixed with roughage and set out as fertilizer for next year's crops. All in all, every job, when put together created for Master Brookshire a self contained community. It ran like an efficient operation.

The twins were fast learners. In no time at all they had mastered the art of separating the piglets from their mothers. Working as a team they were able to complete their tasks in half the time. They did so by distracting the sow after the snatch. They were performing twice more work than was expected. Briefly drawing the sow's attention, they ensured that even if one of them missed a step, the distraction would ensure the other's safety. Absalom enjoyed the creativity and the master was pleased that after assigning the twins, the work production showed, and maintained a marked increase.

This had become the lot for the twins. After some time, into their sixth month on this detail, Master John Bill remembered his friends. After his full day of horseback riding, reading and mathematics lessons, swimming and a visit to the city with his mother, he remembered the fun he had had when he played with the twins. Recalling those good times, barely six months prior, he summoned them from their quarters. They had to appear in the play area, on the west side of the mansion at once. No matter that they were dead tired. They were needed to serve as playmates for their very young master. He smiled as he saw them trotting up the hill, on the approach to the mansion. He was about to greet them with a hug, until he could smell the wretched odor as they neared.

"Stop! Stop right there!" he yelled. He made the most awful, twisted, horridly contorted face any person had ever seen on a child. Any person who had seen masks designed to evoke fear would have believed that his image was far scarier than any of those. The young master could not understand that he had passed the area where the trees, as situated, had formed a blockade from the natural downward draft, creating an upwind effect. He smelled their stench, their horrible odor from the pig sties, a full blend of hog funk, dung and bacterial laden mud, mixed with the natural body musk, sweat and dirt of the twins.

The twins, in full obedience, stopped dead in their tracks. The boy inched closer, their odor growing worse and worse as he approached. They were too strong and at length he was forced to retreat before he could open his mouth to talk with them.

"Esau and Isaac", he strained his vocal chords, the words coming as if in total disgust. "I should be ashamed of myself for even commencing to summon either of you all. You all reek, like the natural heathens that you all are. From this day hence, you all are never to come within sight of me, or the master's house."

His father and grandfather would have been most proud of John William. It was as if the words had come from the very mouth of the master himself. He would not have been so proud because of just how the boy articulated and enunciated, but due to his having learned the lesson that each slave, no matter how young, had to be taught his proper place. Master Brookshire was very pleased when told of how his youngest son had treated both boys, who until six months previous had been his playmates, and close friends on a regular, daily basis. He felt that now was the time to give him a special gift that would befit the occasion.

He took him out to the barn, there to give him the present. It was his prized thoroughbred racing horse. He actually had bought the horse via a trade of two male slaves and three female slaves, and one quarter horse. At one point, his son would take over all riding duties associated with the horse. Eventually, the animal would be assigned to stud. Before then, the handlers were to take good care of the animal. Master Brookshire had decided to train him for the Great Derby, to be held in Louisville. The horse was one year old. He would compete with all comers there in two years. The year following, the race was to move to Jackson, where, again, all comers would be invited. He wanted the highly spirited, skittish mount trained to perform in those major events, and a few other minor events throughout the county, state and region.

On approaching the front gate marking the entry to the Brookshire estate, one was met by the usual statuary that adorned most estates throughout the South. But instead of two black little jockey statues in racing silks, he had four. Whenever a visitor commented about the unusual number, four instead of two, he would reply simply "Don't my little old Nigra riding boys look so good? Ah am so glad ya'll like those little darkies. Ah shore do". Mr. Brookshire was that way. He took every thing for granted about his wife, Janie Ellen, his two daughters, Opal Mae and Janie Ellen, and his other two sons, Noah Maximilian, and Robert Calhoun. He really did dote on each of his children and his wife too. However, he never gloated about how fantastic he thought they were. He didn't have to. The reason was that by his every action everyone seeing his interaction with his wife and the children could see that as far as he was concerned they were the salt of the earth. His "Nigras", as he referred to the slaves on his plantation had to treat one and all like they were religious deities. Townsfolk had to treat them with the utmost respect, as if they were royalty.

Even though no one from the town would dare cross, insult or even look askance at one of the Brookshire brood, their father insisted that whenever they left the plantation that one of his executive staff had to accompany them. They were quite a picture when they went shopping. Quite often the girls went with their mother and the prominent house slave who was in charge of the kitchen. She was even permitted to ride in the wagon with the girls and Mrs. Brookshire. The prominent male house slave sat atop the coach with the driver. At times he was even permitted to control the team of horses.

In the various shops and stores the Brookshire girls simply selected the items they wanted for their bedrooms and the fabrics they wanted with which their outfits could be made. No matter what the occasion, Tamar, the house slave who excelled at dressmaking could fashion the exact garment that they described for her to create. Practically everything the girls wore, no matter the occasion, everyday attire, church going outfit, social event, even playthings was put together by Tamar. Eventually she began to do the shirts for the master and the boys as they came of age and showed a preference for the upper class attire to which their father had become accustomed.

Tamar always had fabric left over. To keep herself busy, she quilted. She also made dresses and undergarments for the female slaves who worked the house and in the fields. Through union with Will, Tamar gave birth to one boy. Then through union with Matthew, a field slave, she gave birth to five boys and one girl. They all worked in various areas of the field or in the barnyard. She also had one other child. Though she would never indicate the identity of the father, many thought it to be Charles Rogers. He was the eldest son of the minister of the Mount Pisgah Baptist Church, the very church in which the entire Brookshire family held membership. That child had remained on the Brookshire estate for only the first two years of her life. Then she was sent to live with Reverend Rogers, Charles' father, and the Rogers family. On occasion, Tamar would see her on visits to town with the Brookshire daughters and/or with Mrs. Brookshire. Though that girl had a light olive complexion (that the slaves called 'high yellow'), curly strawberry-blond hair, freckles and a long neck, there was no mistaking who her parents were. Though no one ever was heard admitting it, she had features more resembling the minister's son than she did her own mother. Be that as it might have been, she carried features of Tamar as well.

Though she was the granddaughter of Reverend and Mrs. Charles, as everyone referred to Mrs. Rogers, they never ever treated her the way they treated their other grandchildren. A bright child, it didn't take her too long to understand that she was indeed a grandchild. On the few occasions that she saw her mother, the girl rekindled those days of nurturing in her mind's eye, never to forget who her real mother was.

It was about that time that the Brookshire girls and the two older boys were to begin their entrances into polite society. This meant that Master and Mrs. Brookshire would be called upon to host afternoon teas where teenage boys and girls would be encouraged to meet, mix, and be initiated into the ways of gentlemanly courtship. After their book-learning activities and religious training, the children of the emerging upper class were taught how children of refined society should behave at such functions. Lessons included waiting to be introduced to a young lady; how to bow and wait for the young lady to offer her hand; how to ask for a dance; the manner of offering to get a drink for the young lady; how to sip tea or lemonade; how to take stronger libation and so on. Both genders were drilled and required to display what they had learned. If anyone had not effected the proper behavior through these lessons, that person was not permitted to attend the social event. By the time the girls were ready to be introduced into formal society at debutante balls they had become well mannered in the social graces and the behavior required in polite society. So it had come to be with the Brookshire girls and the two older boys. Those girls set the standard for fashion every time they appeared in public. Thanks to Tamar, this became expected. Master Brookshire would have nothing less.

About this time, the two older Brookshire boys were given to understand that they had to begin to undergo an earnest orientation into the management of the plantation. During this stringent education, they had to continue all the other activities in which they were involved. These included monitoring of the various work details of the slaves (under the management of specific foremen and work supervisors, all who answered to the overseer); attending their continuing education classes in language, mathematics, music, history, and the classics; attending Bible study lessons Wednesday evenings at church; attending the dance and proper etiquette classes two sessions per week; and animal husbandry at the Grange Society Hall two sessions per week. Now to learn the management of the plantation, they would spend everyday at lunch with their father as their tutor. Training under Master Brookshire would prove the sternest of all tests.

A practical man with a keen business acumen, he was driven, totally committed to his goals. First and foremost was to ensure that his name and memory would be accorded historical significance as the one person whose life had the single, most important influence on the shape of the institutions of the South. The second was to preserve a system of plantation ownership and management so successful that it would preserve the Southern way of life. For this to endure, it would require two elements, each co-dependent on the other. The initial goal would be attained by his children learning to administer the plantation. The latter would depend on the continuation of slavery as an institution. He knew he could attain the former. The second, he realized, would require shrewd political maneuvering on one hand, and if necessary, eventual secession from the Union, on the other.

[I have to make one point clear to you boys. The Master Brookshire was not interested in establishing the Confederacy. That was the furthest thing from his real goals. Personally, he would have favored a compromise that would have maintained the Mason-Dixon line, and allowed, of the emerging states from the Territories, one slave state for every two free states. He figured that the prize among these would have been Texas. The truth was that he would have been willing to argue that every new state admitted to the Union could be admitted as free state under one condition.

That condition was that Texas, as its legislature and president desired, would be entered among the slave holding parties. Master Brookshire was a man of foresight and faith in the future. He evaluated all the arguments in the Northern press, and what he learned was under discussion in the Congress. While he wished that the debate with the abolitionists would subside, he maintained a healthy respect for the competencies of the leaders of that movement. In spite of his keen understanding of events shaping the nation, he was unable to assess the strength of that movement. Like most Southern plantation owners, the real holders of power, he was unable to see that his cause could only succeed through a material preparation for war. Their preparation was spiritual, and since Southerners were convinced that their way of life had been ordained by Almighty God, their spirituality would preserve their way of life if war were to be undertaken. That is what they believed. William J. Moore]

More than anything else, Mater Brookshire wanted John William to become the family expert on equine husbandry. The lad was becoming skilled in judging and assessing racing horses, trotters, pacers and speed horses. He also became familiar in understanding the physical characteristics that made for good quarter horses and draft horses as well. Eventually, with the knowledge firmly learned, the master planned to teach him the rudiments of assessing other farm animals. These included mules, ninnies, jackasses, donkeys, oxen, cattle, pigs, and all kinds of fowl. To his older boys he had entrusted awareness of the physical attributes of their human property, the slaves. Dental strength, musculature, size of feet, thickness of skin, and the apparent slowness of thought, due to ,the master was sure, an obviously inferior intellect. The older boys had also intensified their training in all areas of plantation management. When the youngest son reached the 'correct age', his studies would expand to those areas as well.

One day, late in the summer of 1857, John William was out exercising the prized thoroughbred his father had presented as a gift. Accompanied by David Monroe Trotter, his riding instructor, his brother Noah Maximilian, and the lead caretaker in the stables, a house slave known as Jeremiah, they were on the path leading from the plantation toward the timing area behind the city square. A number of slave children tagged along the whole while they were still on plantation property. They went as far as the end of the path. A stern look from Jeremiah was all they needed to know that that was as far as they could go. The timing area was a track with a grandstand. It was about five miles Southeast of the Brookshire plantation. Master Brookshire had actually purchased it from a group of businessmen in the city. Due to mail order purchases of farm implements from companies up North, and direct delivery from railroad brokers, farm equipment purchases from small entrepreneurs were becoming passe. Master Brookshire awarded each businessman from whom he purchased the timing track and grandstand two female and one male slave. He required that even though the slaves belonged to these men in actuality, that they could not claim them as their real property in legal matters. Slave trading had long since been outlawed and he didn't want to be accused of violating the law. It didn't matter to him that he never would have been convicted in a court of law. He simply didn't want the accusation. The other reason he wanted to maintain this arrangement was that slave ownership was not simply a sign of power; it was power. In some respects it was more significant than legal tender and business ownership. The recorded ratio gave him more power in the state legislature and the Congress of the United States than any single person in the country. Even though parting with as many as half his slaves would not have jeopardized this position, officially he would not part with even one. He would not so much as think of it.

They exercised the horse, rested and enjoyed lemonade, while Jeremiah rubbed down the thoroughbred and gave him a light snack. The horse was doing better as he matured. His clocked time over a distance of one mile and a half was as good as any recorded in the history of the South. The real question would be how would the animal fare in a race, pitted against other equine. Many a horse had timed well in practice only to lose horribly in races. On the contrary, a number of horses that fared poorly in timing trials had done remarkably well in competitive races. Nobody would know just how well John William's prized thoroughbred, the pride of Brookshire Farms, could do. Already judged by the experts who had observed him to be the most outstanding thoroughbred in the country, this claim could only be certifiably accepted after he had bested any and all comers in races.

After awhile the group finished their light snacks and cool lemonade. Now they were to return to the Brookshire estate. All among their group were in the saddle except John William. As had become his wont, and befitting the class distinctions he was learning, this was the order of things. Jeremiah was even atop his mount, but he held the reins tightly of the race horse. Mr. Trotter, at that point, had to alight from his mount and give an assist to young Master Brookshire, boosting him back to the top of the racing pony. Though yet skittish, after a workout, racers like this seemed too much in control and maybe even somewhat tired to expend substantially more energy. Therefore, the group's formation was somewhat more loose on the return, than their usual style.

It was when they were about two miles from their destination when something got into the big animal. It was as if he had been struck by a bolt of electricity because that horse reared up and almost threw John William off the back. The boy held on for dear life because in an instant he feared that a fall backwards with such impact as would have been felt might have killed him. Instantly the other horses bolted as well, though their stirrings were not so strong as the racer's. Each of them headed into alternate directions while the strong mount still carrying John William raced back to the farm in break neck speed. Frightened out of his wits, the lad held on, clutching and pulling on the reins while his legs squeezed at the horse's sides. All was to no avail. That animal seemed possessed, wildly intent on carrying himself and his rider where he wanted to run and run he did. A number of people saw what was going on and they all realized they were too powerless to be of help. Only a fool, many reasoned, would be stupid enough to hurl himself into the path of a horse like that. It could only mean certain death.

Slaves and workers at the plantation could hear the screams of the lad when the horse approached within a quarter mile. Had there not been the usual activity about, then the hysterical voice would have easily been picked up further away.

"Git away from that gate, you li'l niggahs", the pig sty foreman yelled at Isaac and Esau, who, alerted to the boy's screams, ran to help. "They's go be hell to pay, and ah gots to give ya'll twenty lashes if'n ya'll don't git yo niggah asses back!"

The twins stopped suddenly, then turned and looked back. At once they heard the screams again and realized that the Master's son was in mortal danger. Though they had remained their distance from the main house, and John William when he so ordered just a few years before, they couldn't ignore him in his time of need. Their lives had gone totally different routes since that day and he had all but forgotten about the two boys, who began their lives with him as sharing friends. Now they were simply the same to any white person in town or anywhere in the South. They were even more so to John William. To them, that, however, did not matter. The lessons in The Good Book (as the slaves referred to The Holy Bible) had taught them that they were to love their enemy, and treat the person good who had mistreated them. Even though slavery was bad, to hate those who despised them would have been worse than living the everyday hell of slavery. The only hope for freedom was to live the good life, the Christian life, even as a slave, and then to die the right death so that one could go to heaven. Those two boys did an awful lot of hard thinking in the few seconds they had to make a decision. All things considered, it wasn't all that hard after all.

By the time the horse was rumbling past the farm, it was still at a good pace, though tiring. In no time at all, the twins were outside the gate. There they spotted the racing horse with John William still holding on but by now losing his grip. Any second and he would have been off that horse, falling toward the hard turf along the bridle path. Esau, the faster of the twins, began running in a trot away from the gate. Isaac, who was nonetheless, very fast, actually ran past his faster brother. Then Esau ran past him. He caught the horse, grabbed the middle rein and the left side rein, while Isaac, sizing up the situation from behind, caught the horse and timed his leap perfectly. He was astride the giant animal, supporting John William just as he was falling off. He grabbed the lad and positioned him firmly in front of himself, back in the saddle. At the same time, Esau, yelling commands to whoa, controlled the head and neck of the horse. His hands, fingers, and forearms wore raw just from the few seconds of wrestling with the bit and middle rein while running as fast and as powerfully as he could. They helped John William from the horse, as the rest of the group finally caught up.

John William was taken from there by buckboard to the manor, cleaned, cared for, and put to bed. A potion of goose grease and duck fat, concocted by Aunt Sapphire as a curing salve, was applied to the hands, wrists, and to the upper torso and hands of the twins.

In no time at all, the boys were back to work with the pigs. Late that afternoon, just before they were done, Master Brookshire paid a visit to the sty. Then again, later he showed up that evening at the slave shed where the boys were housed with the rest of the young male bondmen.

Skip One-Eye, as the pig caretaker was called, for an obvious reason, recounted to Master Brookshire how the involvement of the twins unfolded, emphasizing that they had violated a direct order not to leave their work area. He had promised them that if they left, he would personally apply twenty lashes with the bullwhip to their backsides. Master Brookshire studied on the matter for awhile because it was much different from the usual occurrence when slaves run. Though the twins had acted valiantly and clearly had no intention of running to escape, they still had disobeyed the most important rule for a slave throughout the South. They had run, nonetheless, disobeying a white authority figure.

Then, to make matters worse, as Master Brookshire and Skip One-Eye saw it, they disobeyed the direct order of their overseer's assistant. So on the one hand, Master Brookshire would thank them for their gallantry and bravery, he would not let the deeds of running, and disobedience go unpunished. This was strictly the law of the South and it had to be not simply enforced, but upheld with a religious zealotry.

Sapphire and Fedderson knew what awaited the boys the next morning before their work day was to begin. Everyone on that plantation knew. They were to be beaten in front of every slave. Any of the white work crew could look on if they wanted. Of course they would not miss this. Those assigned to the house, kitchen, laundry area and even the excavators were to report to witness this before they began their work. Through it all, the boys were told that they could not hate anyone.

In the aftermath, their backs bore deep gashes, with blood and sweat running down into their pants. The sun seemed to create an oily crystal in each crevice of their wounds. Each gash ran for inches from their necks to just below their waists. Strange things happen among boys, so young, as they move into their manhood, and the same strange phenomena were manifest here. Many psychologists, students of human emotion and deep thinkers can't quite put a handle on it. But those black folk always seem to understand. They understand it perfectly. They understand it perfectly well. They also understand why. Both Esau and Isaac, those two little, young boys -

they refused to cry. Though they were too weak to stand, and had even been beaten while they lay on the filthy earth, not one, single tear, not even a little one, came from their eyes. Not one scream in pain was heard from their mouths. All fear, was now gone from their souls.

They knew.

They understood.

They were beaten to an extent that no human being should ever even come close to enduring, and yet they could not make them cry. The boys knew why they could not cry. They understood, with a maturity beyond their few years, why they could not scream. This was their reward for saving a life. It didn't matter at all. This was the harsh lesson of slavery.

> [The reason those boys couldn't cry was that no matter how hard they were beaten, nothing was so bad as being a slave. If born to slavery and being forced to endure the worst of all human degradation could not make a person cry, then surely a severe beating would not do it either. William J. Moore.]

Then Jesus replied: I came into this world to divide it, to make the sightless see, and the seeing blind. New American Bible. John 9 - 39

Chapter IV - Fit Me With Them Wings So I Can Fly

[Please hand me my guitar from the corner, behind the fan.]

My grandfather seemed to be going to his guitar more and more as he grew older. He might have favored it to the Bible, as he continued to read it often. Even though he didn't stop reading it, he just seemed to read it not so often as in the past. He never stopped reading the newspaper. Two additional activities appeared not to be affected. These were his interest in listening to the baseball games on the radio (He never cared much for television, if at all.) and his interest in listening to the various religious and talk shows on the radio. These pursuits maintained him as perhaps one of the most well informed people in the area, if not the country.

He lived by himself in the house that he, my grandmother, my mother, aunts and uncles had shared for a number of years. At one point my younger brother and his wife lived with him. How lonely he must have been living there by himself. On our many visits he would fashion a rather faint smile. I often watched the expression on his face when others would come by. He always smiled and as he grew older, the smile became wider. It was obvious that he enjoyed the company of others. I believe that smile was at its most obvious when my uncle's wife came by. Others said he was hard to read. I think he was easier. No matter, he was a delight in his latter years because he was obvious.

Listening to him strum the guitar, and sing those blues (religious) songs was a blessing. Many he had learned as a child living in Mississippi, and others he had composed there, and still others he had composed in his young adult years in Illinois. We never tired of his singing or guitar playing Looking back, my only real regret is that we never remembered the tunes or the notes and we never recorded them.

(Anything that we sing now from those days represents words and melodies that we re-create, losing most of the words but little of the meaning from our memories.)

I believe that his music, like his epic tales and short stories would have provided a lasting treasure into understanding significant aspects of black culture. We all felt that at some point, we would form a group to simply sit, and orally review the many stories he had related to us. At another point, those of us with musical talent would regroup and recall his many tunes and melodies, transfer them to written notes and, of course, give him all the credit. Again, I reiterate a goal stated by Bernie back then. If anyone had the ability to arrange the tunes and set the correct tempo and music, Bernie was the ideal person to do so.

When ya'll take me home, oh, oh, oh when ya'll take me home.
When ya'll take me home by and by,

When ya'll take me home, oh, oh, oh when ya'll take me home.
Fit me with the right wings to fly, oh, oh fly.

This here old house it ain't my home.
This here old house it ain't my home.
This here old house it ain't my home.
It's just a place to rest by and by.

This here old house it ain't my home.
This here old house it ain't my home.
This here old house it ain't my home.
It's just a place to rest by and by.

So when ya'll take me home, tell them angels I won't cry,
Just fit me with them wings so I can fly.
Just fit me with them wings so I can fly.

That song, like many that my grandfather sang for us, was never performed exactly the same way twice. Oh the music was always the same, and he memorized each note so that there was never deviation. But the words changed slightly each time.

Well, he sang verses from that song until he got so tired and eventually he just sat the guitar onto the floor. I think he saw that we wanted to hear and he wanted to give us more about the twins. It was almost like an instinctive immediacy that controlled the situation. As a result, we wondered whether he or our desires were in control. Maybe, as these types of metaphysical things go, it was neither. Could it have been the elements? Or was it, as the more thoughtfully religious of my cousins used to say, the Spirit? He just picked that guitar right back up and strummed a few more chords, then arpeggios, then full chords again. He found the right notes through this process and went into this timely rendition:

If ya'll, I say if ya'll. If any o' ya'll sees ole massah.
Then tell him, tell ole massah, I's done gone up North.

If ya'll, I say if ya'll. If any o' ya'll sees my wife.
Then tell her, I says tell her, tell her the same thing too.

If ya'll, I say if Ya'll. If any o' ya'll sees ole massah.
Then tell him, tell ole massah, I's done gone up north

If ya'll, I say if ya'll. If any o' ya'll sees my wife.
Then tell her, I says tell her, I be back to git' her too.

Since the song was sang rather slowly, it took longer than the previous one. However, when we left his house that day singing it, we naturally speeded up the tempo. The best thing about that song is that it actually led to the theme of the continuation of his Narration. Even so, there were a few among us who wanted to hear his singing continue.

> I think the very worse thing we can do (and we often do so to our fellow black brothers and sisters) is to make assumptions about people. You can make generalizations about the tendencies of people and what not, but you can never be sure until a person is in the crucible of knowledge, where one encounters a situation where his or her actions can determine the fate of another individual. During the time that this narration occurs, black people are making all kinds of generalizations about each other. High yellow house Negroes don't care one bit about field Negroes. Most field Negroes don't care about all Negroes, but sometimes, just to curry favor from the master, any Negro will sell out another. The more you put your trust into one Negro, the more likely you are to regret it sooner or later. It is true that almost every time a slave was betrayed to the master, that betrayal came from another slave. It is also true that the house slaves, to a person, thought that their lot was better than any field slave and that, therefore, they were better than the field slaves. However, there was always a slave in any situation who would find himself in a position to help another slave. Quite often, this was the very slave who a potential runaway thought would have betrayed him. We now turn to look at one such slave, whom the others thought would have been the betrayer. William J. Moore]

The Reverend John Calhoun Rogers lived with his wife and youngest son, Ephesus Rogers, on the North edge of the city, just about a mile from downtown. He had assumed guardianship and ownership of Plumpsie, when she was eight years old. They taught her to clean house, cook, sew, and all in all, serve as a personal attendant to Mrs. Rogers. The elder son, who had moved from the house, was rumored to be the father of Plumpsie, having had his way with one of the slaves from the Brookshire plantation. Truth be known, he had his way with more than one slave from that plantation. More truths: he had visited a number of plantations from Mississippi to Alabama and Georgia and did the same thing. Plumpsie had more sisters and brothers than she could have imagined. The elder Rogers had more grandchildren, sired by their son Charles, than they could have imagined. In the South one didn't have to tell another who one's parents might have been. Somehow, everyone seemed to know. Maybe it was the color of the skin, but that didn't always prove anything, for sure. Maybe it was the size of the nose in ratio to the whole face, or the way the mouth curved at the top, and the size of the slope of the bottom lip. Still other factors might have concerned the texture of the hair. No matter what, slaves always seemed to know, and this was a lesson learned at an early age. What was so telling about black people that slaves knew who belonged to whom? It was the mannerisms and the temperaments. Plumpsie didn't look a lot like her mother, Tamar, one of Will's progeny, but she did possess a few of her physical features. For that matter, she didn't bare a great resemblance to Charles Rogers, but she did have more of his physical attributes. The traits that clearly defined Plumpsie as Tamar's and Charles' child were her mannerisms. She walked with an assured gait, her head held high, and her back straight, just like Charles. When she smiled, she showed pride in learning something new, in being a person of worth, like her mother. When she talked, she seemed to take her time to articulate each syllable carefully, often curling her tongue up distinctively like her mother. Nobody had to say it, and she was the first to realize it; her mother was a house slave at the Brookshire Plantation. Her father had grown up in the very house she now occupied, albeit as a slave, not as a family member, nor as a free person.

Her treatment certainly was many times better that that accorded her many cousins, aunts and uncles, and her sisters, who had to live a horrible life on a plantation that was worse than a sentence of hard labor for life. In many ways, her life could not even be compared with that of other slaves. This concerned her activities of daily living only. Added to this was that on Sundays she could accompany the whole Rogers family to church. She was allowed to sit on a small stool behind the white children of the community at Sunday School. At the regular church service, she was permitted to stand beside Mrs. Rogers at the end of the pew on the first row. When she grew tired of standing, she was permitted to retire to the back of the church and sit there on her small stool, which she had to return to the basement at the end of service. She was permitted to sit for no more than ten minutes or so at a time. When Reverend Rogers nodded, she had to return to her place, standing at the end of the pew.

The Rogers provided her three pairs of shoes. This was one pair more than any other slave. She had three outfits, one for church on Sundays;

one for her work about the house during the week and for helping to clean the church on Monday; and a final third one for attending Mrs. Rogers at formal functions. As the wife of the minister she had been invited and was accustomed to invitations to all kinds of events. This was entirely befitting the wife of the pastor of the most prominent church in the state.

Plumpsie's life was also different from those of the other slaves in other respects too. Though she rarely had a free moment, she seldom was required to perform the laborious work of the plantation slaves. For example, she didn't have to pick cotton or attend to animal husbandry. Once in awhile she would be required to wash down, feed, or exercise the horses, but she truly liked horses and even at a young age asked to assist in birthing mares at foal. The other stark difference between Plumpsie and the other slaves, even the house slaves on the various plantations, was that she was never beaten. She was never stripped of all her clothing and placed onto a stake to be administered the most dreaded of all punishments, whipping until your backside looked like a pack of hungry dogs had had their way at sup. Mrs. Rogers had taken a switch to her from time to time, if for no other reason than she thought she was carrying out the will of the Lord.

Plumpsie was different, even when comparing her treatment and standards with other favored light skinned slaves of mixed parentage. Astoundingly, she knew that she was different. The difference with Plupmpsie was that that made all the difference. She recognized that all slaves in the region had taken to believing the stories from the sermons preached on Sunday mornings. She recognized that they had come to love those who held them in human bondage. She saw a change in behavior where they began to show evil, unrestrained hatred of each other. She recognized that this change coexisted with the greater incidence of maltreatment to the slaves. She believed that due to this growing torrent of unrestrained hatred, but for one slave's being the property of the white master, many most assuredly would have killed another in anger.

Plumpsie also saw that all other slaves had social and personal relationships that had more meaning than her relationships with them, and certainly more than her relationships with her owners, the Rogers family. They knew who their fathers, mothers aunts, uncles, sisters, brothers, and cousins were and could so acknowledge. She lived with her paternal grandparents but could never even think of referring to them as grandmother and grandfather. Her father, Charles Rogers, used to visit this house occasionally in his travels but she could never call him 'Daddy'. He was always Master Charles, and his brother, who was her uncle, had to be referred to as Master Ephesus.

Plumpsie had no idea what Charles did for a living. Neither did his parents. Word about town is that he went off to study theology at a seminary and now served the Lord as a traveling evangelist. He rode in the finest and most elegant of riding coaches, with a driver, assistant driver and personal valet, all in his employ. A few others believed that he was a secret agent in the cause of the South's effort to preserve its way of life. Others believed he was a speculator, seeking to purchase and control vast reaches of real property in the West and North for political purposes. The last rumor about Charles' real line of work had him as a slave trader, still active in an occupational activity that the Supreme Court of the United States had outlawed. Plumpsie had heard all these and believed each to be true. Little slave girls, or grown slaves for that matter were not even permitted to entertain ideas about the business of white people. They were not even to so much as listen when white folk talked of such. Theirs was to do as told, quickly and without question; speak when spoken to; and above all else, know when to and how to show due respect for anybody white.

When Charles visited his father's house, Plumpsie had to show his employees to their quarters. They took care of their master's clothing and items of personal toiletries, then attended to their own needs. On one such visit, Charles had a meeting at the Brookshire Plantation. Coincidentally, Mrs. Rogers was to attend a meeting of the women's auxiliary at the Brookshire's. This was the first time Plumpsie had been inside the coach owned by Charles. Careful not to so much as even crease the fine soft leather seating, she let herself ease down very softly onto the seat. Charles uttered a few words about having a slave within his coach but one cross stare from his mother shut his mouth. It wasn't so much a reminder that the very slave upon whom he looked so derisively was his daughter, as a reminder that Plumpsie had become the personal assistant of his mother; in effect she was the chief slave in waiting. Mrs. Rogers referred to her as 'My Little Negress'. But, strangely and artfully, by now, Charles seemed to have forced himself to erase from his memory the very advent of his having fathered a daughter, by having raped her mother. Though the girl shared many of his physical features and nuances, down to the color of her crimson hair, his denial had attained such a state that for him, fatherhood was out of the question.

Charles' business that afternoon was with Master Brookshire. They met near the stables on the Northwest corner of the plantation. After exchanging the usual pleasantries, they walked toward the entrance gate and began to talk in earnest.

"Ah really want to know exactly, Ah say exactly, what them damn Yankees are thinking. If that scalawag, Abraham Lincoln gets elected, we might just all be in trouble."

"Well, Mister Brookshire, Ah can attest to you that he ain't gonna get elected", Charles reassured him in as calm a voice as he could have measured. They walked back toward the house as he continued. "To the best of what my sources point out to me, that niggah lover ain't gone git enough votes to carry the electoral college with a majority. The House of Representatives will have to decide and what most of those fellers fear is the secession."

"Boy, Ah says boy, Ah can only hope that your resources are telling you the right way. The moment that niggah lovah do get in, war go be inevitable. What do your sources say about that?"

"Oh Ah wouldn't worry bout that either, suh. Them damn Yankees ain't got the stomach for a long war. A war is gonna cost the South a lot, but we can win it. That's a real fact."

"How can you all be so sure?"

"Well, Mr. Brookshire, suh, all we got to do is hold out. We don't have to win outright, although we can. If they want war, the North will definitely bite off more than they can chew. Of that Ah am sure."

"Is that what you all learned traveling up North?, cohabitating with them damn Yankees?"

"Oh Ah see, Mr. Brookshire, suh; you all have done your homework well. Therefore, Ah know you have already evaluated my assessment."

"Ah just wanted to hear it from your mouth, first hand, shall we say."

"Ah don't mind letting you in on all the gory details, suh. It's what you all payin me for."

"No thank you all, Charles. That information, all the details, is best left in the confidence of you and your cohorts. Now let's walk back toward the barn and discuss that deal we talked about making."

They walked about two hundred feet along the estate's main road, then turned to circle around back. There they stopped to watch Isaac and Esau exercise the horses. Their conversation concerned the boys. By now, they had become even more valuable assets to the farm. Having continued their work in the hog pens, they also helped out in the mating and training of the mares and stallions. The younger, and thinner of the two had become an expert horseman. Master Brookshire had entered his name to ride his prize thoroughbred in the Great Derby at Louisville, instead of his son. The older twin who stood one-half inch shorter and four pounds heavier was a natural horse trainer. He seemed to be able to get any of the prize ponies to obey his every command, sometimes, it seemed, by the way he simply looked at them or winked an eye. He was the major subject of the discussion.

The ladies' auxiliary meeting was closing about the same time as they had stopped along the path. Charles and Master Brookshire had paused midway the main road to continue their 'business discussion'. Plumpsie, waiting at the trail, noticed the pair emerge from the shadows of the Magnolia trees dotting the road. It didn't escape Plumpsie's notice that when they stopped along the road, the whole time they leaned against the white painted fence, their gaze never left the twins.

If you had tried to explain the concept of female intuition to Plumpsie, she never would have caught on to what it meant. She didn't understand clairvoyance and she didn't believe in seers. Those were the few concepts that many a slave brought over from Africa, and held. Something about the entire episode with the two men just didn't sit too well with her. Just based on what she had seen, her father, and Master Brookshire must have been up to no good. Worst of all, she imagined, it probably involved the twins. She watched them carefully, and every time one or the other looked her way, she would look the other way, before they saw what she was looking at.

"It's not good to look in the direction of Master Charles and Master Brookshire when they are talking, Plumpsie." Mrs. Rogers startled her as she came upon the child from behind.

"Why, Mrs. Rogers, Ma'am, ya'll scared me just like when I catches me a little ole June bug. I was just admiring them big old trees, how beautiful they absolutely looks." The lie worked. Right away Plumpsie knew that it had worked. This was the first time she was in a situation where she had to tell a lie and in spite of all the lessons on right and wrong that she had been taught in church and in Sunday School, and from the discussions she had had with Reverend and Mrs. Rogers, she felt no guilt on lying to her owner. In fact, she found enjoyment in it. "I is so glad that God created them trees."

"Oh, dear, those are magnolia trees. I am glad you noticed." She patted Plumpsie on the head as the two men reached them. They stopped to make conversation while Charles explained to his mother that he would be ready to leave after he signed a document in Master Brookshire's study.

Before returning to their home, Charles and his mother enjoyed pork chops smothered in gravy and onions, hominy, green peas, and biscuits. Plumpsie, although accustomed to enjoying her meals with Mrs. Rogers, understood that when in the company of other white folk, she could not have meal with her owners. While this might not have set well with other slaves who attained that level of familiarity with their owning family, Plumpsie was not upset by the arrangement one twit. In fact, she preferred the opportunity to interact with her darker skinned cousins. There was true love and fellowship when she had occasion such as this to spend quality time. Most of them had completed their chores for the day. This accorded time for singing, dancing and just enjoying the company of each other.

> [Quite often, I observe these phenomena during three activities. These same factors can be discovered at family reunions, funerals and gatherings of the extended family. These latter occur on holidays such as July 4th, Memorial Day, and the times when a group, or someone simply decides to have a big get-together. There doesn't have to be a specific reason; we just want to celebrate each other because we feel like a celebration. This is a characteristic, a positive one, that commenced during slavery when there was a lull in white folk's activities and slaves could get together and have a good time. Oh they ate 'from the bottom of the hog' but they felt good. And the

lemonade had to have apple cider added to it for everybody to have a little, but everyone had some. Back then, the children had their places and the adults theirs. However, they were always under the watchful eye of an older teenager or another adult.

When white folk sponsored these events, Master Brookshire, like all the Southern slave owners, often paired slaves against each other to see who was the better fighter. Then he would match his best fighters against the best fighting slaves from another plantation. This is the truth. Those boys would fight each other until one, near death, simply couldn't go any further. Winner and loser, were brought back to their respective plantations to sleep it off. Both were too tired and too weak to eat. Even sleep was difficult due to pain and excessive bleeding and bruising. That never did matter to the master. All those boys who fought the night before, had to be out in the fields or down at the working stables in the morning, before the crack of dawn.

Well, there was never any of that at the black family get-togethers. Slaves ensured that there was no behavior that was harmful to another slave. They caught so much hell from the master and the overseer that they just didn't feel like giving it to each other. As far as I'm concerned, personally I would not care if all black folk commenced to never using the word overseer again. It should not be reverted to in any context. It conjures up the most hurtful memories about abuse our forebears endured, of any kind in memory. Certainly it brings back more bad memories of any kind I can imagine, just from their descriptions. Well, I shall tell you more about that later, but now, let's get back to Plumpsie.

Oh yes, just one other notion before we return to Plumpsie. It is this: Another thing, no slave ever referred to a family outing, or a family get-together, either during slavery or after it when they were freedmen, as a 'picnic'. William J. Moore]

Plumpsie was in awe of Charles' coach. It was the most elegant thing she could ever imagine riding in. Her cousins, aunts, uncles, and many slave friends watched in envy as she stepped onto the running board and then into the chamber after her owners. They envied so much about Plumpsie. First there was her appearance. As the child of a dashingly handsome white man and a physically beautiful black woman, she seemed to have inherited the most attractive and strongest physical traits from both parents. Like her mother, Plumpsie's facial features were perfectly symmetrical and her wide eyes and long thick eyelashes made her the envy of every girl, or woman, white, black or mixed. Whoever laid eyes on her marveled at her beautiful features. She was just a pretty young lady. Then there was her living situation. Nobody made any mistakes about it - she was a slave. Like all the others, she was not a free person; nor did she entertain hopes of freedom. She would always be the property of a white person. However, she could accompany her owners and interact with a number of whites. Her living situation, as far as they could see, was so much freer than theirs, that they all longed for that type arrangement. But, the singular trait that they all loved about her is that she treated every slave that she saw like she or he was her sister or brother. This girl truly loved her darker relatives and fellow slaves. She identified 100% with them. Nobody ever really was concerned about how she felt about her white relatives and the people in town. Everyone simply assumed that she loved them too.

Maybe she kept her feelings about them to herself. Maybe she didn't need to show them overtly. The truth was, and she kept it to herself, she absolutely loathed them, with a hatred so strong that she would cry herself to sleep every night, praying that the Lord would forgive her because of this one sin. No matter how she rationalized it, it was still a sin to hate the oppressor. If nothing else, Plumpsie had become a survivor. She was not frail, or timid or weak, as everyone believed. If the opportunity presented itself, there would be no doubting of her inner strength and courage.

When they returned to the Rogers', the very first thing Master Charles wanted to do was take a bath. Since the evening temperature had not settled to its usual level, the air was still heavy, muggy, hot and musty. Charles had Plumpsie to draw him a cool bath. He handed her some perfumed beads of soap from his carrying case. She never could understand why white men used such perfumes. To her, they smelled sweeter than the ones the women used; she didn't like women's colognes and their perfumes either. Master Charles took off every stitch of clothing he wore, right there in front of the girl. She had to sit on the foot stool, waiting for each garment, and then take them back to his bedroom. As soon as she returned to the bath house, he remembered that he left his briefcase in his riding coach. That case contained a number of important papers. They were so important that if they fell into anyone's hands, including either of his parents, he would suffer great embarrassment. At once he jumped to his feet from the cool comfort of the tub and was about to rush out to the coach dripping wet and wearing not a stitch.

"Why, Master Charles, it's still daylight out", Plumpsie reminded, before she took her seat on the stool. "Please sir, don't go out like that. For heaven's sake, please put something on." She had lost the embarrassment for herself of white folk's nudity. Actually, she never remembered having any of that, or shame either, for them. Of course, even looking upon a nude man, the sight stirred no emotion in her. His genitals, as far as she was concerned, were as natural, and as insignificant a part of him as his neck or arm, or any other part of the man.

"Oh yes, Plumpsie, you all are quite right. How foolish of me. Ah don't know what Ah was thinking", he drawled, slinking back into the tub. "Ah need you all to do me a favor, Plumpsie, dear. Can you all do your lawd and master a favor?"

"I can do anything for you, Master Charles."

Her response was more than the answer he wanted. It displayed the right attitude as well, and for the Southern aristocracy, slaves had to always display the proper attitude. As Plumpsie had learned, it wasn't just slaves who had to display the proper attitude. Every person, white, black, freedman or slave, who was not a member of the Southern aristocracy, the ruling class, had to display the proper attitude. Any man who needed blessings from someone like Reverend Rogers, or Master Brookshire soon found that by conducting personal or even mercantile business was a risky business without the proper 'good' graces.

"All 'rat' child, that is exactly what your lawd and master wants to hear", he continued, pulling her close to him. "Your lawd and master left a valise near the inside seat on the 'flaw' of the coach. It is composed of a dark brown coloring with black markings. On it you will see the initials C. E. R. in capitol letters. Please go to the coach and bring that valise back to me."

"As always, Plumpsie wishes to please her lord and master, but Master Charles, I cain't read, and I dudn't have the slightest idea what a valise might be."

"All 'rat', child. It looks like a small suitcase. Now do you all understand?"

"I understands exactly Master Charles. But as you know, the Master Reverend Rogers got his servants, and you got your servants back there in the carriage house. They won't let me near that coach and well they should not."

"Damn black nitwit", he muttered under his breath. That he lowered his voice was of no consequence. Plumpsie's hearing ability was exceptional. She heard and understood exactly what he said. Now he yelled toward the carriage house. "Hey you all men out there. Ah am sending a little darkie, a pickaninny out to retrieve something from the coach. Be sure to do exactly as she asks. Now git to gitting."

His voice carried well when he wanted it to. They were waiting for her. Though daylight barely yet remained, the trees surrounding the carriage house created the effect of darkness with the deep shading. There, she could not see, so the slaves led her by hand. Plumpsie was coming of age, but she didn't yet feel comfortable touching a man in the loneliness of the carriage house. Therefore, she asked that the candles be lit. Since a number of female slaves, including Lucy who was assigned to the Rogers' kitchen, had 'stolen' away to the carriage house, they were reluctant to turn on a single candle. She reminded them of the orders from her master and at once six different candles were ignited all about the large ground level room. She could easily see the ante rooms and the loft, fully encircling on the upper level. The smell was like that which occasionally emanated from the bedroom of Reverend and Mrs. Rogers. If there was a difference it was not due to subtlety. The acute smell of sexual activity lit up the room in a manner other than by candlelight, or any other light, that what they were doing would have been obvious and it was. As the candles shone more brightly, it also became obvious why they didn't want them lit.

As with most slaves, Plumpsie's first orientation into the sex act was by visualization. This experience was so different than that accorded by whites, who were lectured on the aspects of human sexuality. Slave children, poor whites, and even the aristocracy had been exposed to various animals and therefore, they all had a general idea. Plumpsie stopped and looked at two couples who were 'making out' just underneath the coach. She knew them both. She also knew the others, but spoke not a word to anybody. Charles' valet, who also attracted a slave from a nearby plantation, actually used the top of the coach with his favor. Plumpsie wondered how that slave, a woman she had seen a number of times, had been able to get away, this far from her master's house. Even more, she wondered why she would risk the severe beating she was likely to suffer if her absence were to be discovered.

The valise was exactly where Master Charles remembered leaving it. As she pulled it by its straps, it opened from the top, exposing one sheet of paper, which fell to the floor. As she lifted it she couldn't help but notice the letters, the words, and each phrase and sentence. It was on letterhead parchment with Charles' complete name, and home address. It noted that the business of his company was trade in fine coaches, household goods, and rare gifts from Europe, the Far East, New York and Boston. She looked at it closely and tried to read the printed document that was on it, at the bottom of which bore the printed names and signatures of Master Brookshire and Charles. This was the wording on the paper:

> Uriah Brookshire agrees to enter into solemn contract this twenty-third day of May, 1858, in Lauderdale County, Mississippi, with Jacob C. Fairfax, of DeCalb County, Georgia to deliver one Negro boy slave, an eleven year old, well bred, high performing and mannerable Negro, to Mr. Fairfax' plantation.
> The name of said Negro slave boy is Esau Brookshire, soon to be

> known as Esau Fairfax.
> Jacob C. Fairfax agrees to deliver to Uriah Brookshire, as fair market value, in exchange, three female slaves. Their names being Jezebel Fairfax, soon to be Brookshire, a highly fecund, sixteen year old mulatto; Lula Belle Fairfax, soon to be Brookshire, a fourteen year old octoroon, soon to be fecund, with perfect teeth; and Zula Mae Bee Fairfax, soon to be Brookshire, a thirteen year old high yellow Creole Negress, with high cheek bones and green eyes.
> Charles E. Rogers, who acts as agent for both Messers Fairfax and Brookshire, shall be remunerated his usual and customary fee for this transaction.

Plumpsie was a smart girl, maybe even too smart for her own good, but then again, maybe not. She had learned so much secretly, but of all the things she had learned, nobody ever taught her to read. That was something she learned to do herself. The greater lesson, much greater than the gift of reading, she had learned, was that she could tell no one, not a single soul, that she knew. This had been forbidden of slaves, and now she saw why.

For the moment, everything was crystal clear. That document explained why Charles and Master Brookshire had stopped at the pig sty and later at the stables to look at Esau. The master had made a deal to transport him to Georgia in exchange for three female slaves. They would work, but their primary need was to ensure that male slaves had more reasons not to risk running away and to produce more slaves for Master Brookshire.

That was just one of many opportunities that confronted Plumpsie where she would have to decide whether to help a fellow slave. The document ended with the understanding that one year following the transaction of this business, both parties, and the agent would destroy their copies. There was also a line for the signature of Jacob Fairfax. In another compartment of the valise, which Plumpsie saw, were two more identical copies of the document.

Plumpsie had heard the rumors about the Underground Railroad. She knew she had to get word to them but she didn't have any idea how. As she hurried back to the bathing house, just off the rear pantry, she wondered, and wondered what would be necessary to do. How could she get word to someone who could help? Who would help? Who could be trusted?

"Did you look inside that bag, you little pickaninny?" Charles demanded of her, even before her foot had reached the floor on her first step into the bathing chamber.

That form of address, like most others to which she and all slaves had to endure and respond was the reference for which she, and all slaves had learned, by necessity, to perform their most accomplished acting. Like all black people, slave or free, she hated the term and was gradually developing a strong hatred to all who used it. Yet, she always answered as if she not only loved the reference, but adored the person using it.

"Why, Master Charles, you is the man I obeys the strongest and the fastest", she answered, masking her voice in a nasal singsong effect. He didn't even catch on. "You knows what, Master Charles, I knows we ain't suppose to read, but I just prays, I jis gits down on my knees and I prays that the Good Lord, he allows Master Charles to teach this here darkie how to read books. I certainly does. But then again, I knows it be a sin for me to learns how to read and all whatnot, so I's accepts that fact and keeps my old ignorant self to myself. And I bees happy wif dat, Master Charles."

"You all had better be happy with it. The main thing you all have got to remember, Nigra, is that God never intended for you all to read. Now, fetch me that towel over there and then git your black ass into the house! Ah'm sure Momma got something like some chores for you all to do."

The night was still young. Yet due to all that she had taken part in, Mrs. Rogers was somewhat more tired than usual. As a rule, anytime that she was away from the house was a time that her needs for attention and service were greater. This day was no exception. She waited for Plumpsie to complete her work with Master Charles before she made any effort to prepare for the evening. As Plumpsie helped her remove her clothing, she noticed that Mrs. Rogers wore no under-drawers. Plumpsie would not have made a big deal of it, but Mrs. Rogers explained that the day had been miserably hot, and she preferred to go without them. She cautioned Plumpsie that it would be their little secret. Not even her husband, was to know.

Plumpsie had to heat water in the heavy pots on the hearth, and deliver it to her bedroom. Then, as soon as she helped Mrs. Rogers out of her clothing, she had to retrieve more very hot to warm water when all the various pots would create the perfect temperature for her. The wash and bathing linens in place, she dampened, rang out, and gave her each towel. She reapplied soap, as ordered and then helped Mrs. Rogers to wash her buttocks, back, and other difficult to reach areas.

"Ah just don't know what Ah'd do without you all, Plumpsie. Of all Master Reverend's slaves, it is you all Ah trust the most."

"And I is so glad you holds me in such esteem, Mrs. Rogers. I sho' is. Now I goes out and empties this water."

Plumpsie knew that her grandmother liked to sit on the edge of the big chair after she had taken her nightly ablution. It was during that fifteen or twenty minute period that she never said anything to anybody, unless Reverend Rogers happened to come into the room. However, he had learned not to enter their bedroom on these occasions. Plumpsie knew she had a little time. She needed someone she could trust to get a message to Old Fedderson, and Aunt Sapphire. She also knew that if she failed, and were found out, it would certainly mean the gravest punishment she could face. Her very own father would rip off every garment on her back, tie her to a stake in the public square and beat her, beat her, and beat her with a belt, then finish with a bullwhip. Finally, he would beat his own daughter some more with a horsewhip, opening up wounds all over her until she could breathe no more. Then he would continue inflicting more wounds onto her already dead corpse. All slaves, from all plantations, near and far would be summoned to view the spectacle. She knew what would happen if she were to try to save her cousin and fail. Plumpsie knew she didn't have time to think too long. In the end, she simply decided what she needed to do as she would have wanted done for her, were she in his shoes. She tried to tell herself that she didn't care about the risks. But she did care. In the final analysis, she had to risk her life. She had to try it anyway.

Plumpsie had seen it herself. Somehow, she always feared that that fate would befall her, just as it had happened to many a slave who ran away or helped another run away. The plan formed quickly in her mind. More than anything she had ever wanted, she wanted this to succeed. She would use none other than Louella,, the slave from a plantation three miles North, following the main road. Her plantation was within two miles of the Brookshire estate. She would have to gain her confidence, convincing her to get word to her relatives at Brookshire. Louella had been in the carriage house only an hour earlier. Plumpsie hoped to intercept her before she attempted to return to the estate owned by Farmer McGuire. Farmer McGuire had a reputation as the harshest slave owner in the state of Mississippi. (Of course this meant that he was the harshest slave owner in the country, if the rumor was true.)

Plumpsie was in luck. Louella was rearranging her clothing as she carefully surveyed a path leading from the Rogers' carriage house. She thought the path was clear. To her amazement, just as she jumped from the rear window Plumpsie was waiting for her. She grabbed the major arm of the older, stronger woman then quickly covered her mouth so that she could not yell out. In matters of human confrontations, struggles where life or death hang in the balance, one can often attain strength never before realized. Such was now the case with Plumpsie, as Louella felt overpowered. At first she thought it was Josie, a white woman in the employ of the Rogers'. Josie, it seems, loved having sex with black men, and would attack any slave who tried to involve herself with one of the Rogers' slaves. Plumpsie's pink skin showed in a pale hue underneath the now clear moon light.

"Shut your mouth, Louella. It's me, girl, Plumpsie."

Louella was startled, and even more afraid. Her heart must have raced at breakneck speed, because she felt the strength of the person, who she thought was white, upon her. She knew that anybody who would tackle her like that in the pale moonlight of early evening had had to be someone who would follow that with a beating. Her heart began to accelerate less as she realized it was indeed Plumpsie. "Why Plumpsie, Girl whut you doin' out chere this time o' night? Why I knows Ole Master Rogers go beat your butt sho nuff."

"Louella, don't you worry bout my butt. It's your butt, you just better worry bout."

"Why I knows it. Soon as I saw your lil' half white self, comin out, into the carriage house, I tells myself this go be a whole heap o' trouble. I tells myself, this here lil' half white heifer, she go up and tell my master."

"So that's what it is, Louella? You don't want me to up and tell your Master? Well, you listen here. If you don't do exactly as I tell you, then you ain't never go have to worry bout' your master beating you again. I promise you that." It was a promise Plumpsie certainly couldn't keep. However, she knew that Louella could be swayed. Most of all, she knew that Louella, like almost any slave, was in dire fear of a beating to be administered for leaving your quarters without permission. Slave masters saved their worst floggings of their human property for that offense. Such punishments never ended in death, but many a slave so wished. "Louella, I know you got to git back to the McGuire Farm quick, so I won't keep you much longer. Tell me, who on that farm can you trust to deliver a message to Ole Fedderson and Aunt Sapphire, early, fore the morn?"

Louella thought for a few seconds. Of course she could get the message to the Brookshire slaves, but she worried whether even with Plumpsie's urgency, that it could be delivered with the utmost haste and security. She knew the exact person to trust with such a responsibility. She decided on Barabbas. He would be the nearest to perfection for the task. Farmer McGuire purchased milk, feed and fertilizer from Master Brookshire. Every morning Barabbas hitched up the mule team and loaded the empty milk barrels to deliver there. He had to complete this job well before dawn. "Barabbas, he be the one. I can git Barabbas to do this for me."

"I know that old coot. Is he reliable? What I mean is this. Can you trust the old coot with your life? Your very life?"

"I can make him reliable."

"Now, Louella, just how do you aim to do that?"

"Don't you worry none bout that. I takes care o' that part. Now whut you wants me to tell him?"

She raised up on her toes and looked Louella eye to eye. Plumpsie had never been so physically close to anyone before. The whole scene to her was actually frightening. Yet, it was educational, in a transitional sort of way. She felt a keen sense of power, almost enlightenment because she knew instinctively that Louella feared more than just the potential for grave corporal punishment. Plumpsie's effect was like that of an angel, an angel that could evoke fear, as well as faith. It was as if Louella's very soul would be at risk if she didn't obey Plumpsie. To that time, these two had seen each other many times. They knew of each other, but they didn't know each other. Perhaps the single most important factor that won Louella over was trust. She could trust Plumpsie. It was interesting that Mrs. Rogers, her husband the Reverend, and her son, Charles also trusted Plumpsie. Was she a good actor, or did she simply have that type personality? As far as Louella was concerned, it was genuine trustworthiness, straight from the heart.

"Okay Louella, here it is. You tell Ole Barabbas to git this message to Ole Fedderson and to Aunt Sapphire. Tell them that Master Charles is a comin'. He is a comin' to git young Lil Esau. Master Brookshire, he go send him to Alabammy. He go trade young Lil Esau for three women slaves. Tell them they knows what to do."

"That be all, Miss Plumpsie?"

"That be all, Louella. Now, are you sure Ole Barabbas is reliable enough to remember all this and deliver the message?"

"I makes sure he be. I will takes care o my part!"

When Plumpsie returned to the house, Mrs. Rogers was asleep, sitting just as she was when Plumpsie left. By the time she awoke, Plumpsie had emptied and cleaned the wash basins and dressed her in her night gown. Plumpsie was tying her hair back when she awoke, briefly. Mrs. Rogers said nothing. The pampering she received from Plumpsie was her due in life. As was her job, the young slave girl was permitted to perform her tasks, to take good care of Mrs. Rogers.

Nobody knows how Louella could cover the three miles from the Rogers' house, through the center of town, and back to the McGuire farm so furtively through the night as she did. For a slave who could almost past for white to accomplish such a fear provoking endeavor was beyond the comprehension of most people. But every time Louella had done it, it had become all the more easy for her. Even when her consort would try to accompany her for some protection, she would decline the offer. On that night she was back to the slave quarters in time to attain her usual due sleep. This night, on the other hand was to be different due to her pledge to Plumpsie. Sleep would not elude her so much as she eluded sleep.

Barabbas awoke at his customary time, two and one-half hours before dawn; hc washed, as was customary, then pulled together his team of mules and hitch. As he led them out, she was there to greet him. Even more strange, she looked well rested, full of pep, vigor, and energy.

Although he was old enough to be her father, Barabbas had always wanted to make love to Louella. Through the years, he had fathered a number of children. Now, the word about the McGuire farm was that he could no longer satisfy a woman. For that reason, Louella had steered clear of him, as far as a romantic liaison was concerned. But now, the need for direct action was different. Far and wide everyone knew of the twins Esau and Isaac. There was not a soul in the entire states of Mississippi, Alabama, Louisiana and Georgia that had not heard of Will and Cassie, particularly Cassie. There was no need to exaggerate her story either. As a fitting heritage, it seemed that every slave throughout the South had developed a deep affection for the twins. This sentiment was so strong that any slave would have done anything, including sacrificing his or her own life to prevent anything that could separate or bring harm to either. It followed that if they were separated, then the breakup should not involve transfer through the slave trade to another plantation, even if it were local. The time had come for the Brookshire Plantation to be visited by a group of people, black and white, who were among the bravest that ever lived. The group was known as the Underground Railroad.

"Why, what you want Ole Barabbas to do, out here on this here fine morning, and you ain't got a thang in the whole wide world to do?" Due to his past as a primary favorite of Farmer McGuire, as Will had been for Master Brookshire, Barabbas still tried to flirt. Immediately Louella knew that the things she had heard, about his interest in her as a sexual partner had been true.

She pulled and tugged at the bridle of the mules to get him to stop the wagon. Since she didn't want to awaken anyone in Farmer McGuire's house, or to alarm any slaves, she didn't yell 'whoa' to stop the team. She jumped up to the side, then hoisted herself to sit beside him, exposing underslip, underpants and dark vibrant skin from her ankles to her sandaled foot on her right leg, and from her knee to her foot on the left leg. "Barabbas, you gots to git a message to Ole Fedderson and Aunt Sapphire. Can you do that for me?"

"Well now that all depend."

"Good. That be real good. Now you listens here Barabbas. This here ain't no time to be all depending. This be time for you to do zactly as I tells you."

"I's listnin'."

"Good, when you arrives at the Brookshire Plantation, fore you does your chores, you gits to Ole Fedderson, and Aunt Sapphire. You does that first thang, you hear?"

"Barabbas, he sho nuff hear."

"You tells them both, that Master Charles be coming there early. You tells them he comin to fetch the twin boy, Cassie's son. He go take young Esau to a plantation over in Alabammy. That be all you gots to say.

"Barabbas be sho to gives them that message."

She jumped down and headed away, exposing drawers up to her thighs. Then she turned. "I gives you your reward tonight, Barabbas. You just does what your job is to do." She then headed back to her quarters, very quietly. Burning inside that she had done her part to prevent the sale of Esau, she couldn't get any sleep. It didn't matter. Louella was that way. She would've given up hundreds of nights of sleep if it meant that one slave could be freed. Truth be known, she would have given her life.

"Barabbas give you his word, he go do his job, cain't you see that young woman?" he declared to himself, pulling the team away from the farm. "Old Barabbas, he a gone done this and she ain't got to give no reward or nothing to Old Barabbas. She ain't got to give him nothing. This a matter of honor. This be all bout' pride."

Chapter V - Ham Bone

[Between that narration and our next visit we were away for a week. By then, word of my grandfather's story had spread beyond the community. At various times, there were seventeen more boys in our party. Looking back, I figure that he knew the audience would expand. As soon as we were settled, a number of stomachs would literally squeak from hunger. At least two were so loud that immediate laughter was evoked. He asked me to run into the kitchen and return with assorted crackers, cheddar and longhorn cheeses, hog head cheese, Braunschweiger, and iced cups with two large pictures of fresh squeezed/prepared lemonade. There was also another real treat, three thirty-two ounce bottles of his favorite drink, Double-Cola. My grandfather was ready for us. Strangely, we had lost not one from the original group.

Since the narration had been communicated from its inception to newcomers, Big Daddy never had to return to the central theme. It seemed somewhat strange that the concept was so easily picked up. Some among us might have heard distant variations from somewhere else. But, it seemed like my grandfather had lived it. Indeed, he might have, and this was not due to his having grown up in Mississippi. It was in his blood. He was talking about none too distant relatives. In a way, it seemed so sad because he would never see many of them, ever again. However easy it might have been, nobody was willing to speculate on how the narration might have progressed. We wanted to hear it directly from him, and every single word.]

Please pass me my guitar.

Oh Freedom. Oh ohhhh oh freedom.
Oh Freedom, over me, mee me.

And before I be a slave
I be buried in my grave, and go home
To my God, and be free.

Oh Freedom. Oh ohhhh oh freedom
Oh Freedom, all over me, meee me.

And before we be your slaves
We be buried in our graves, and go home
To our God, and be free eee free.

[Sing us another one, Brother Moore. Please sing us one more song before you begin the Narration. You know what? It was unanimous. You know something else. Big Daddy knew my friends would ask for one more song, and he was ready. He was always ready. The next song was among my favorites, 'Shall We gather at the River'.]

Barabbas delivered his message to Old Fedderson and Aunt Sapphire just as he had promised. Like so many slaves, Barabbas had heard of the Underground Railroad. However, he had not known of any activity in this area to assist runaways. Barabbas didn't have much faith in too much of anything. That was his nature. He knew of the role that his namesake had played from The Bible. For him the whole concept seemed unbelievable. It just didn't add up that anyone who shared his name would want someone else to suffer for his wrongdoing. Likewise, considering the plight of slaves in America, he didn't believe much of what was taught him about The Bible, especially those matters dealing with slaves' enjoyment of their plight. On the way to the farm, he seemed more self assured than he ever had. That little slave boy, carried the hopes and aspirations of Barabbas and those working to free him. If successful, he would carry the hopes, dreams, and aspirations of all the others as well.

They would all find inspiration and a stronger will due to his freedom. Barabbas' sense of relief and well being was as deep as it was strong. It was as if he opened his very soul on that trip back to the McGuire Farm. When his soul opened, it was as if the actual Spirit of Almighty God entered and proclaimed:

You have done exceedingly well, my son.
I am pleased with your work.
You will not be disappointed.

It is true. Barabbas thought he heard those exact words. From that day, until the last day of his life, he recited those words.

Back at Brookshire, Aunt Sapphire and Old Fedderson wasted no time. They went to the rear of the barn and awoke Esau. During the commotion, Isaac was awakened too. In fear, he feigned a return to sleep. It was all so quick. So fast. Esau had no time to be afraid. Out back, they removed his clothing, bathed him in fresh water, and applied colognes and deodorants that they had taken from the mansion. Those items still would not be missed. Then they put fresh clothing onto the boy.

Ham Bone, Ham Bone, where you been?
Round Dat Whirl and I'm gwine again.

Ham Bone, Ham Bone, whut you go do?
Run one due East, and come back two.

Ham Bone, Ham Bone whut you do nex?
Run one up North and Come Back three.

Ham Bone, Ham Bone where you been?

[Many of us stood right up in the floor and did the hambone. I think my brother, Raymond, was the best. That's something that had been in our culture for years, even centuries, if not eons, and we never knew the origins. Slaves simply brought it over from Africa. We never knew it had served as a secret code to organize flights to freedom, and eventually slave revolts. Its most effective use was in communal dance and just plain old communication.]

Immediately after Old Fedderson and Aunt Sapphire did the hambone, they gathered twenty-three field hands who could run like the wind. They rubbed the clothes that Esau had worn, all over their garments. With that scent very fresh these field hands ran a circular route stretching two point five miles East of Brookshire, and three point six miles North. Then they continued two point four miles West, and finally finished three point six miles due East of home. The runners were stationed at strategic points so that no one had to cover a distance of more than four miles round trip.

The plan was to give the hunting dogs the most dogged, unconventional quest for a run-away that the state of Mississippi had ever witnessed. Aunt Sapphire and Old Fedderson's plan was that they would absolutely run in all directions but that not one could get onto the trail of the little boy slave.

[Okay. I will commence to tell you boys about the
hambone. Slaves had a number of unique ways to
communicate. Each way involved a secret code.
In the Mother Land, Africans had developed a rather
intricate means to communicate with one another. They
used terminology peculiar to their native languages.
The most intricate and effective means was the drum.
Drumming became the primary means of planning escapes,
planning to assist slaves in their attempts for freedom,
and simply to beat out rhythms for the sake of dance.
Eventually, through an act of betrayal, a house slave
told his master about the significance of using the drum.
All the drums had to be destroyed. Anyone caught using a
drum incurred the most wretched of all penalties. He was
burned alive. This penalty was actually initiated in the
State of New York, before slavery ended there. However,
by then, all slave masters used it in the South by 1850.

The slaves were ingenious. They commenced to solving

that problem and it was remedied in no time. The slave turned to making the steel used to fashion horseshoes, and carved that steel into metal taps that could be fitted onto their shoes without any nailing. Then they commenced dancing out their communication rhythms to the sounds of the tapping. Again they were betrayed to the master, and tapping, or tap dancing was outlawed.

This just served to test the creativity of slaves all the more. Freedom was just too important a cause for the slave to accept defeat. Two new forms of communication were used to express their plans and goals through coded messages. These involved using the hambone, whereby the slave would beat out the tapping and drumming messages on his chest, head, mouth, knees and feet. The words one used to sing out his message in a rapping beat were meaningless. The other slaves, ever rapt listeners, learned to ignore the words and concentrate on the cadence and words formed via the beats. This form of communication was used that morning to plan Esau's escape. One other form of secret communication involved singing 'Spiritual' music. When the slave began singing about praying, heaven, and being saved, those few who commenced singing had no concern about those words. The 'Spirituals', to a song, carried hidden meaning that permitted many an escape to succeed.

There was one more language pattern that the slaves used and its base was the English language. So effective were the slaves that the white man never knew what was going on. I even hear it used to this very day by young black people here in East. St. Louis and across the river in that cesspool of slave trade, St. Louis, Missouri. We can get to all that later. You all probably know it better than I do. William J. Moore]

By the time Master Brookshire and his family were awake, dressed and ready to attend to their affairs, they had no awareness that a slave had escaped.

To ensure that the news of the escape would not be betrayed too early by one of the favorites of the master, Aunt Sapphire decided to tell it herself, with some help from her partner in 'crime', Old Fedderson. He had actually been awake since Barabbas had brought the urgent call to action. Getting on in their years, he and Aunt Sapphire certainly needed their sleep. Be that as it was, they were not the least bit interested in catching up on it. As they saw things, they would have an eternity to sleep, before too long. "Well, if that ole woman don't look 'lack' a whole mess o God's chillens upset and whut not, then we is all in a whole mess o' trouble. Ya'll go out there and help your Ainny Sapphire. Go on now, all ya'll chillens. Gwine. Git to gittin."

Old Fedderson was yelling at the top of his lungs. He just didn't want the young people near him to fear. They knew what to do without even hearing his instructions. Old Fedderson was making sure that the master and his family would hear his rumblings.

At that, about nineteen of the young people, men, boys, and girls began to run toward her as she returned up the main trail. These were some of the same young men among whom they had enjoined to assist the escape earlier. The beat of Old Fedderson in his hambone routine was clear, crystal clear, still in their minds. Oh yes. They were tired too. But at that point they were putting on a new show for Master Brookshire, his sons, the overseer and the working crew, not to mention the rest of the slaves. There were field and house slaves looking on, and Aunt Sapphire and Old Fedderson simply didn't want them all to know. With each young man carrying a piece of the garment Esau had worn, they had scattered a trail for miles through the woods, in all directions. They had covered the town and main roads too. Before dawn, they had returned, dipped in the lake themselves to remove whatever scents they might have carried. Now they had come from their quarters, as if they had slept all night.

"Ya'll git your filthy hands off me. Where de master? I says, where the master be?" What a natural actress. Aunt Sapphire was pulling it off. Even the slaves who had helped began to wonder whether they had been in a dream.

"Why Ainny Sapphire, here is your lawd and master. Ah am rat here." He still had no inkling what was going on. If he and the others had looked closely into the eyes of the slaves, they would have discovered quite easily that few wore the contented, rested eyelids of people who had had a full nights sleep.

"I jis go sits right here on this here stump of a log by the side of the road, Master, cause I is a heap upset." She struggled and struggled to catch her breath. Aunt Sapphire was a physically fit woman. She didn't need to go through all this, but she had to make it look convincing. She had to make it look as if she would have given her life on behalf of the master. Of course every slave now realized what was up.

"Make way, let her sit. Cain't you all see the poor old woman is about to faint or just die. You all rest there. Somebody get her some water."

"Thank you Master Brookshire. You is such a decent, God-fearing man and all. Lord go sho nuff bless and keep you." She kept huffing and puffing. To make it really convincing, she even threw in a few wheezes.

Usually, Master Brookshire was most impatient, not just with his slaves, but with everyone else. It escaped no one's notice that for the moment, he was most gracious, uncharacteristically patient with Aunt

Sapphire.

"Here, Ainny Sapphire, you all just let this here cool water roll down your throat. Now you all just take your time and tell me all about why you all come running up the Main road lack you all been all the way to Tennessee and back."

"Well, Master Brookshire, you knows Aunt Sapphire be a God fearin' woman. You knows Ainny Sapphire, she don't like no ugly, cause God don't like no ugly. That's whut Ole Fedderson be sayin on Sunday mornings. Ole Fedderson, he be sayin it come from The Good Book." She continued to pant, wheeze, pant, huff and gasp for more and more air as she related her story.

"That be right, Ainny. Ah am glad to hear Ole Fedderson is doing the right thing too. Please now, continue on Ainny Sapphire. He squatted in front of her, reassuring her that everything was alright, that she should feel comfortable to continue.

Now she panted more, heaved, and coughed, struggling all the more to catch her breath. By now, every slave on the plantation, every worker, and every person who had business on the Brookshire Farm was there. They encircled the brave black woman as she finally appeared to regain her composure and continued speaking. "It done be the boy, Esau, Master Brookshire. He done up and scaped. He just upped and run away", she cried, her voice quivering as she related what had happened. No slave had ever escaped from the Brookshire Plantation and lived to tell about it. Mr. Brookshire's punishment, that he personally rendered to runaway slaves invoked such fear that for the past seventeen years, nobody had dared to even try it. "I bees feared for that lil ole boy, Master Brookshire. I bees most feared for him. He ain't got no call to run off and scape lak dat. That be why I jis be runnin after that lil ole boy. That be why I wants to bring him back, bring him back fore anybody know even whut be happenin."

Right away, before anybody could get a thought out, before anybody could get the first word of a thought out, before anybody could get the first letter of the first word of a thought out, Master Brookshire's face turned beet red. Why it was as red as the hot fire. His eyes changed too, right there, in front of everybody. Those eyes seemed to form into a yellow ball. Somehow, he knew how to continue showing care and comfort to Aunt Sapphire, while at the same time he displayed his anger to the extreme about the escape. No sooner, it seemed, had those words come from Aunt Sapphire's mouth, did the hired crew jump into action. The assistant foreman scurried to the stables to saddle work horses and the day laborers went to the dog runs. Without even so much as being directed they knew what to do. They unleashed those dogs. They were in the slave house at the extreme rear of the plantation, sniffing the place where Esau slept, and the foot stool on which he sat the night before for his evening grub.

"You all must be very tired, Ainny Sapphire, and Ah want you all to know that your master does appreciate the effort you all made to do the right thing. Now you all go git some rest. You all can start your work at ten o'clock sharp." Brookshire was respectful to her due to his belief that his rules were supported by Aunt Sapphire. It was no show that he was putting on.

Aunt Sapphire, on the other hand, played out the full routine as if she were in a traveling minstrel show. However, she didn't want to hold him too long. If a rain came, the many trails the dogs would follow could be lost. "I be mighty obliged to you Master Brookshire, and everything. But, if it be all the same to you, there be a whole heap of work to be done on this here farm. I needs to work."

"Well, you all decide what is best for you all."

The boy was well hidden. Aunt Sapphire, for her part, didn't need to return to the field. She really was very, very tired. Her task, as she saw it, was among the slaves. It was to ensure that the will and spirit of nary a one would be broken. Many had had a part in the concerted effort to hide the lad. In just a few short hours everything would be completed. Their task was to simply hold on. There was a prize, and they all needed to keep their eyes on the prize.

There is a place for me,
That's where I be goin to.
All God's people can come and see me,
Cause it's good for me and you.

Cousin Esau be on his way.
See him there tomorrow noon.
If we all do what must be done,
We will surely see him soon.

Every slave on the plantation beat out that rhythm to the words with a hambone. Some didn't know the interpretation word for word, but they all understood what it meant.

Within minutes the hunting party was gone, fast on the trails that so many running slaves had left. The dogs were excited and the start was so quick after Aunt Sapphire's return that the Brookshire family and the whole lot of the workers were sure they would catch him and those who had helped.

Three hours later, each dog had returned, leading a different tandem back to the exact spot where they had begun. It was only after the last group, led by Master Brookshire's oldest son returned, and realized what had happened. The escaped slave was the very boy who was to be sold in exchange for a cash sum and three female slaves. His father had been betrayed. Dejected and angry, the master decided that he would get to the bottom of this before the day was over.

Shortly after eight that same morning, Charles Rogers appeared at the front gate. He was stopped there. Word travels fast. Word about an escaped slave travels faster. Word about a slave, escaped from the Brookshire Plantation would travel faster than anywhere. Its reputation was that no slave ever escaped and lived to tell about it. Charles knew. He also knew that Master Brookshire would suspect everyone, even him. When he insisted on passage, exclaiming that he knew about the escape, and that he had information that would be vital to the master, they let him through. He had his driver to deliver the coach all the way to the central house, the primary mansion, the official residence of the Brookshire family. He had to load some materiel that Master Brookshire had earmarked for the militia in Tennessee and for pro-slavery factions in St. Louis, Missouri. In addition to his many functions, Charles was also a gunrunner.

The two men whispered as the slaves loaded the undercarriage to conceal the weapons. What a pity. A pity on both of them. Neither Charles nor Master Brookshire realized that one of the narrow boxes contained a living, breathing human being. It was none other than the lad, Esau.

Now would begin the most dangerous aspect of his journey. Indeed, each leg would be fraught with danger. He had been told to stay put. He had been told to utter not a sound. Simply put, he was ordered to stay put, for as long as he could, longer than a human being could possibly endure. He faced a long and arduous journey and he had to be strong. This would take him away from his loved ones, his twin and all that he knew as family. This would be the most difficult journey that anyone would have to endure. Aunt Sapphire, Old Fedderson, and an aunt of his, Brownie Rose schooled him well in those few minutes. To settle his nerves, Brownie Rose promised that they would all see each other again, and that it wouldn't be long.

In a way, this journey was like the ordeal that free Africans endured two hundred, one hundred, and maybe as few as fifty years earlier. The only difference was that they didn't have the pleasure of being seen off by loving family members. Aunt Sapphire and Old Fedderson recalled the accounts of parents, grandparents, aunts, uncles, cousins and friends describing the terror of being kidnapped, literally stolen from their land, to be chained and thrown into the hulls of ships. Their quarters were such that a pig sty would have been a big improvement. They could only hope that Esau, that one little boy who carried the hopes and aspirations of six generations of slaves would make it to freedom, and succeed.

Chapter VI - Freedom's Journey

So then, brethren, we are not children of the bondwoman, but of the free. Galatians, 4 - 31.

The slaves worked hard that day. They sang. They thought about Esau's success. Master Brookshire was so angry that if anyone had wanted to stick a thermometer into his mouth, he would have registered as a sick man. The slaves, working as they were, should have filled two purposes. The first is that by their singing and whistling, the master should have been happy that they seemed so happy. The second purpose was that the boy's escape had succeeded. They were most happy about that. Unfortunately for them, they were not getting through to the master. They might not have cared.

Master Brookshire had talked with Aunt Sapphire again. All she could remember, as the only 'admitted' eye witness, was that he was "in the company of one or two white gentlemens" as she put it. "Or was it three?"

When quitting time came that day, Master Brookshire ordered all work among the slaves and the crews to continue. Not one slave, house or field, no matter sick, with child, or near fainting, was even permitted to eat so much as a morsel of a piece of cornbread. Strange thing. Not one slave was hungry that night. Slavery did that kind of thing to a black man. Freedom, the thought of freedom reigned in their hearts. The effect of the mere thought of freedom, it was argued, could free one's mind from the needs of the body. In truth, the slaves didn't want to eat until the final good news of Esau's escape was reported. They didn't miss the food. Before then, they would not have known that they could have been so strong.

Fedderson's advice also served them well. He told them that Jesus spent forty days and forty nights in the wilderness, traumatized by Satan. He said that if the slaves wanted to be like Jesus, then they had to endure a full day without food. He prayed for them. When he finished praying, he got up announced that every person who stayed the fast would someday be reunited in heaven. Not that they needed that assurance, but it certainly didn't hurt.

That night there was a lot of praying at the Brookshire estate. First, Master Brookshire, all his family, Reverend and Mrs. Rogers, and many members of the church gathered there to pray for the capture of the escapee and his return. They prayed that he would be taught a grave lesson on his return, and that those who helped him would be lynched.

Meanwhile, the slaves prayed too. They asked God to deliver Esau to a safe house in Illinois, his destination, and that he would forever be out of harm's way. Following their prayers they sang, making up the words as they sang. These very words ushered the wagon with the boy through Mississippi, Tennessee and Kentucky, praying that he would reach Illinois Town, the primary and most well known destination for runaways. Most cities and towns

South of Illinois Town held strong pro-slavery sentiment. The common will of the slaves was that their singing and emotions would be strong, that the angels of mercy would protect the boy, and his escorts, fulfilling the destiny as manifest. Their joyous singing and celebration, which Old Fedderson described as the triumphal dancing described by David in First Chronicles, Chapter 15, only without the horns, and music leader, went this way:

One by one, we going to Jerusalem
One by one, we going to Jerusalem
We say one by one, we going to Jerusalem
and you be taking us there, You don't know it,
But you be taking us there.

The first one be going like a son of gun
The first one be going like a son of a gun
I say the first one be going like a son of a gun,
and you be just a going there too; Yes, you be just a going there too

First box top heaven it be loaded so full
I say the first box to heaven it be loaded so full
I say the first box to heaven it be loaded so full
And you can go to heaven too, some day; And you can go to heaven too.

Next box to heaven it be loaded full too
Say the next box to heaven it be loaded full too.
Say the next box to heaven it be loaded full too.
And you can be in one of them boxes too, oh yes;
And you be in one of them boxes too.

I be loaded in the next box too.
Oh yes, I be loaded in the next box too.
Say I be loaded in the next box too
Cause I can get to heaven too, oh yes.; Say I will get to heaven too.

The white horses, they go take me up there.
The six white horses they go take me up there.
Six big white horses they will take me up there.
And you can just hop on too, oh yes. I say you just be a hopping on too.

Children, don't be afraid to go to heaven.
I say don't you be afraid of going to heaven.
Children, God will take you by the hand.
Children of God, he will lead you to the land.
Then we can all be in God's heaven. Oh yes, we all be in God's heaven.

I'm gonna catch that train up to heaven.
I say I'm gonna catch the train up to heaven.

Don't you know, I done punched me a ticket.
I'm leaving this world of all the wicked.
Cause I be up in heaven too, some day. Cause I be up in heaven too.

As that evening wore on, Master Brookshire asked Ephesus Rogers to go and check on his slaves. He wanted to know exactly what they were doing. The presence of Ephesus did not influence the slaves one way or another. He just walked among them, paying attention to more how they looked, having been denied food. The slaves sang their song as they continued to add verse, harmony, rhythm and melodic music, building on the basic tonal concept all night. As he walked among the singing throngs, Ephesus' footfalls betrayed an affectation from the strong, driving force of meter. His body swayed to the music as he walked and felt the force of the slaves. He maintained that movement, totally influenced by the music's beat, as he walked throughout the slave gathering, finally returning to his prayer band. He reported that the slaves were indeed good 'nigras'. "All they seem to want to do is sing and dance about going up to heaven. They don't have their minds on that little slave boy one whit. If you all ask me, Ah'd say they believe that if they disassociate themselves from that escape, God won't hold them responsible. They are all very, very unhappy that that boy escaped."

Down through the next few years, to white people, and a number of blacks, that song was simply another ditty that slaves made up to amuse themselves. On many a hot day, toiling in the masters' fields throughout the South, and in areas up North where freedmen picked cotton for a lowly wage, such as Illinois, Missouri and Indiana, slaves and former slaves seemed to gain encouragement from their singing. That one began on the Brookshire Plantation and became rife through every glen, dale, cotton field, cotton processing yard, and farm yard from Mississippi, on up through Tennessee, Kentucky and Illinois. Then, like so many other 'Negro Spirituals' it traveled to Louisiana, Georgia, and Alabama. A few claimed to have sang the song in the Carolinas.

Soon every slave who understood the code of Negro Spiritual music and every freedman and white abolitionist who secreted through the Mississippi Trace from Natchez North knew exactly what was happening and the secret of the escape. When slave owners would eventually learn of what the real meaning was, the penalty for singing it became twenty lashes on the back of any black man, slave or free. Even white people were warned that 'good, God fearin' white folk would not take too kindly to hearing it from them either'.

Charles Rogers was carrying a load of weapons from the deep South to sympathizers in Illinois. The shipment was to reach, eventually, the militia in Tennessee, as well as Southern sympathizers in Illinois and Missouri. That was not the only secret that this Southern spy carried. The second secret, of course, was the one of which he had no idea. The slave boy, Esau, had been stowed in one of the crates. Charles, Master Brookshire, and the gun smuggling cabal were symbolically delivering him to 'heaven'.

In the box a ventilated air pocket had been formed and Esau was given a few items of food to nourish him on his way. Though young, and uninitiated, he knew exactly what was going on. He trusted Aunt Sapphire and Old Fedderson. They had reassured him that he had to go because this departure would be much better than his being sold into another family. They told him freedom was better even than heaven. They had him convinced that once he reached free country in Illinois, the network would have alerted friends of freedmen. If he could just hold on until then, he would have all his worries behind him. To ensure he maintained cooperation, they also told him they would try to get his twin out of Mississippi. Of course they knew that after this escape, Master Brookshire would see to it that preventative measures would be in place to make another escape attempt far more risky. As things were with Esau, he would have to hold out much less than he thought.

When Charles reached the Tennessee state line he was met by a group of men. They were on horseback. They seemed to know of his mission. The three strangers, all white, and all well dressed for horseback riding, looked as if they had been in the saddle a good while. Unbeknownst to Charles and his group, situated about thirty yards diagonally from them, in a thicket, was a coach and horses, pulling what was surely a heavy load. The men spoke some words to Charles. Those men with the stranger, could neither hear nor understand what was said. What Charles believed is that he had come upon fellow spies from Southern states. Their accents and manner of speech gave them away as Alabamians and Georgians. They warned Charles that the area in which he was headed had recently become a haven for abolitionists and enemy agents. To ensure the safekeeping of his goods, he would best take off and head due West from that spot. This would take him to the 'Great River', their term for the 'Missouri-Mississippi'. Convinced they were truthful, he followed their advice. Playing it safe, Charles and his party watched them as they headed Southward, until they were out of sight.

Charles traveled about twenty miles more and darkness descended. They shot and cooked rabbit and quail, then bedded down in bedrolls and pallets from their workings.

As they slept, one man, crawling on the ground, so quiet, yet so efficient, made his way to the coach. He was among the party that had recommended this route to Charles. Deftly he opened the first crate from underneath the coach. Esau certainly knew what was going on now. But, just in case, he made no noises. Recalling the advice from Aunt Sapphire, he would not betray those stern words. He had no fear, however, as the man worked. One by one, each repeating rifle was removed. The men, from what Charles had thought was a spy party, had joined twelve others. The total, fifteen in all, formed a work line. Quietly and determinedly they passed along each gun. They refilled the crates with sand bags.

The second crate also had guns. However, there was human cargo as well. They knew there would be. Freed from the tight box, Esau knew exactly what to do. He moved furtively on the ground, crawling in the direction they showed. Without a word, as the circulation returned to his body, he retreated to the line and helped, ferrying the weapons from Charles' carriage. Then he would ferry the sandbags, as good as the rest of the bigger, stronger men. When their work was completed, they moved on, through the night, heading back across the Great River, going from there Northward. They didn't let sleep tempt them until they were miles and miles away from Charles.

That morning Charles and his fellow travelers were well on their way by the crack of dawn. By now, due to the detour, he was one hundred thirty miles from his destination, Cairo, Illinois. He had made a lucrative deal for the guns, and on delivery was to be handsomely rewarded. If all went well, they would arrive by midnight that very night. Of course, to make the time in that distance required changes of horses in two places along the way. The first of these towns was a place called Brains, in Arkansas. Northerners, and many Southerners wondered whether it got that name because they needed to attract people who were intelligent. More nearer the truth was a meat processing plant known for its hog brains. Said to be a delicacy, this part of the pig was the primary ingredient in their sausages, and also packaged for its singular consumption. There they rested briefly, and ordered fresh eggs, scrambled, of course, with hog brains. Ready to continue, the drivers rotated and they were on the way.

The next stop was Jericho. It was named after the city of Biblical fame. There, again they rested, changed horse team, and ate a light meal. It was their final stop in Arkansas. They wanted a steak for late lunch at the way station, but all they got was raccoon and opossum belly. This left them hoping for better fare at their evening stop.

On they traveled, headed North by Northeast, leaving a trail of dust in their wake. They worked that team of horses like there was no tomorrow. Though they worried about the horses, they had no concerns about Charles Rogers' wagon. Exquisite in every detail, it was also able to withstand rugged terrain and the worst of conditions.

Their next, and last stop before Cairo was to be Walnut Log, a sleepy community just South of the Kentucky state line. Due to the warning from the people they had met the evening earlier, and a warning Charles had received before he left Mississippi, they knew they had to unload their goods in Illinois, as soon as possible after entering the state. No matter what their personal needs, the payload required attention first. The reason for this was growing anti-slavery fervor in Southern Illinois. As recently as 1850, a bill was introduced in the state legislature to allow slavery in all areas of the state South of Springfield. It had only failed by two votes in the lower house, and therefore, didn't make it to the state senate, where it would have been likely to pass. As a testament to the growing sentiment for abolition, a number of towns had grown with recognition of the roles that blacks had played in the revolution. These included monuments to black militia men who had performed heroically in every war to that point. Charles, as a result, had been warned to get into the city, and get out as fast as he could. Usually he stayed around for awhile to buy and sale information, make other deals to deliver slaves, goods and just learn about the political situation from his usual associates. Now he could not do that.

Due to their hard riding, and Charles' determination, they did arrive in Cairo about 11: that night, Charles' noting in his diary. He had also entered his meeting the night before with whom he believed to be fellow spies.

He found safe haven at a livery stable near Hatchett Road, the only real road in and out of Cairo. Most goods, coming or going, were carried by barge or laden boat along two rivers, the Missouri-Mississippi and/or the Ohio. The city, which was a bustling business port, enjoyed trade, commerce, and recreation from both waterways. With the stage lines adding more passenger travel, dirt roads, some fortified with brick or mortar and rock, were coming into greater use. Assured that his goods would be well protected, Charles checked into the most expensive hotel in town, a real saloon, with men carrying weapons at their side, games of chance with cards, dice, and pool, played with large sums wagered gentlemanly and mannerly.

Like Charles, all the patrons were well dressed, and clearly among the elite of society. They seemed to come from all areas of the country, conducting many varied business dealings and associations from religion to banking, trading in human flesh, to trading in animal flesh. There were no limits. Everything could be on the table. If you could name it, then there was somebody hear who could make you a deal. Nobody questioned anybody's politics and no one seemed perturbed when some men clearly represented opposing sides of the gravest issue now facing the country - slavery.

A floorshow began onstage just as Charles joined a few others at the table for a round of poker. Not very good at cards, nor lucky, his only interest was the conviviality with other men of means. Card games, other than poker, were considered the sport of poor knaves. As always, he only wanted to socialize with and meet men who were already possessed by fortune, and therefore, able to further his attempts to attain wealth. All in all, he retired not having made any connections of worth.

The following morning, Charles rousted his team very early. A couple of his white cohorts had found lodging in less expensive hotels. The two slaves, and one other white person had slept about the livery area, guarding the coach during the night. After his own good night's sleep in an elegant, comfortable hotel bed, Charles was anxious to obtain money for his contraband, and then exchange that for silver certificates. As always, these would be insured and then forwarded to his bank in the Delta. As he walked to the livery stable, he was surprised to see that the very same men, who the evening prior, had sent him on detour to his roundabout destination, were there. Immediately Charles sensed that something was afoot. They had headed South, and were well on their way to Mississippi. Why, he wondered, were these very same guys in Illinois, now?

Cairo, as far as he knew, was a good place to transact business, especially if the transactions could benefit the South. He knew that based on the wide open rules that applied to Cairo, if they were Yankees, he had no cause to fear. Yet, something just didn't compute. Maybe they had doubled back because if the rules of engagement in Cairo had changed, then they would certainly support Southerners in any kind of confrontation. Or would they?

Inside the livery, when they looked at the crates, his driver wondered whether the crates had been disturbed. He observed that the packing formation had been rearranged from the way they were loaded at Brookshire Farm. The change could not have been due to the rough nature of the ride. Those crates had been packed solidly. There could have been no movement, no shifting during transport.

Charles was a very matter of fact person. He didn't believe in speculating at times like this. When you needed to know something, you simply look into the package and make sure you have it. "Well, the only thing to do is open the damn things and take a look to see what is in them. Since you all boys were here all night, and the company had it guarded on top of that, Ah can only assume that nobody was able to so much as touch our goods."

Charles was right about that. Surely, he surmised, nothing could even have come close to happening here in Southern Illinois. Nor was something likely to happen. The sympathies for the cause of the South ran strong and deep in this land, no matter that it was Lincoln's adopted state.

One by one, each crate was opened. The highwaymen had done their work well. They had weighted down each crate with stones, in sand bags, save one. That one contained the clothing that Esau had worn when he escaped from the Brookshire plantation. One of the drivers recognized the trousers and identified it as the little boy's. Also inside were morsels of crackers, cornbread and bits of bacon on one end. The other end of the box contained a bottle with long neck. Inside the bottle, a cork cap halfway plugged, was the most powerfully smelling urine they had encountered in a long time. Charles remembered the bottle as one in the vicinity of the piggery at Brookshire. He saw it and others just like it when he struck the deal for Esau with Master Brookshire. Angered, bewildered, he bolted from the stable. There to meet him was the entire group of strangers he had encountered the night before. In front, staring him face to face, and of all things, making eye contact, was none other than the little slave boy.

"Ah just got to know one thing my friend, if you all don't mind telling me, Sir. You all used me to bring my own property out of slavery to freedom, this little boy, this little nigger. Then, you all led me into a trap and stole my guns and ammunition. Sir, what is your name?" Charles looked at him in respect, then with disdain. Charles felt that good brains were wasted unless they worked for the benefit of the South. He wanted to save that face, that height, that gait, that physique, to imprint their memory onto his brain. He wanted to remember the man's mannerisms, the way he sat, so tall in the saloon, so proud in the saddle. He wanted to meet the stranger again when he could exact a heavy toll of revenge.

"I know what you are thinking, and I don't blame you one bit, you varmint. I am the kind of man that don't speak ill of another man, as a rule. For you, I shall make an exception. The only thing worse than a person of your ilk is a cold blooded snake in the grass. And even he has some degree of honor. You, my Southern bag of pond scum, have none. Your kind really is not worthy to even mention my name, you tainted son of a rascal of a preacher. I am a preacher too. I shall have you to know that, and I am a member of the same faith as that low down bastard of a daddy of yours, the Baptist of America. And my name, why it is James Butler. If I have my way, our paths will keep crossing. I know you to be a spy. Therefore, I know you will return back up here. Your lowlife kind will do anything to anybody for a dollar. You will be back up here, and when I see you, I shall tell you what I'm gonna do with you. I plan to take whatever is yours just like I did this time. Only next time, don't expect me to be so generous with your life, you yellow bellied skunk."

The whole while the man insulted Charles, the whole while he stood there, accepting it. He even whimpered, when the man stared him down, during the insulting, intimidating tirade. Even Charles' crew felt the rage from the stranger. There were times they too wondered whether bodily harm would be thrust upon them, in addition to the verbal tongue lashing. They also wondered why Charles, at the very least, didn't argue back at the man. Even though they had the 'jump' on them, a true man of the South still would not permit himself to be berated like that. A real man would have to say something. Otherwise, he risked losing the respect of his own crew.

"The next time I see you, I am gonna take the clothes off your filthy, stinking back, down to the last garment you have on. Mark my words, you liverless turkey. And this little nigger, as you call him, I prefer a different name, he has my permission to shoot to kill you next time he sees you. What you had planned to do to this boy brands you as a traitor to all of human kind. Now we will take our leave of you until the next time. Vaya con DIOS, gringo."

On up the road they made their way, each man carrying guns and ammunition they had stolen from Charles. That day was the worst day in the life of Charles, to that point, anyway. Only the future would tell whether there would be more like this.

Chapter VII - Esau in Illinois

Come along with us. Let us lie in wait for the honest man. Let us, unprovoked set a trap for the innocents. Let us swallow them up, as the nether world does, alive, in the prime of life, like those who go down to the pit! All kinds of precious wealth shall we gain; we shall fill our homes with booty. Cast in your lot with us, we shall have one purse. (Proverbs 1: 10-14)

Still impressionable, but aware that a new reality had taken place for him, Esau made friends fast with the protectors, the Butler family. He was treated most kindly by Mrs. Butler, who met them midway their journey in a place known as Kaskaskia. With her was her teenage son. A serious lad, he was tall, handsome and quick witted. The only thing that seemed somewhat incongruent about the boy was his hair. It was blond, a flowing blond and it was well below his butt. The long hair, the peachy clean face and his slight build actually made him appear to be a girl. The lad was quick on his feet, and even quicker with a gun, a rifle, or drawing a knife from his belt. Esau, like everyone who knew him, took an immediate liking to the boy. Esau wanted to know all about the prairie and life as a free person, how to make a living and to hear about travel wherever one wanted to go. Young Mr. Butler warned him that the area was not all that safe. In fact, if he were not careful, it could be downright dangerous. As far away as New York or Boston, black people were quickly shanghaied back into slavery by profiteers and nefarious scoundrels, as evil as the devil, just like old Charlie Rogers, as the Butler youth referred to Charles. Though young Mister Butler was named after his father and a great uncle, two men he admired and respected more than any other, he insisted on going by another name. He adopted that name, or rather it adopted him, and he became known more popularly as Wild Bill Hickock.

[That is a true story and a fact. It was attested to by Joe Lewis in 1966, at a dance sponsored by the Government Association for Better Services. Joe Lewis was William J. Moore's brother in law.]

[There were many songs about Wild Bill Hickock and his father. Here is one of my favorites. William J. Moore]

I lived up North where I tell you, man; Reaping the Wind and the Gale.
Where I was friend to none other than, The bravest soul, ever walked this land; Reaping the Wind and the Gale.

The Union cause did he serve well; Reaping the Wind and the Gale.
Tis true my friend, he never fell, His story I can clearly tell.
Reaping the Wind and the Gale.

Oh Bill, you son of a preacher man. Oh Bill, you son of a gun,
You do whatever you can, man. Doing whatever you can.

He saved some people from slavery. Reaping the Wind and the Gale.
You'll never see such bravery. This man was a such a rave, was he
Reaping the Wind and the Gale.

He went out West to stake his claim. Reaping the Wind and the Gale.
The best gunfighter by any name. It was he, who had all the fame.
Reaping the Wind and the Gale.

Oh Bill, you son of a preacher man, Oh Bill, you son of a gun,
You do whatever you can, man. Doing whatever you can.

Reaping the Wind and the Gale. Oh this is true I haven't lied.
His true story cannot be denied. I was with Bill, that day he died.
Reaping the Wind and the Gale.

His story has endured I must confess. Reaping the Wind and the Gale.
Of this country's true patriots, He was the very best.
His heart was pure and mind at rest We are sure his soul's been blest.

Wild Bill, you son of a preacher man. Wild Bill, you son of a gun
You do whatever you can, man. You do whatever you can.

[My grandfather truly liked those parts of the Narration where he could intersperse anecdotes about famous people. In so many ways, they played an integral part for the abolitionist cause, without whom, we would not have succeeded. Wild Bill Hickock was one among many.

Perhaps, the most renown person to play a part in the cause was the woman who directed the Underground Railroad. The Butlers surely would have been involved with her. To free Esau, Aunt Sapphire had needed to contact a person, who could contact another person, who could get word to Sojourner Truth. Word had it that she was miles away when the escape occurred. Though that might have, or might not have been a fact, one fact was clear. She knew about the effort, and apparently approved the assistance to be provided by her network. His favorite quote from this true life 'savior' was from her mentor and friend, Harriet Tubman:

> I have conducted many one-way railroad trips from the South to the North. Do you know one thing? I have never lost a passenger.

One of our group asked him why slaves sang so much, when their lives were filled with such misery. He explained that the black race brought so many gifts from Africa, and no matter what the white race would try to do, there were some things they simply could not remove from our culture. He used to lament that this was such a strength, and today, so many of our people simply put that concept to rest. Here is one just way that that bit of self hatred manifested itself. Dear reader, you: Have you ever heard someone make these comments or statements?

1) You can take the boy away from the farm, but you can't take the farm away from the boy.

2) You can take the boy out of the country, but you can't take the country out of the boy.

3) You can take the Nigger out of the country, but you can't take the country out of the nigger.

No matter how you verbalize these concepts, dear reader, remember this. You are referring to your own people, people with the backbone to withstand more pain, suffering, and abuse than you or I can even begin to think about. What they endured is beyond our imagination. Yet they were able to sing and hold on. In fact, the black slaves in America (North and South America, both continents) endured more extreme physical, mental, social, and cultural abuse than any group in history. My grandfather wanted us to be aware of the suffering and pain they had to endure. By comparison, even though things are still bad for us in so many, many ways, we are having a party, by today's standards. I share in that belief. If we had continued the fight, which those brave slaves, and abolitionists started, we wouldn't still be having some of the problems that we have to this day. Well, you didn't buy this book to read my sermon. Let's get back to Esau in Illinois.]

The Butler's destination for Esau was another city on the Mississippi. Located immediately Southeast of St. Louis, Missouri, this place went by the moniker of Illinois Town. Illinois Town enjoyed a reputation as a wide open city. It had become attractive for runaways, as escaped slaves were called, due to the many opportunities for former slaves to provide cheap labor, and perform many of the jobs that even white folk on the prairie were loathe to do. Esau's care was entrusted to a black family. The head of the family was a man who went by the name of Reverend Omer. Himself an escapee from Kentucky, a plantation just outside Columbus, he held the distinction of being the only slave to escape, then return to his old home and lead his wife, brother and his three children to freedom.

In all, the Omer family had accepted thirteen escapees into their home. All but three of these had been led to safety by the Butlers. These former slaves were from Tennessee, Kentucky, Mississippi and Georgia. The Butlers, and the former slaves on their land held a reputation of being God fearing people. They were law abiding in Illinois, learning from Mr. and Mrs. Butler, their children, and every former slave. Reverend Omer modeled his life on the Butler's. It followed that his wife, children and adopted children would have to be the same way. Esau was the youngest of all the escaped slaves when he joined the household.

For Esau, life with the Omer family was better than anything he could have imagined. In so many ways, it was a dream come true. Mrs. Omer saw to it that he washed properly every morning and gave him, all the other 'children' and her own children the kind of breakfast that as far as he knew, and the others had known before life with the Omer family, had been reserved only for the family and close associates of the master and his family. His first day there was so unusual. Though greatly hungered, he made no move to reach for the food at the breakfast table. Before they could dig in, they had to wait while Reverend Omer prayed over the food. When asked the blessing from God, he did something that Esau and the others had difficulty comprehending. He actually referred to God by name. For this, and other religious habits, some people had begun to refer to Reverend Omer as spooky. That kind of familiarity with The Deity had not found acceptance in this hemisphere. However, it meant nothing to Esau. Even when Mrs. Omer offered him food, he simply sat there. As far as he knew, the only way black people enjoyed fresh eggs, bacon, sausage, grits and biscuits with gravy was through thievery, not to mention chilled orange juice. Not until she actually placed the food onto his plate would he begin to eat. Strangely, though he started eating later than the others, he had finished his food before all the others. After all the food was gone, everybody waited before leaving the table. Reverend Omer prayed again, thanking God for having provided them with good, fresh food for breakfast. Again, as before, he referred to The Deity by name.

Esau's job on the Omer Farm was not very different from what he had performed in Mississippi. The only change was that he also had to tend sheep. The work was hard, but the pressures of being a slave were gone. The workers didn't have to worry about beatings, about rape, or about competing against other slaves to curry favor from the foreman, the overseer, or the master. What competition existed was against oneself. Reverend Omer would never use one worker to demonstrate a task for another worker to perform. He never did the demonstration either. He would take the worker aside, and explain what was to be done. Members of this extended family also knew they would eat well, each day. The most important concept they learned was that the Omers and their children cared about them as human beings. That was a wonderful feeling.

The evening meal each day was a powerful gathering. That hour and one half, at day's end was worth more, far more, than anything money, riches or any kind of wealth could have provided. They developed a sense of belonging, rich with the accompaniment of knowing that they were loved. Each escapee, and this included Reverend Omer, his wife and their children, was encouraged to discuss their families and friends still in bondage, and the goings on at the old plantations. The Omer family believed in keeping alive the memories of past associations. Perhaps the reason he did this was to maintain the strengths associated with the past. Perhaps it was due to his belief that slavery would end. This way, at the reunion, all former slaves would recognize each other because the fond memories of good, wholesome association would be rekindled daily. Perhaps he knew that would singularly represent the happiest day of their lives. He never told why.

Reverend Omer had felt a longing for his African heritage. His forebears had been kidnapped from their agrarian community in Nigeria. He remembered how his parents, before they were sold off to other plantations, and his grandparents, who suffered the same fate, rekindled those idyllic lives, before the betrayal, not by members of their tribes, but by people whose none-Christian religion, they had adopted. He recalled, that even as a slave on that large plantation in Western most Kentucky, his sadness truly began when the history of his family was plucked away. He had been a man whose parents spoke various languages that were peculiar to his people from Southwestern Africa. He had learned those languages and English, as a child. However, with the selling of his parents, first to separate them, then the speculative dealings for ownership of his grandparents, separating them to different plantations, the cultural heritage of religion, language, family values, sense of self, and sense of worth, were taken away. To make matters worse, his owner assigned him and his brothers and sisters to different tasks on the plantation. As a result, even though they were on the same plantation, they could never see each other again, except for Sunday morning church service.

Esau and each of the others had to talk about the good times and the bad, offering a different anecdote every evening. Eventually, their stories would be repeated. This gave rise to the gift of story telling, making up tales as they went, so prominent among many black people of that day. The talented tale spinners learned to make up these tall stories, as they became more adept verbally, and then grew more into maturity to allow their being related them with a straight face. Here is one made up by Eli Stewart, a runaway from Georgia.

> *When I was a boy o' two years old, maybe two and one-half, my old pappy, he take me and three older boys fishin in the pond. Now the name o' the ole pond where we bees fishin be called, The Old Pond. Zactly. The name o the ole pond be 'The Old Pond'. One o' the boys in the group, he be a natural born trainer. He able to train any cat, horse, pig, dog, even gator to do tricks. He even able to train wild animals to act like they house pets. I seen it wif my own two eyes, cause he trained a rattle snake to live wif one family.*
>
> *Well, one day, we be down at the ole pond, he commence to*

talkin. That ole boy go by the name o Rufus. He catch him a fish, a real lil ole fish, ya'll know, the kind we throws back. Well, ole Rufus, he say, I be danged if I cain't train this lil ole baby fish to think he a dog or cat, to be a pet, round the plantation. Ole Rufus, he jis worked, and worked, and worked a lil more wif that fish, (all the time, that fish be growin bigger). He git frustrated, but he don't give in to no fish. He say, I knows I can make this here fish think he a real pet dog, cause they say fishes be smart. They say fishes brain food. Make you smarter you eat a lot o' it. Rufus, he commence to have that fish breathin out his brain, after he put just a lil bitty ole hole up there. He say put the hole in the brain cause he ain't feel no pain. That be whut he say, that day. He give that fish a name, call him Oily, cause he be oily. Pretty soon, he jis call him Oil, and that fish answer to that name.

Then he teach that fish how to stand up straight and walk around on them hind fins. Then he haves Ole Oil rollin over, playing dead and all sorts o' tricks like you teaches a dog, or a cat. Pretty near soon, he had to tie that fish up when he go to the field to work; don't, that fish take to followin Ole Rufus. Now one day, Ole Rufus, he up and decide he go go fishin again, back in that ole pond. He kiss his dog, his cat, and that ole fish goodbye. By now, that fish, good gracious, think he ain't nothin but a dog, but he be naturally smarter. After all, he be a fish. Rufus set out for that ole pond. Dang if that pet fish don't figure out how to unties that rope. He set out after Ole Rufus. Well Ole Rufus, he look up, and he see that fish a' walkin towards him. And, that fish, he see Rufus. That fish, he just jump wif joy, he be so excited just like a dog. But, in his excitement state, that pet fish commence losin his balance. Right there he fall backwards, and he tumble right into The Old Pond, right there on that spot. Rufus, he be so sad, he heart broken and everything. He know his pet, he be in a whole heap o' trouble. Rufus ain't never taught that lil Oily fish to swim again. By now, he be thinkin he ain't no fish, so he done forgot how to swim. By time they pulls that fish out that ole pond it be too late.

That pet fish done drowned. They bury him out back.

Of course that produced great big, side splitting laughter. It seemed that they were still laughing ten minutes later when Absalom Grayson, a runaway from Natchez, Mississippi, decided he could top that:

The farm I comes from, it be located in the deep South.
It be so far South, they runs out o' space on the map.
Them boys wudda been done put us in the big ocean.
Well, a po slave, he couldn't git no kinda break on
the plantation. Massah, he grow all kind a meat there,
yes he do. We used to cure that meat in the smoke house,
way out back and Massah Grayson, he consider that meat
his pride and joy. We cures all that meat, and we
smokes bacon, pork, ribs, a whole side o' hog, sausage,
ham, pork butt, beef sides, beef ribs, turkeys, guinea
fowls, squab, pheasant, gator, chicken, wild boar,
deer stags, and bear. We smokes and we cures
everthang. Lawd chile, we smokes your hide you don't
be careful.

Massah, he use it on special occasion at that plantation.
Otherwise he sell them meats to the top bidder. Course,
they don't meet his price, he don't sell that meat. In
other words, you wants to buy, then you money gots to
meet the meat. Ya'll know what I'm sayin. We learnt how
to pack that smoked meat to send all over these here
United States, even up here to the North. Well, Massah
Grayson, he never allow no slave, or no po' white trash
to eat none o' that meat. Why he used to smell our breath
at the end o' the day, to make sure he don't smell no
flavor o' that meat. That meat smelt so good, sometime it
be too hard to resist. We bees smellin that hickory, that
birch, and that apple and pear wood, and all them different
flavors Ole Jim, the cook be done rubbed on that meat, and
all them different whiskeys he be throwin over them coals.

Some o' us slaves, well we commence to sneakin round d smoke
house in d hope o' us pickin up a lilbitty piece when
it all fall from the packin. It got so that them dogs
round that plantation, they scare us from it, from pickin up
that meat. We gits so mad, we figger out whut we go do.
We studies on that whole process, on how that meat be
fallin off, and we learns to move so quick, we catches

that meat fo it hit the ground.

(Of course that brought uncontrollable laughter but Absalom tried to quiet them all. He was not finished.)

Ole Massah Grayson, he always be a quick thinker. They says he never wanted to be out thunk by no slave. So he do this. He figger out how to keep them meat scraps from fallin off. Yes, suh. He sho nuff do that. Pret soon, me, my cousin Obadiah, my cousin Noah, and my brother Daniel, we finds out how to sneak inna that smoke house come end o' night and we takes to eatin that smoked meat. One night we all be in there eatin meat, when Jonas, that po ole white trash foreman hear us in the smoke house. He run fetch Ole Massah and they cumma runnin. They there, fo we can git out.

Ole Massah, he say, who there? If anyone in here Ah'm gonna shoot him dead. Ya'll know how Massah be talkin. He mean that too.

I says MEOW.

Now ole po white trash Jonah, he say Oh, Massah, it be de cat. Ya'll know how that old fool talk. Massa and po old white trash Jonah, they leaves.

My cousin, Obadiah, he eat one mo' bite, then he leave.

Po White Trash David, the foreman, he ain't permitted to eat no meat there either. Yet and still, he be the prime protector for the massah. Well, a week later, he hear Obadiah in that smoke house. We all be there, but he hear Obadiah. He call Massah, and Jonah. They cumma runnin. They says, who here?

I says MEOW!

Ole po white trash Jonah, he say, it be that darned cat again. You knows how bad he talk.

They leaves, and my brother Daniel, he take one mo bite and he commence to leave too. Well, they hears Daniel, but he be gone. They hurry back, and they says, who there.

I says MEOW.

This time Massa, he say, it's that cat again. You knows how they talks. Them hunkies cain't talk English too good. They decides to leave. They leaves jus me and my cousin,

Noah. I says to Noah. Noah, I says. Your black carcass better commence to go wi me. Noah, he really done took too good a likin to that smoked meat. He ain't near bout ready to go. He say, boy, you go on back to the slave room. I stays here just a lil bit longer. I eats more meat. He say somethin. He say, I takes care o' myself. Well, I tries to talk some sense inna that boy, but his head be too hard. He just don't pay me no mind.

So, Po Ole White Trash Jonas, he hear me leave. He call ole massah, and they cumma runnin. Now I done gone. Massah Grayson, he say, somebody is in there. You know how they talks. He say, Jonas, if I catch whoever be in that smoke house, Jonas, you has my permission to tan his hide, fifty lashes up and down his raw, naked backside. Now massah, he say out real loud. "Now who is in there?"

My cousin Noah, he be real quiet. He don't say one blessed word. Then he remember what happen last time and he say. It be the cat again!

Reverend Omer and his family had never heard tales like this. Actually, he wondered whether they were really true. After the third escapee gave his story, the Omers actually believed these were just jokes. But, even if they were not, there was great moral value in each tale, great humor, and interesting activities. The third tale came from David Appleby. He had escaped by row boat first, then by a 'borrowed canoe' through the swamps of Louisiana. David had been a trapper, of renown and fame, on the Bayou. He knew every inch of the swamplands throughout Louisiana and Mississippi. This was his tale:

On my plantation, we had us a bad man. He be bout the baddest man this side o' the Alligator Mountains.

"Wait a minute, David, ain't no such place as no Alligator Mountains down in Louisiana." He was challenged by Luke, one of the Omer children. Luke had learned book reading so he thought he knew a lot.

"Listen here Luke, you don't know everthang. They is some Alligator Mountains. They is back East, in Virginny, and they runs all the way down to Louisiana. You can look it up." David sited a source, an imaginary book. He was always quick to retort to, you 'can look it up'. The truth was that he couldn't read.

The name o' this bad man, it be Bad Sam. Kin folks, they

up and they calls him B.S. He be a lil ole man. Ain't no bigga than a inch. He so bad, even white folks don't mess wi him. Here be the reason why, and this ain't no bull stuff. Actually, the truth be that this boy be just three inches under fourteen hands tall. He be real, real short. But he bad. Truth about it is, ain't nobody evu even seed this boy fight. He all the time be talkin bout how he go commence to beat hell out somebody. This here boy, he be talkin so good, ain't nobody go mess wi' him. Now they's got themselffes a plantation bout, oh bout eight, nine miles up the road. Massah White, he own that place, yes he do. He own a big o slave go by name o' J.W.. He be six feets, six inches tall in his bare feets. That boy big. I ain't lyin. He weigh in at zactly sixteen, I says sixteen stone. He a big o bad man. On top o dat, boy be black as de ace o' spades.

Well, whut they all does, they decides they go have a fight. B.S., he be a lilole guy; he spose to fight J.W., he be the big ole boy. That boy J.W., he be so big, he got muscles everwhere. That boy, he got muscles on hisself where he ain't even got places.

Day the big fight, Ole B.S., he slip out back, and he go up the big house. He a sneaky lil devil. He walk right up to Massah Abernathy and he say, I just wants to see the man who brought this boy up here so I could whip his big, black butt, good. He look at old Massah White, and he say, if you don't say a word to nobody, just go down to the field, then I won't beat that boy too bad. I leaves him just enough strength so he can work tomorrow. Then B.S., that slick rascal, he put cotton balls in both Massah White's ears. Ole Buzzard, he cain't hear nuthin.

Then B.S., he so slick, lak a fox. He do same thang to that ornery ole Massah Abernathy. That be a cold fact. I sees it myself.

He run down to that field where they go fight. He run real fast. He gits there fo' they does. That boy, he run lak the wind. He see both them massahs a cummin. So he commence to cussing both o' them. He call them two white men all kinds o' insults. They jis keep on a cummin. They don't say nary a word.

> *B.S., he act like he real mad. He know they cain't hear. He still be cussin. He know they cain't hear, but don't nobody else know that. So by and by, he be talkin louder and louder to them two ole mens. Them words be so bad, I cain't repeat them in this here good company. That how bad them words be. B.S., he say to them two white mens, I gots the power. I gots the power o' the Good Lawd, right heah, in my hands. That boy be so slick. He done took them cotton balls out o' they ears and they doesn't even knows it. B.S., he say, the Good Lawd, done told me to bring back yo' bility to heah. He say, right now, ya'll jus heah me. Now when I hits bofe o' ya'll in the face, Lawd, he say, don't ya'll git mad, ya'll just thank B.S.. He doin jis whut I tells him to does. Bofe o' dose white men, they jis nods. Cose, we back down by the fight field, and we be lookin at all this.*
>
> *J.W., he be lookin too. We sees, when B.S. commence cussin out dose two white mens, ole J.W., he commenced shakin a lil. We thinks that boy be gittin scared. Then, everybody be lookin rat at ole B.S.. We sees that boy haul off and slap ole Massah Abernathy. Then he turn around and he slap ole Massah White. We seed it with our very own eyes. Then he turn real slow, and he be real mad. Just a look at that face, you see how mad the boy be. He madder than a sissy they done told he cain't go to prison. Ole B.S., he look right at J.W.. J.W., that boy shakin like a leaf on a stiff breeze in winter he so scared. He take off a runnin in the oppsit dye-reckshun, fast as a bolt o' lightnin on a greased rod o' steel and iron. Ain't nobody done seed that boy ever agin and that be a fack, a hard fack.*

Eventually, the Omers actually encouraged the boys and girls they accepted to not only tell the old stories that were true, but they also gave them favors to make up tales sitting around the table after the evening meal. In all, the Omers accepted forty-eight runaways, all from various abolitionist sources in Illinois and Missouri. However, about one quarter of these came from the good efforts of the Butlers. Yet more came from the Underground Railroad. And a few were brave escapees, with no help. They made it to freedom based on their wit, determination, and fearlessness.

Reverend Omer paid a good sum for forged papers of manumission for each runaway at his home, and for those escapees who went to live in other homes. Even though they were 'ostensibly' free, he taught them to be careful in their comings and goings, in Southern Illinois, in Indiana, and most importantly, in St. Louis, Missouri. If they were to express themselves freely, they also had to pay the price for living freely. They had to be ever vigilant. They also had a role in seeing that new arrivals from the South learned to be vigilant. They had to look in front, to both sides, and anticipate trouble. Reverend Omer told them to walk a safe distance behind others, to make sure no harm would come from the rear. After a certain distance, always look back, for your friend's safety because nobody has his 'back'.

The essence of freedom, the quality of being free, is the most precious commodity on earth. It is the consummate blessing of waking up each morning of your life, knowing that you are not owned by another human being. It is the joy of knowing you have the opportunity to work hard and expect to receive, and do receive, due remuneration for that work. It is being able to live with a family where you will be fed, and know that you have a future that contains diversity, that provides the opportunity for personal growth and development, where you can learn to read, write, and handle money, and most importantly, to learn about life and the wonderful lessons it teaches. It is caring for your family and having your family care for and nurture you. Esau and all the boys and girls, new to the Omer family took to freedom like fish take to water. They were in their element. There were routines, chores, and responsibilities, personal and with a team. These were somewhat like those they had on their plantations in the South. But here, they could buy things on their own. They opened bank accounts immediately. Early on, they learned to save more money than they spent. Eventually, Reverend Omer reduced the income he paid by a fair amount, taking out modestly for their rent, upkeep, and food. He did the same with his own children too. He even took them from his farm to other areas of Illinois Town so that they could see how much more they would pay if they roomed and boarded somewhere else. However, more important than the money they saved was an intangible that they could not have been provided anywhere else. The Omers truly loved them. They loved every person in their home as much as they loved their own children. It was not incidental that their own children made no noise about receiving the same treatment as the others. That their parents had enough love to show each of them, and other children with no place to go, fitted in very well with their own nature and temperament. Stated simply, they were just down to earth, basically good people. They did make one very simple difference in their own children. They were required to save more money from their earnings. This actually inspired their other 'adopted' children to save more too.

Mr. and Mrs. Omer owned a number of horses, among their livestock. Skilled in animal husbandry, Reverend Omer kept each one of his mares in foal at regular intervals. The young animals were exercised regularly. His horses were the most highly prized in Illinois and the immediate area to the West. As a result, he earned a fine penny selling to the Unites States

Army, various local militia, breeders, and show enthusiasts. In addition, each resident of his farm, owned at least one horse that was his or her own. He would give the first as a present to one of his children, or the other 'adopted' children. Any beyond that, they could purchase from him at fair market value. For every mare that produced a foal, he would pay his son or daughter fair market value also.

One of the boys on the farm was a naturally gifted portraitist. He drew pictures of each family member, and also of the farm animals. These came in handy, because with the horses, markings and physical traits which were captured on the course woods on which he drew, were better than the markings made by branding irons for displaying ownership. If they ever needed to show ownership due to rustling or to settle an honest dispute, his records would be the deciding factor. Of course these were supported by notarized documents bearing every descriptive detail of the animal. Eventually, everybody there began to recognize all the different traits. Then they associated certain behavioral characteristics with the farm animals, such as aggressiveness, color, awkwardness, strength, agility, endurance, speed, gait, size, and so on.

Back at Brookshire, Isaac had not been permitted to ride. That started out as a pleasure for Esau, but would soon turn into something else. It would become demanding, and perhaps even dangerous. For now, sitting in that saddle, controlling those reins, and riding through the countryside, sometimes all the way to the river during the early evening was the most appreciated blessing that freedom now provided. As was the rule with Reverend Omer, Esau was not permitted to stray more than two miles from home in any direction, unless he was in the company of at least three foster brothers, any of whom might have been one of the sons of Reverend Omer.

After approximately one year in Illinois Town, on a Saturday afternoon during late spring, Esau, John and Luke, foster sons like Esau, and Reverend Omer's son, Ishmael rode down to the levee's end. There, traders laded ferries and barges, filled with goods for trade across the river in St. Louis and points beyond. They filled other carriers for trade up and down the river, and Westward to hook up ten miles Northwestwardly with the Missouri River.

The boys had been warned never to tarry in that area because, though beautiful and picturesque, it was notoriously dangerous. Many a drunken brawl took place there, and at times, groups of men would set upon younger men, usually just a stranger traveling through. Local folk said it was just hometown lads having a good time. It was more than that. There were a number of harsh truths about the exact reasons for what appeared to be wanton, unplanned violence. Foremost among these harsh realities was that men often lost their hard earned cash on games of chance at the local saloons. Others were victimized by the growing trade in human flesh, where young men and young women proved equally adept at separating anyone foolish enough to spend too much time in the area from his money. Quite often these young locals would set upon an innocent young man, waylay him, and take his money. The hooligans, in turn, would lose their ill gotten cash to gaming tables and prostitutes. Worse than that, they in turn could be preyed on by stronger criminals or stronger groups of criminals. Another danger applied primarily to young white men. If they hung around too long, and were by themselves, they risked being shanghaied to serve as hired hands on the ships, barges, pleasure craft, and trading vessels along all the rivers in the region, East to Ohio, South to Tennessee, West to Nebraska Territory and North to the territories reaching Canada.

The greatest danger of all was meted out to careless black men and women. They had no means to defend themselves from the most dangerous game. This game was not limited to the levee, but preyed upon them for miles in all directions. When one fell prey as victim, the effect was for life.

A number of men made their living by kidnapping freedmen, runaways, and manumitted slaves. For a handsome bounty, they were delivered to agreed upon sites in St. Louis, Missouri, and Freeburg, Illinois, for delivery to the South. A new life of bondage, or re-bondage awaited these men, women, boys and girls. The bounty paid for runaways was the highest. On return to their former owners, many were not given a chance to return to productive work in the fields. Stripped of their clothing in broad daylight, in front of every soul at the previous plantation of servitude, tied to a stake, or tree stump, they were beaten to death, the last few lashes coming from a slave. Reverend Omer warned them to be extra careful and ever vigilant again, and again, and again, lest this fate befall them.

Chapter VIII - Recaptured, Back to Slavery?

My son, walk not in the way with them, hold back your foot from their path! For their feet run to evil, they hasten to shed blood. It is in vain that a net is spread before the eyes of any bird. These men lie in wait for their own blood. They set a trap for their own lives. This is the fate of everyone greedy for loot. Unlawful gain rakes away the life of him who acquires it. (Proverbs 1: 15-19)

Don't let the sundown catch you, down on the levee
Don't let the sundown catch you, down on the levee.
Don't let the sundown catch you, down on the levee.
Coming to take you down will be in pursuit a chevy.

Watch your step when you down there.
I say, watch your step when you down there.
Boy, watch your step when you down there.
Don't somebody be caught and bound there.

At the levee, my dear papa was taken.
At the levee, my dear mama was taken.
At the levee, my dear sister was taken.
Now I'm all sad, and forsaken.

Don't go down to the levee.
Now don't ya'll go down to the levee.
Stay away from that levee.
Or on your heart, that burden lies heavy.
Yes, on your heart the burden be too heavy.

[Like most of my grandfather's songs, this one prepared us for the inevitable. Only this one betrayed no subtleties. A terrible stroke of bad luck, maybe more than one stroke, would befall one, or a few of the boys. Up until this time, after weeks of Narration, and using his songs, a number among us believed he made up most of the lyrics as he went. My problem is that I can only remember these tunes after years of their record only in the recesses of my personal random recall access imagery system. However, when some among our group were overheard by their parents, uncles, aunts and older family members, they wanted to know exactly how we young people had heard those old Negro Spirituals and Folk songs. Their recollections of these songs reaffirmed to me the truth - no, my grandfather did not make up these songs. He simply remembered his relatives and friends singing them from his youth. No doubt, these and hundreds others - that I shall never be fortunate to hear, are out there - and they also go back hundreds of years. As always, when he entertained us with narrations about the struggles in slavery, the great blues wars, the Race Riot in 1917, and his concept of religion, we were torn between enjoyment of the narration and enjoyment of the song.]

The boys had heard about a duel to the death. It was to take place near the road leading directly to the central part of the levee, down beyond Front Street. It was just on the other side of where the flop houses, saloons, and inns lay. Fighting duels at this time was an accepted fashion for gentlemen to end their quarrels. In this case, the gentlemen in question were members or greats of high society in St. Louis, Missouri. Their families lived in mansions just beyond the flood plain. These two rivals actually came across the water in the same large steamboat. It moored about one hundred feet from the river's edge. As if in a formal processional, they were watched by the boys, and many others as they headed from the shore. First came their seconds. Each second carried two cases. Inside each case was a weapon. Each second carried weapons that were certified fit for a duel. The seconds opened each case, and inspected each gun painstakingly. A coin flip would decide which protagonist would select first. For each protagonist the first gun to be used was a single barreled pistol, with six bullets, one per chamber. In each of the second cases there was another gun, just like the first gun, but there was also an epee in each case. A third case, left back on the steamer, contained a Bowie knife and a scarf, for each.

The boys had heard of duels to the death, but they had never seen one. Such matters had become the norm, regularly occurring in Illinois Town. There was a law against dueling, just as there was in every city and town for miles around. The difference was that Illinois Town was the only city where this law was not enforced. The boys were very quiet, taking pains to call no attention to themselves. As the road became more firm and their horses' footfalls became more prominent, they alit, tied the horses to a tree, and walked the last fifty yards till they were atop a slope, thirty five yards upwards on a slight angle from the place of action. Though they remained quiet, they were not aware that every move they made was being watched. It wasn't that they were the only blacks at the duel. There was one more. It was none other than a freedman who had been owned by a French family in the Southeastern Missouri Boot Heel. His name was Paul Montmartre.

Initially, Montmartre's interest in the duel was as keen as anyone's else. He wanted to see every last detail. A ruthless man, he took extreme joy in witnessing the death and the pain and suffering attendant of violence on another man, or innocent beast. This Paul Montmartre was one of the men who had been with Charles Rogers when he tried to smuggle contraband to the Northerners sympathetic to the Southern cause. He had unwittingly helped to deliver Esau, two years earlier to the North. Nothing would give him greater pleasure than to collect the bounty for his return. He figured he would collect that bounty, a handsome reward, and get paid extra bounties for delivering three new slaves to the Brookshire Plantation.

He quickly left the duel, and canoed across the river to report his observation to Charles Rogers. Charles was there, once again, to support the cause of the South, and to make as much money as he could in a number of deals he was making. During the time since Charles' earlier failure, he had grown more bold, but more careful. He was gaining a greater reputation as the South's most effective intelligence agent. He also improved in his other area, and became more adept at smuggling 'goods' across the mid South to be used by those who wanted slavery legalized throughout the country. Charles had two reasons for continuing this line of work. Like most of his fellow Southerners, he believed the country was headed for civil war. He had hoped to fortify those who shared his values, with weapons, money, leadership and direction sufficient to fulfill that cause, or at least, inflict heavy damage upon the enemy, from within, if and when war came. His second purpose in carrying on clandestine counterintelligence work was to increase his personal wealth. By far, at that time, through his efforts, his personal income was greater than that of any single man in the South, who didn't personally own slaves or participate in agrarian business.

Ever since he raped the mother of his acknowledged only black female child, Charles preferred the sexual company of black women. Having used the ruse that the lady allowed into his hotel room would attend to his needs of clothing arrangement, food preparation, and filing of his personal and business papers, he was involved in his usual dalliance when Paul knocked on the door. Paul knew what they were doing, and he knew that his employer of this week, would be extremely angry for this interruption. Downstairs, the clerk had told him that he should not disturb Mr. Rogers because he was 'at work' with his personal aide. Paul simply brushed him away, responding the he knew exactly what kind of work his boss was doing. Having worked with Charles, and other such agents, Paul knew when he had a good bit of information. Besides, the drive of personal ambition is only superceded by the drive for revenge.

Paul knew how much Charles desired for revenge. It was a craving that had to be satisfied. That they, and their cohorts could turn a profit in the endeavor was all the more befitting. Yes, initially, Charles would be angry. It would have to subside, Paul reasoned, when told of the information. Paul sat in a chair and explained the situation. He was directly across from Charles and his lady friend. They did nothing to conceal their sex act, while Paul looked on, making conversation with Charles. Although Charles could have made use of a room divider, he wanted this to remain in view of Paul. Paul didn't object, didn't want to either.

Preparation for a duel involves a great deal of pomp, ritualistic behavior, steps which had become standardized pursuant to an unwritten code. These had been adopted from the European code of honor, and become more refined in the Americas. It had become recognized as the gentlemen's manner of participation In the basest of man's desires - the killing of another man. Although the foes here had gone through training in the art of fencing, fighting with knives, and target practice with firearms, neither was well skilled in any of these matters of combat. In duels to the death, the fate of the victor or loser was usually decided not by skill, but by luck. As many times as not, the firearms user who was the more accurate shooter, would lose. There is a big difference in taking aim at another person, than shooting at a still, lifeless target, or a dumb, defenseless animal, than at a living, breathing human being.

By the time Charles, Paul and their crew, returned to Illinois Town the affair of arms was just getting underway. The men had taken ten paces and had turned to face, and then to fire at each other. The first shot, from each man, was errant. The second barrel was cocked and each took aim. These shots were also errant. At once, the duelers were attended by their seconds. Their brows, heavy with sweat, were towel dried. Each gentleman shook like a leaf. At the distance, one would have thought that each man, firing simultaneously, would have been wounded, at least. To steady their nerves, the seconds poured a four ounce glass of brandy for each. They were also given advice on the advantageous deployment of their aims, to create better chances of results. Once again the combatants moved to a line, toe to toe, then at the command, performed their 'about faces' together. For some reason, maybe a detraction to the French Code of Combat, the referee was known as the homme d'affaire. He signaled the men to take aim, waited a few seconds, while each man raised his weapon, cocked it, and tried to avoid shaking. Then he gave the command to fire.

The boys made no noise, and continued watching the duel from their spot above the levee. They had no idea that Paul, Charles, and Charles' crew had come to accost them. The first to be attacked was Esau. He was clubbed directly on the back of his head from Paul's makeshift stick. He fell immediately, like a ton of bricks was dropped on him. Another of Charles' men then struck John, the largest of the group. He used the butt of his hardened riding crop. Ever alert, John could not elude the full effect of the blow, but he did adroitly bend away from its full impact. He took a marginal hit. As he turned, he saw Esau out cold on the ground.

"Run, run, run and get the horses", he yelled to Luke and Ishmael. Dodging another attempt to 'crown' him, he delivered a telling punch to the forehead of his would-be assailant. "Don't worry about Esau and me. Bring back the Reverend and help."

The millisecond, in time, that he caught his attacker with an effective blow, just as he was alerting his brothers what to do, John was pummeled by two other heavy, black men. Within thirty seconds he was subdued under their relentless attack.

John had fought valiantly but there were too many. In the resultant melee, Luke was overpowered. The only member of the group to flee successfully was Ishmael. Unable to reach his, or one of his companions horses, he was able to take one belonging to the attackers.

The three captives were bound with cord and tied to a flatbed that Charles had hired. It was about one mile South of the duel sight. He sent advance word to other spies in his network to await their arrival at a cove of the river in a little town known as Danby.

Due to the type of struggle waged by the boys, Charles was determined not to untie their bindings until he had them safely returned with him, inside Mississippi. He couldn't afford to take any chances. Due to his failure to deliver the boy to Alabama, he wanted to clear this one blot from his reputation.

Back at the Omer residence, Reverend Omer calmly listened to his son explain the circumstances that had occurred at the landing on the levee. This was quite an unusual man. His behavior, his response, and his demeanor confused and surprised his son. Most importantly, he showed no anger. In fact, there was no outward emotion of any kind whatever. He appeared so calm and so cool that a disinterested observer might have believed that nobody he knew had been harmed, let alone abducted. Then he quietly had his wife to prepare a sandwich for the boy while he went out, through the neighborhoods from his home.

He returned with three men, and two of his foster sons. They were heavily armed, and all appeared as quiet in demeanor as he. Ishmael could take the silent treatment from his dad no longer. He put the question directly to him. He even made eye contact with his dad, for the first time since he could remember. Reverend Omer made his reply short, plain, and simple. He said he was angry with neither him, nor his brothers. Now, the explanation went, was not the time to be angry, or mad. Now was the time to bring back his family, to rescue at least one, if not all, from the very clutch of hell. Slavery was a living hell. In a way, taking extra precautions to maintain freedom was also like fighting against the minions of hell. He knew that having lived free, his boys would die if remanded to slavery. To lose them now, was to have them lose their lives.

Reverend Omer framed his thoughts as if to put himself in the heads of the boys' captors. He had no boat, and worse, no means to obtain one. Even if he had been able to commandeer a water craft, he would not have followed them by water. They were at least two hours ahead of him. His hope and prayer was that Charles would misjudge the river current, always tricky, but even more so during this time of year.

Thinking as the kidnappers might have been, and knowing that they would find safe haven in Danby, he planned to meet them just one mile North of their destination. The truth was that his plan, at best, was his hope, which at worst, was a prayer. The place he believed they would have in mind was a cove. Many a settlement had been attempted there. Due to the nature of the river currents, no one had succeeded in establishing even so much as a trading post in the direct area of the cove. Reverend Omer knew every inch of that river, and he remembered that if the currents were unusually wild, water craft had to strain to keep away from the cove. Any crew, whose craft ran ashore now would have to leave it, and proceed by foot, or horses if they had them on board.

The currents were diametrically different in the cove than in the great, mighty, muddy river. Ship and crew unlucky to venture into the calm waters of that cove required extraneous effort to return to the pathway on course. Yet, they had to venture close to the cove's mark so as not to lose valuable time in the river's course.

Along the way, Reverend Omer explained every step of his mission. He planned to use strong rope to slip a knot onto the edge of the flatbed or whatever craft was carrying the boys and their captors. With the initial shock, stopping the craft's progress, their plan was to set upon the kidnappers and in the confusion, overtake them. They knew that the kidnappers would have more men than they. The element of surprise would have to work for it would be their only chance.

The rescue party was in luck. The cove was even more calm that they had anticipated. This meant the river currents, just beyond the mark, would be dangerous. Even better for them, there were no local fishermen in sight. One of the group was given the mission of intercepting the kidnappers, and hoisting the rope over the boat's fittings. Then, after the initial jolt, they would all set upon the craft, yelling as loud as they could. They hoped their noise and the suddenness of their attack would instill such immediate fear that their adversaries would not even think to fight back. Reverend Omer also wanted them to think that they were being attacked by a party of Southerners. Ordinarily, he would never have disdained to portray himself as a white Southerner under most circumstances. However, as he saw it, this was an unusual occasion. His sons had been kidnapped, and the crime demanded the most expeditious means to save them, with as little harm as possible.

The plan could not have worked any better. There was minimal resistance. In a few minutes Charles, Paul, and the entire party that included the mob that had set upon the boys and two additional white men were bound in rope, the very same rope that had been used on Esau, Luke and John.

Then they stood up the group of kidnappers, one by one, in a row, all next to each other. One by one, the members were asked what they thought should be done with them. To a man they said nothing.

"What you do to me, if I had kidnapped you, and taken you to a place where you would be horsewhipped, beaten to death?" he asked Charles, the torch only a few inches from his face. "You don't have to answer that, you stinking piece of Southern trash. I know zactly what you would do."

Enraged by a black man's using that tone and that manner to a white man, Paul Montmartre tried to break away from the group and loose his binds. That rope was not very tight, but it was secure. The rescue party knew how to tie a person or animal without harming the circulation of bodily fluids. "Why you stupid nigger, you gots no right to talk to Master Charles like that. If my hands wuz loose, I'd beat the livin shit outta your black ass right heah", Paul swore at the Reverend. It was clear that he wanted to grab him and have his way with the smaller man. Paul could understand the desire to save family members from a return to slavery for two, and death for one. But he could not understand or accept such behavior toward any member of the white race. He believed that was far too out of place for a black man, no matter what the circumstances.

Reverend Omer looked at his sons, then looked back at Paul, before addressing his sons. "Luke and Ishmael, ain't this the nark who sneaked up behind yon Esau, and clubbed him from the back, like a weasel?" he asked. At the mention of the word 'nark', Paul struggled all the more. That was about the worst insult one black man could hurl at another, a term that when ascribed to a man, he never seemed to outlive. When so called, the only means to redeem oneself was to take it by revenge, in a fistfight. Reverend Omer knew this would outrage Paul even more than his treating Charles as the man he truly was. They walked up closely and took a good look at him.

"Yeah, Pa. That be the man who done it", answered Luke. "He cold conked him like a sneaky snake in the grass."

"A snake has more honor than this nark. And you, Ishmael, what say you?" he asked directly to his son. Ishmael studied Paul carefully, because he knew exactly what was in store for him. He didn't want to accuse an innocent man.

"Yeah, Pa. He be the lousy pond scum. He be the very coward who cold conked Esau from behind. That po boy ain't had no chance."

"Pond scum ain't dirty as this idiot. Okay, Mr. I loves white folks so much that I haves to defend they honor', you go git yo chance to own up to them crazy words the devil made you utter from your very mouth. Esau, I want you to untie this boy's hands and feets. Eer body go git a chance to see how 'Mr. I loves white folks so much that I haves to defend they honor' do defend they honor."

More torches were lit, illuminating the still darkness of the night, and providing a sense of warmth. Without hesitation the ropes were loosened and removed by Esau. The bigger man charged at Reverend Omer, who stood at the center of the barge. As Paul dove at his adversary, the smaller man, who was also much quicker, swerved, eluding Paul Montmartre. Paul tumbled to the warped, well worn wooden floor. All he gained for his effort was painful splinters thrusting into his back. He was allowed to return to his feet.

Poor Paul. That rascal should have known better than to continue. Having had his challenge met at once, he should have known he would be no match for his short, strong, muscular adversary. Paul was never known for using his intellect, or what little of that he had. He swung at his opponent, but

The Reverend ducked. Then Paul lunged, but all he caught was air. He kicked at him, with a move so powerful that when he missed, he swung his entire body high into the air, landing flat on his back with a resounding thud. These futile efforts to inflict bodily damage by Paul, were to no avail. He seemed much wearied and spent, until he could not even raise a finger. Then Reverend Omer made another suggestion to his sons. "Luke, Ishmael, come here right now."

In a split second the boys stood with their dad. He didn't have to tell them what to do next. They knew. Without the utterance of another word, seemingly without even a thought, they lifted Paul and held him there. All Paul could do was breathe. Next Reverend Omer looked at Esau. Instinctively, like his brothers, he knew exactly what was expected of him as well. One of the boys splashed water into Paul's face. Though now fully conscious, he finally began to use the brain power he had remaining. He realized that to struggle now would only mean the infliction of greater pain. To increase what would become a painful punishment could mean, perhaps, death.

"Do you know where to hit this big windbag of shit, Esau?"

"Why no, Pa, Suh. Ah ain't never hit no man before."

The Reverend pointed to a spot just underneath Paul's left ear. "Here, boy. Right here is where you got to hit this crocodilian. You hit a man here with your fist as hard as you can. You hit him here, you stops the flow of blood to the brains. You stop the heart from pumping blood for two, three seconds. You hit a man here and you make his whole body twitch. Best thang for you though is that when you hit a man here, the harder you hit him, the less it hurt yo fist. You understand?"

"Ah understands, Pa; yessuh ah shos understands."

Reverend Omer told Charles and his men that he never wanted to see them in Southern Illinois again. If they ever returned to within fifty miles of the area, or if anybody who even resembled them were caught in the area, they would kill them. Charles believed what he had heard. He knew when he had lost. He resolved that after this encounter, his second with Esau, he would stay away from the boy. It just wasn't worth it, was what he finally decided. Esau whispered into his father's ear that Reverend Butler had also given fair warning to Charles. Reverend Omer decided that warning or threats against this man were not sufficient. He had been warned and apparently scoffed at that. He didn't kill Charles as promised by the Butler group. Maybe what he did was worse. Charles was untied, and ordered to sit on the bottom of the flatbed, and remove every stitch of his clothing, garment by garment, piece by piece. They not only took his togs, but his papers, his information about efforts to extend slavery beyond Missouri into Kansas, and his efforts to recruit more Northerners friendly to the cause of the South. Worse yet, he had a list of prominent Northerners, from Western Pennsylvania to Missouri, anxious to help the South. In the face of such failure, the honor code of intelligence required the spy to commit suicide. If he did so, his death would be reported as in service of his cause. Charles was given the chance to die honorably, therefore, from his own hand. He didn't have the guts.

"You know what Charles Rogers, yo po carcass ain't even worth a laugh. I, for one don't know why they gave yo weak spine that name. Seem like to me, that a man who ain't worth a laugh, they should've given his po carcass the name of chuckles. Chuck, chuck, chuckles. That go be yo name from now on, Chuck Chuckles." Reverend Omer was serious. He used the term derisively. Thing about it, whenever he, and other black folk gave nicknames to white folk, whatever the name, it was applied derisively. No honor was meant in bestowing that nickname, to displace the given name of Charles Rogers. No honor was meant in applying a nickname to any white person.

Immediately after striking Paul Montmartre as instructed, the pain in Esau's skull subsided. The welts on his arms, wrists and legs, embedded though they were, caused no more pain. And Esau, once again, was a happy fellow.

And Paul Montmartre: Paul was never the same after that. He did return to Illinois Town, a ghost of the mean rascal that he was before. He couldn't remember why, or understand the significance of his own behavior. But every time he ever laid eyes on the Reverend, or any of his sons, or any member of the rescue party after that fateful day, he would cower in fear. He would literally beg them not to harm him.

Prior to that night, Paul cast a fearsome shadow throughout the area among black folk and Chippewa, Cahokia, Seminole, and Lakota who also lived in the area. They would just as soon cross the street, when he approached. Nowadays those were long memories and those who never knew him found it hard to believe that he had had the reputation of being a bad man, a man who invoked fear into others. On one occasion, one man from the rescue group met him on the street in the area of the black settlements and ordered Paul to eat fresh dog excrement off the street. It got so bad that other men who had a score, or more, to settle with Paul also began to take advantage of him as well. The last time Paul was seen, one such fellow, with another score to settle from their youth, ordered Paul to his knees. There, he was made to open his mouth wide. He used Paul's mouth as a urinal and a spittoon. Mercifully, Paul died two weeks after that. His family, unaware that Reverend Omer had had a fateful encounter with him only two years prior, asked the good Reverend to say a few Christian words at the funeral. Of course The Reverend accommodated them. Based on what he said, and how he said it, it appeared he really did love the man.

Beat your plowshares into swords. and your pruning hooks into spears: let the weak man say, “I am a warrior”. Joel 4: 10 The New American Bible

Chapter IX - A Great Jockey

Woe to them that devise iniquity, and work evil upon their beds. When the morning is light, they practice it because it is in the power of their hand. And they covet fields, and take them by violence; and houses, and take them away: so they oppress a man and his house even a man and his heritage. Therefore, thus saith the LORD, Behold, against this family do I devise an evil from which ye shall not remove your necks; neither shall you go haughtily: for this time is evil.

In that day shall one take up a parable against you, and lament with a doleful lamentation, and say We be utterly spoiled: he hath changed the portion of my people: how hath he removed it from me! turning away he hath divided our fields. (Micah 2:1 - 4)

And he shall judge among many people, and rebuke strong nations afar off: and they shall beat their swords into plowshares, and their spears into pruning hooks: nation shall not lift up a sword against nation, neither shall they learn war anymore. (Micah 4:3)

After the escape, and for years continuing, just the mention of Esau's name in the presence of any white person on Brookshire property, or in the presence of Master Brookshire was taboo. Any slave overheard by any of his family, or any white employee of the plantation who did so was reported. The overseer promptly administered corporal punishment when this was done. As usual, the slave, or offending white person was tied to a pole and ten lashes from the bullwhip were administered. This tactic might have worked but for another secret form of communication learned by the bonded class at Brookshire.

This was in the form of a pronunciation application that was based on the English root word. It was quite simple after the basic concept was understood. As they tried to become more complicated, they actually engineered more applications that were subtle. Here is how it went at the beginning.

The sound that was made by pronouncing the letters I and Z were simply added after the initial letter of the word. To ask the question, 'How are you today?', the slave would say 'Hiz-ow ariz yiz-ou toiz-day?'. The answer might have been, 'fiz-ine, aznd yiz-ou'.

After they incorporated these basics, then the slaves added another sound, this time at the end of a word. The question then became 'hiz-ow-ku ariz-ku yizou-ku to-iz day-ku?'.

[I remember visiting Tennessee State University in 1964 with a good friend, Dr. Charles Means. Charles had learned of the basic rules - or I should say, some of the basic rules - when he had been a student there. I was ever amazed at the command of this interesting communication form by young men and women, most in my age group at the university. The words had a form and rhythm that were absolutely captivating. Even though I never could quite attain the mastery of the lilting phraseology as my friends, including Charles, I did understand the basic rules, due to the Narration. Charles and some of the other students simply dismissed my inability to capture the correct technique as a lack of true soul. (I still don't know how to have taken that, but I do believe Charles was right and I was not insulted. He provided information that I needed.) At any rate, I asked the fellow who everyone seemed to believe was the expert in its application where it originated. Actually, for many days, I had heard it on my campus in Illinois also, but not to this accomplished degree. Of course I had first heard of it in my youth from my grandfather.

That fellow simply used creative logic (In other words, he lied). He claimed he made it up himself. It was a creation of his mind, he stated with as straight a face, I suppose, as was registered by historians who incorrectly proclaim that Columbus discovered two new continents (so-called America). I ran into that fellow years later. The occasion involved travel to what I believe to be the most fascinating city in the lower forty-eight. It was when my job carried me to New Orleans, Louisiana to conduct a training conference. There I met him briefly and asked him to recall those days. Of course he remembered the language and those days at Tennessee State University. He remembered Charles and some of the other people, like Robert Reed, Ernest Murphy, James Claiborne, Franklin Mosley to name a few from Illinois.

Of me, however, he had no recollection. I realized that he was not a good liar, for this time, when I asked him from whence the language had come, he admitted learning it from his great grandfather, whose father was a slave on a plantation in Cottonport, Louisiana. That man had taught him, and others the language in a narration just as my grandfather had described so much of it to us.

I also asked the fellow why he never admitted the truth during his undergraduate days at Tennessee State. He looked me directly in the eye and answered, "If those Negroes at your school, my school, and many other colleges and universities in this country, had realized they were learning a secret tongue used only by slaves, they never would have so embraced it.

Just like you."
Actually, that fellow was so right. I can bump into my friends from that period to this day, and they can recall that process of applied syllables so well that they can speak it now, with no loss of detail. In its most complicated form the slave would even apply Pig Latin. This increased their fun, and according to this fellow, slaves would use it with this form of expression simultaneously. Oh yes, here is how they would pronounce the name Isaac. "EYE-IZ-ZACK", and incorporating the Pig Latin "EYE-IZ-ZACK-AY.]

Isaac had trained to become a jockey. For his first race he was outfitted from head to foot in new gear, made by Tamar. Everything was measured and tailored down to the thirty-second of an inch including his silk riding cap, silk pants, silk shirt and light cotton under drawers. Now thirteen years old, he had become proficient at riding and handling all the thoroughbred horses at Brookshire. Plantation owners were a competitive lot. They could find so many ways in which to compete. Obviously selecting those slaves who mastered the sweet science of fighting was the most impressive means. Slaves on many a plantation were required literally to beat each other in fighting so that those most highly skilled at protecting themselves, while simultaneously inflicting grave punishment on another were the most highly valued possessions. They simply pitted slaves from one plantation against slaves from another.

[I can't even count the endless number of times I have had to prove my mettle in neighborhood fights, continuing to display proudly that I too can excel at a meaningless game borne out of white folk's having fun at the expense of black folk's inflicting pain and suffering upon each other. Of course, most times, I was on the losing end of these fights, and was rescued by my younger brother, Raymond.

Slave owners owned slaves who could fight, in the very same fashion that boxing promoters own fighters, or the rights to fighters today.]

Those were sometimes contests to the death. The master, having lost a wager on the outcome, did not find it unusual for the losing slave to lose more than the fight.

There were also other means that slaves were pitted against each other. There were contests involving foot races, weightlifting, and high and broad jumping. The most glorious contest though, after boxing, was horse racing. Slaves who trained cocks for fighting were a distant third. Those selected for the horse back riding contests really could travel far beyond the home plantation. After winning his first race in Collinsville, Isaac was selected for a number more in cities and towns much farther away. He enjoyed great success in all his early contests, taking four titles and six second place finishes in his first ten races. A good judge of horses, he had accompanied Master Brookshire and his youngest son on their travels to purchase new horses, and to negotiate stud and broad moor services. At auctions, conditions reached the point that Master Brookshire would not purchase a horse until Isaac signaled that the animal was worth the investment. Isaac's place at such events was at the back of the room in a location where his master would have no trouble seeing him. Likewise, he would signal when broodmare or stud services were involved or indicated.

In matters of purchasing female slaves, and female horses, slave traders and owners like Master Brookshire bandied the words broad mare, broodmare (symbolizing a horse) and broad (symbolizing a black female slave) as if there were no difference. Eventually, the word broad became more commonly associated with the slave and broad mare, with the equine.

At length, Isaac was selected to represent Brookshire Farms, as Master Brookshire preferred to call it at the Great Derby in Lexington, Kentucky later that summer. He was excited beyond belief. Although he was still under the harsh reality of bondage, he fared somewhat better now as far as the requirements of slave labor were concerned. Still an active trader in human flesh, Master Brookshire had more than doubled the number of slaves on his property since that day, seven years earlier when Esau had escaped. He could afford to extend some slack Isaac's way. Lest he become 'spoiled', however, they would have him perform minor chores each day - morning before the horses were taken care of, and evening, before the horses were retired for the day. He also trained other slaves to handle horses in much the same manner he was doing. Isaac was a good teacher, making sure they acquired every skill he had attained, and giving them pointers on how they could go even further than he. He was a poor sap. There was but one reason his owner wanted to ensure that other slave boys were learning the nuances of horsemanship. Master Brookshire had received an offer to trade Isaac away from the plantation. Nobody simply found out about this decision the way that Plumpsie had come across the information about Esau.

It was actually easily through the process of deductive reasoning that Old Fedderson figured out what was going on. There could be one, and only one reason, he decided, that Isaac's tutoring of five thin, young, strong boys had attained paramount importance. Master Brookshire must have decided to get rid of one of them. Simply due to their quick learning, and their youth, it was clear that any one of them would be more valuable than Isaac after they completed their apprenticeship. For now, the commodity for which he could reap a handsome price had to be Isaac. As with Esau, years before, he consulted with Aunt Sapphire.

Due to the bit of detective work by Plumpsie, years earlier, they had secreted Esau away just before that fateful morning. Another factor that made them suspicious was the frequent visits of late from Charles Rogers. He and Master Brookshire had exchanged a number of handwritten notes. They had been prepared on the Brookshire's exquisite parchment, bearing his seal, and his proxy signature in script. Unlike other official and unofficial papers, these were maintained under lock and key. Security was so strong that full loads of dynamite would have been required to remove those written documents from the fortified wall safe in the parlor.

Old Fedderson and Aunt Sapphire came to the conclusion that if Isaac went to Lexington, to compete in the Great Derby, he would never return to Mississippi. Recalling how the mother of the twin boys had suffered, only for them to see one lost to the slave trade, they could not bear the same fate for the next. Though Esau was free in the North, and hopefully living a good life, it was the slave trade that was the cause of his separation. That very day, Aunt Sapphire and Old Fedderson began to hatch a plan that would deliver him to the North as well. They would use the Underground Railroad, just as they had done with Esau.

They got word to friend's of the Butlers, the very same friends who had worked with them on Esau's behalf. The work of these white abolitionists had been nothing short of amazing. They used assumed names in every part of the South where they traveled. A number of times they encountered the same people in one state, they had met in another. Till now, they simply used assumed names, and faked their accents to avoid detection. So far, so good.

On the morning they were to meet with Aunt Sapphire and Old Fedderson, they actually passed right by Charles as he was leaving. For a moment, the man feared exposure. But as he passed by them without batting an eye, he continued. Maybe it was due to the glare of the sun in the early morning. Or maybe he was simply too weary. Or perhaps he figured that no person would be so brazen as to walk into the land of his worse enemy and plot to rob him of valuable property. Perhaps, even so, the courage and conviction of the friends of the Butlers, Mr. and Mrs. Samuel Pennypincher were the very principles motivating them to take such chances.

The Pennypincher couple, due to some notoriety, would not take an active part in the scheme this time. They wanted to teach Master Brookshire a lesson, a painfuln and an expensive lesson. The man to handle this job had no limitations of apprehension when it came to the abolition of slavery. He had even less patience. His name was Rex Cotton. A tall, well built man, graying about his temples, he appeared somewhat younger than his given age of forty-one years old. His graying temples, and the whisk of a thick mustache gave way to an air of sophistication; he looked distinguished and aristocratic. His attire was appropriately befitting his demeanor, as he acted and looked the personification of European erudition and charm. He was a sophisticate, and those in his company always wondered whether their action and behavior met his standards.

The ostensible reason for Rex Cotton's visit to the Brookshire Estate was to arrange a deal for the purchase of raw cotton to a manufacturer in Sweden. This was one of a few ruses used to gain the trust of Southerners. The phony Nordic accent didn't hurt either. As far as Master Brookshire was concerned, it was similar to other Nordic accents he had heard before. He had his youngest son to take Mr. Pennypincher and Rex on tour of the grounds, all around the vast property he owned. As planned, they spoke briefly with Aunt Sapphire and Old Fedderson, when the opportunity came. They described the boy, and the type clothing he would wear for the race. Angry that their master would do this, Aunt Sapphire and Old Fedderson asked that they remove the boy even before the race. They wanted to deprive him of even the brief victory on the race track. The Pennypincher response was that they would seize the boy at the most appropriate time. This was their way of saying that it would be too dangerous to take the boy at that point. The best opportunity would be to complete their task in the jockey quarters when the race was over and the exercise people and Master Brookshire would be in the paddock. They did allow that this time, they would take the boy in full view of Master Brookshire.

As a minister of the Gospel of the Christian Faith, The Reverend Mr. Pennypincher didn't believe that it was proper for one in his position to enjoy the frivolity of a horse race, where money was wagered. The greater sin was that most of the people who wagered, and lost, were hard working people, unable to ill-afford such recreation. But, he was a practical man and he knew that all men, no matter how greatly committed to the cause of Christianity, may suffer such a shortcoming. For him, he had seen the greatest of man's shortcomings to be the sin of gambling. Even his own brother, also a learned minister, had proclaimed that gambling was not a sin because there was not one indication in the Bible that man should not gamble. Reverend Pennypincher always had a snappy comeback. He would simply say 'The Bible never says: Don't take strychnine either'. When he happened upon an area where a number of horse races were to be run, he would permit himself to watch no more than one race. Although he detested the way horses were trained to race for man's folly, he did enjoy the communication and mastery of the beasts by the short, thin, powerful riders. They were black lads and they looked as if they had been born to their tasks.

If the opportunity to take the boy in Lexington presented itself early, before the race, there would be no looking such a gift horse in the mouth. If there were no such early opportunity, they would enjoy the race, then take the boy.

The visit worked like a fine jeweled watch. The boy, whom the Pennypinchers and Rex saw would never be told of the plot. Both Old Fedderson and Aunt Sapphire believed he would show reluctance to leave Brookshire Plantation. The phony letters of introduction and references by 'the King of Sweden' succeeded. What was all the more unusual was that the deal for the cotton was for twenty thousand, doubled bales of cotton more than Brookshire could deliver. He had the largest production capacity in the world, but the order, which he agreed to deliver was not only unlikely to attain, but impossible. He was due favors from growers, not just in Mississippi, but beyond. There was not a cotton farmer from Illinois and Missouri North, and all the way to Virginia in the South, who didn't owe him more than one favor. He would simply squeeze them. This deal was too important to be lost due to morality or ethics.

Rex Cotton offered him a check for Twenty-five Percent of the total amount of the agreed on purchase price, as a good faith offering. The Butlers had done their research well. They suggested to the Pennypinchers, that they recommend to Master Brookshire that he deliver the check to his bank, in Jackson to prove its authenticity. As a gentleman, doing business with gentlemen, the master declined. But, also as a gentleman, the Reverend Mr. Pennypincher insisted. At that point, the Pennypinchers would bow out and leave everything to Rex Cotton for carrying out their plan. Rex agreed to meet whomever Brookshire appointed. The meeting place was the Veal-Loin Restaurant and Bar, across the street from the State Capitol in Jackson. They were to meet after Brookshire's representative left the bank, the following day. The time for their appointment was at noon, the following day. Brookshire would send his two older sons. Once the check was confirmed, they were instructed to treat the Cotton/Pennypincher party to a lavish afternoon, a six course meal at the Veal-Loin. They were to spare no expense and all this would be on the master.

Rex Cotton was a man who left nothing to chance. He had been introduced to the bank's expert on international currency by a mutual friend only months earlier. Due to his manners and attire, people often assumed that Rex Cotton was 'funny'. He was anything but. The bank officer made the same assumption. Mistakes like that could lead to the ruination of the party making the error, or the party who had been erred. Although Rex wanted nothing of that sort to do with him, he did lead the fellow on. Soon he was encouraging the man, and even allowed that if he assisted him in a certain scheme, he would have the young man accompany him to Europe.

The Brookshire boys arrived at the bank at 10:AM and asked to see the bank's president. They were announced, and went directly into his office. They described their business and the bank officer summoned one James Knox Singleton. A man of slight build, and balding about the top middle of his head, Mr. Singleton was extremely formal, though polite. He was relaxed enough for the Brookshire lads to understand and accept that he appeared the expert in every way.

He examined the check, and exclaimed that he had never seen one for such a large sum of money. He added that it met all his criteria for authenticity, but he wanted to make a trip to the local telegraph office to secure higher verification. The older boy accompanied him up Market Street to that office.

The telegraph wires in Jackson extended Northeast in one direction and Southwest in the other. All messages Eastward went through Philadelphia, Mississippi, the next station. Reverend Butler had two of his experts on the wire, stationed midway. They intercepted the message before it could reach New York City for verification. From that point, they returned a message verifying the authenticity of the check. It was deposited into the Brookshire account immediately. Without a doubt, based on that one deposit, the Brookshire holdings in the Mississippi State National Bank of Jackson, Mississippi elevated him to the richest man in all the South. At the rate he was amassing wealth, his personal fortune would challenge the holdings of the super rich owners of the railroads and the steel manufacturers of the North and East.

Lunch at The Veal-Loin was more a culinary feast than Rex Cotton or the Brookshire lads, no strangers to lavish parties, could ever have imagined enjoying. Even the place itself was a veritable palace. It was far more elegant than any home in the South, and this was the section of the country that wanted to displace New England as the personification of elegance.

After the afternoon meal and they were set to depart, Rex Cotton approached the two Brookshire lads with a special request. He complained that owing to the wonderful time he had had in the South, and all the money he had personally invested, he would be unable to replenish his personal or corporate account until his return to New York. By rail, he hoped to be there in three days. He asked whether he could prevail upon them to advance him a loan until he reached New York. Since the amount he requested was only a fraction of the vast amount he had just secured to their personal account, it was difficult, in matters of business, for the boys to say no. He also knew that the boys would be somewhat reluctant to make the loan without permission from their father. The two young men huddled, and decided that it would make good business sense to provide the money. They even concluded that as men of honor, they could not, and would not, seek the prior approval of their father.

Rex Cotton now needed time to think; then he made his decision. "Also as a man of honor, I cannot accept such terms. A loan from such honorable people as bear the Brookshire name requires the full approval at the highest level. I implore you to seek approval from you dear old daddy."

The boys never expected such generous terms. They went directly back to the telegraph office and wired their dad. Since the cable would require printing and hand delivery, they knew the response would take a bit of time. The party retired to the veranda of Veal-Loin for mint juleps and lemonade.

The response, ostensibly from Master Brookshire, but actually from friends of Rex Cotton, in consort with The Butlers and Rex' cohorts, admonished the boys for refusing to immediately agree to the loan. A request for a mere million dollars was an insult, and the response was to increase it by another million. The boys returned to their bank, and issued an approved check for 2 million dollars in silver certificates to be paid to the bearer.

When this encounter was completed, Rex Cotton and the Pennypinchers were on no train headed East. They changed clothes and by horseback and four-team coach headed due Southeast to New Orleans. There they disposed of the cashier's check at the Home and Grange National Bank. They had actually obtained empty valises for the money from the Southern National Bank and Trust, located a scarce two blocks up Royal Street. At that location, they deposited ten percent of the money, and wired the balance to accounts the Butlers, and the Pennypincher duo maintained in Illinois, New York, and Pennsylvania.

As a final insult, they forwarded the original message regarding the true value of the check to be drawn from the National Bank of Sweden, to the International Monetary Exchange in New York City. Two days later, the president of the Mississippi State National Bank of Jackson received a response. The message was stamped urgent. It read:

> Stop. Check drawn for account of Rex Cotton,
> from National Bank of Sweden is worthless.
> Do not honor. Stop. Alert Authorities.
> Detain Rex Cotton, a known confidence man, for
> U.S. Government agents.

Due to the nature of these events, and follow up investigations, the expert from the bank was removed as a suspect. The blame for the breakdown was placed squarely onto the shoulders of the telegraph company.

To add more insult to injuries, even after the theft and scam had been discovered, the fellow who gave his name as Rex Cotton reappeared at the Southern National Bank and Trust to withdraw the final $200,000 from the account he had opened three days prior. He simply vanished into thin air immediately afterward.

We are soldiers, in the army. We have to fight, although we have to die. We have to hold up the blood stained banner. We have to hold it up until we die. You know Old Fedderson , he was a soldier. He had his hand on the Gospel Plow. But one day he got old, and he couldn't fight anymore, He said I'll just sit here, and fight anyhow. (A song from the times)

Chapter X - A Negro Leads the Attack on Fort Sumter
The Civil War Begins

You shall not deny one of your needy fellow men his rights, (Exodus 23:6 [The New American Bible])

Thou shalt not wrest the judgment of thy poor in his cause. (Exodus 23:6 [The King James Version])

The sweat rolled down Isaac's face into his eyes, meeting the pockets of perspiration in the folds of the oversized, wool shirt just above his waist. He breathed hard and fast, just as the horse underneath him panted. He worked him into a full gallop, a hard run, each toning the other for the hard race ahead. The small, slender, yet solidly strong jockey was on the timetable that Master Brookshire's head trainer, Morris Phillips, had set for the colt. Isaac jumped off the horse, and in one continuing motion, the lead rein was grabbed as quick as a wink by the trainer. He handed this to an exercise boy, who ran the colt over to the enclosed pen. There they permitted him to run even more, but at his own controlled pace. This served to gradually cool down the big animal, while burning off excess energy at the same time. All the exercise boys at the track at Lexington were slaves. They were owned by the family that controlled the track. When the horse was ready to relax, both jockey and trainer met their prized colt and took the rein from the exercise boy. Working as a team, they removed the bit, bridle, reins, saddle, blanket and weights.

"Well, Isaac, my boy, how does he look? Ah say, how does he look and how does he feel, my animal, how does he feel underneath you?", Master Brookshire questioned the lad. Before the horseman could answer, the trainer spoke. As a member of the old school, he never could understand why a white man, certainly of his employer's standing, would even ever think to talk to a slave. More assuredly, the trainer, Morris Phillips, never wanted to hear a slave's voice in his presence. The voice of a freed black man, or a free black woman he disdained even more.

"You all got yo self a fine piece of horse flesh here, Commodore Brookshire. All them other owners ought to just pack up and go back home. Well, Ah guess they do want to see who is apt to come in second and third place."

"Well now, Mo, you all say that lak it's in the bag."

"It is. But that is the main reason we need a strategy. Why Commodore Brookshire, Ah bet ya right now, them other boys is plotting just how they go pull a fast one to beat yo horse. That is why this boy yo got to do yo riding got to be on his toes to win this here race. If he be runnin, like I be teachin, ain't no horse on God's green earth go beat yo horse."

"You all sound mighty sure, Mo."

"Commodore, Ah am so sure bout this here one thang, that Ah tells ya whut. This here hoss don't up and win this race, you ain't got to pay me my fee fo trainin. That be how sho Ah am."

Not yet one to totally believe the trainer, he still turned to Isaac. "You all think this here boy know what he be talking about, Isaac?"

"Ah reckon he do, Massuh Brookshire. He feel like he ain't never feeled before. Dat he duz. Dat old hoss, he go up and he go run de race o' his life. Sho nuff."

In his thirteen years, Isaac had learned to answer directly and to the point. He always answered when he was spoken to, and never volunteered to offer an opinion, even when he knew another person, whether white or black, wanted it. The youngster had a natural politeness about himself, and this inured him well to everyone he encountered.

Until then, the biggest city that Isaac had ever seen was New Orleans. However, even then he had to remain virtually out of sight, almost invisible to the goings on there. However, he had been permitted to see a bit of Natchez, when, due to weather conditions, the race was postponed one day, then a second and a third. On those trips he had learned a very important aspect of horse racing. It was to assess what appeared to be the skill levels of the rival jockeys when they had down time in the stable areas. Concurrently, he wanted to prevent their assessing his abilities, strengths and weaknesses. Generally, they threw dice, bragged about their prowess at making love, and bragged even more about their prowess at fist fighting. Never saying much, and never thinking of participating in the games of throwing dice, Isaac listened and learned. His greatest asset, what made him so smart is that he was able to learn how to learn. He could detect when someone was bluffing, and who would deliver his strongest competition simply by how they interacted with each other. He also understood voice inflection and modulation as means to detect character, and inner strength. This, for many a slave was a key to survival. Eventually, after those first ten months of races, word had spread throughout the region that Master Brookshire had a natural to command his entrant at the Great Derby. Clearly for his first big day at the track, Isaac was established as the jockey to beat.

Isaac's plan for the race was going to take some calculated risks. Something about the mannerisms of these boys told him that this event would be unlike most others. He detected minor, more subtle changes in their behavior, their temperaments. What was very different now was that they simply ignored him to a jockey. Previously they would try and engage him in some conversation and just to show that he could be a regular guy, he would warm up to them, if only slightly. Now, on the eve of the Derby, they wanted nothing to do with him.

The other boys had a plan for Isaac. He knew it. Based on their plan for him, his plan for them was perfect. Every racer, each black, and representing a major Southern estate or farm, knew that Isaac simply didn't have the best horse. He was also the most gifted jockey. They could see his confidence in the way he walked. They could recognize it in his mannerisms, how he stood in the saddle, the determination, the inner strength, and the will, the all consuming, all powerful will to win. Clearly the Brookshire team was in a class all to itself. This is the reason that the other jockeys had conspired to have the quick horses pin Isaac in. They knew that he had the strength and the skill to maneuver his mount to the outside and then reposition himself for a strong finish. The key was recognition. What the others hoped for was that this small lad, still a babe in a wild, though cunningly brutal sport, would recognize only too late that he had to make a major modification to his race plan. That was their only key to victory for any one of them. This was to have its place in history as another of the best laid plans of mice and men. The reason was that the race that year, slated for Friday, April 13, 1861, never took place. Believing that it would be bad luck to start atrocities on Friday the thirteenth, the South attacked Union forces at Fort Sumter, in the harbor of Charleston, South Carolina on Thursday, April 12. The race was cancelled the following morning, the 13th.

Ironically, the general in charge of the loose band of soldiers and marksmen was none other than an acknowledged Creole. As such, he was a man with traceable amounts of recent 'Negro' blood. How ironic that the first general to lead the cause of the Confederacy in battle was a Negro.

By all information and accounts, though speculative, in newspapers throughout the South, the attack at Fort Sumter came as a big surprise. By now, people like Master Brookshire and all the power brokers throughout the South knew that war was imminent. Due to his slipups, Charles and other spies were left out of the loop. The North did learn of the attack on Fort Sumter thirty six hours prior. This accorded no time to affect a proper defense. On the contrary, prevailing wisdom in the North had the Southern first strike taking place in Virginia, or Tennessee. Fort Sumter was selected due to symbolic reasons. The South wanted to begin with a resounding victory. That type of message, the South believed, would invoke fear, and define the newly seceded states as a potentially dangerous adversary.

The news reached Kentucky quickly. The newswire story went as far as to detail a victory for the state militia of South Carolina even before the Union garrison accepted defeat. It was also noted that a number of black soldiers participated on the side of the state militia. The news of the takeover met mixed receptions in Lexington. The primary reason was that Kentucky was a state that did not favor secession. Officially, the state believed that slavery could have continued without resorting to civil war. Most of the leaders were pro-slavery, but pro-Union also ran. The Governor wanted the state to enter the war on the side of the Confederacy. However, the legislature prevailed, and the state maintained its status, for the record, as neutral.

Young men and boys from Kentucky would fight for both sides.

When the Confederacy established forts and strategic points in the state, they were run out by the state militias. Later, however, when General Grant established posts in the state, the same militia forces looked the other way.

When the race was cancelled, Master Brookshire, and all the other owners moved away from Lexington as soon as possible. As many as 11,000 people had trekked to the city for the Derby that year. By that evening, all the travelers had departed. In addition, more than half the population of young men and teenage boys had departed. Most of these moved northward and eastward, to join northern forces. The others moved to Richmond, Virginia, and Jackson, Mississippi, joining forces with the Confederacy. A few others, wanting no part of the pending war, and fearing forced conscription, headed west.

Chapter XI - Deliverance

For I know Whom I have believed, and am persuaded that He is able, to keep that which I have committed unto Him against that day. (II Timothy: 2 - 12)

The trip to Kentucky, at great expense had been for naught. Not only did the bettors not retain their wagers, they were billed for other 'expenses' due to the organizer's not meeting their costs. As men of honor, they were 'compelled' to pony up. Brookshire had actually hoped to begin to recoup the money the abolitionists had swindled from him. He did not deplore the abolitionists for wanting to fight against slavery. But, he did believe that to rob a man of his own money through a game of confidence, using his immature sons, was despicable. He never believed, however, that his continuation of the slave trade, and support of slavery in 'free' states and territories was not right, morally or ethical. Now with the war imminent, he planned to take it from the banks in the North, and more, by force, after a victory for the South.

The beginning of the war signaled the great difference in the way all slaves were treated. First, the major underground freedom routes were discontinued. Slaves continued to make attempts to escape and some succeeded. Accounts actually demonstrated that while attempts to flee decreased, the percentages of successes went up, and the real number of successes also increased. The greatest reason for this was that Confederacy resources were stretched more thinly. It simply became more realistic to use those resources to fight the war than to run after escaped slaves, at a time when the escapee was not faring well in the North either. Since the South was so convinced of its ultimate victory, as a condition of peace, they would demand that all blacks throughout the North be forcibly driven to the South, as repatriation for one of the costs of the war. There would be more conditions but this would be the first.

> [One escapee was an uncle of mine. His name was
> Jeremiah Noah Cash. He made it all the way to Chicago,
> a city founded by a black trader. His reward for attempting
> to settle there was death at the hands of an angry white mob
> in 1862. The reason: He was accused by a group of drunken
> workers from the milk factory of being the very person for which
> young white men were being conscripted into the Union Military.
> My uncle was one of many throughout the North, treated so
> shabbily by whites. Senseless slaughter of dark people in this
> country began well before Mr. Lynch lent his name to the act.
> Another fact of life in Illinois, particularly Southern Illinois
> was that in Illinois Town a powerful political family emerged
> after the war. Its power grew out of direct relation to the war.

That family was active in politics of East St. Louis (the name given to Illinois Town when the city leaders changed the name in 1861, the year the Civil War began). Its members didn't appear to give up that power until the 1950s. By then terrible damage had been wrought against the fiber and social structure, due to which, this city will never recover. In fact, the East St. Louis police headquarters, located on Main Street until it was razed barely still in this generation, bore the name of the mayor prominently on its center stone. His name was Jim Crow.

That area, Southern Illinois, had a reputation for lawlessness, hypocrisy, exploitation of poor people and racism. Elijah Lovejoy, a newspaper editor in Alton, Illinois had been assassinated on the front steps of his newspaper printing office in 1833. His killers, who bragged about their deed, were never brought to justice. Editor/Publisher Lovejoy had written an editorial deploring slavery in the country in general, and in Southern Illinois in particular. Another strange fact about the murder of Jeremiah Cash was that, like any lynching and murder in the South, this one, up North, was witnessed by black men. Just as a black person identified Emmett Till for his killers, so it was also with Jeremiah Cash. The name of the black traitor escapes me. But one thing is sure: that kind of lawlessness has always been a part of the fabric of America. I have always believed, and still do, just as my favorite Biblical Scripture attests in Second Timothy, Chapter 2, Verse 12, I know whom I have believed and am persuaded that he is able, to keep that which I have committed unto Him against that day. It was said that Jeremiah Cash and Old Fedderson came to believe in the truth of it too; each asked that it be read it at his funeral. William J. Moore]

Will someone hand me my guitar, please.

You'd better watch out for Jim Crow and his men.
You'd better watch out for Jim Crow and his men.
If you gits caught by Mr. Crow's henchmen
Then you just go join the other lynched men.

Jeremiah got caught by Mr. Crow and his men.
I say Old Jeremiah got caught by old Crow and his men.
He got too careless with his life way back then.
And he done joined all the other dead men.

You'd better stay away from Mr. Crow and his men.
You'd better stay away from Mr. Crow's henchmen.
If you gits caught by Mr. Crow's henchmen

Then you just go join all the other lynched men.

Jim Crow's men thought they caught Junior Phillips.
Yes they thought they had caught Junior Phillips.
A lynching they had planned, but Junior shot them down.
And he scared them boys out of Illinois Town.

Junior taught us that we should fight Jim Crow.
Junior said that was the only way to go.
Black settlers followed his advice.
The whites began to think twice.
Fewer blacks were killed, fewer yet were maimed.
The Jim Crow disciples we had tamed, yes Lord,
The Jim Crow disciples we had tamed.

[Of the many songs that my grandfather sang to us, I believe our group enjoyed this most. It had so much action to it, and the time changed, the key changed, the tempo would be altered, and, as one can see, there are no limits to the number of words and verses that can be added.

We also had heard about such bravery from freedmen and escapees, that we all seemed to develop our own greater resolve. Personally, I had a fear of white men because I thought deep down they would rather maintain us in a socially weakened state. Worse yet, they had the power to do so. In my many years of working in private and government concerns, I am more convinced, personally now, than ever before that that concept still abides in their hearts. Looking back, I received great inspiration from a number of people who have helped me to overcome this fear. Foremost among these were my father and mother, my uncles, especially William Henry Moore and his wife - Aunt 'Mike' - and my other aunts, notably Marvine and Jane and Doris Jean; my brothers and sisters, my teachers (notably Jean Allen Faulkner, Lillian Parks, Homer Randolph, who, along with so many others were the true inspiration for so many young black men and women and my friends, most especially my close friends. I have been truly inspired by, and learned so much from narrations (such as this one, and others) and the examples and confrontations of a few, notably Julian Kelly, John 'Sprint' Robinson, Zee Massey, Leland Seaberry, David King, my brother Raymond, his best friend, Vaughn Jackson, Carolyn McGilberry and nine most unforgettable sources - Aunt Essie, Louis Moore, Isadore Chambers, Wyvetter Young, Ethel Scott, Homer G. Randolph, Elijah Owens, Will McGaughy and my wife. I have heard many anecdotes from them, and witnessed some of their experiences. I know quite well that everyone whose name appears here, and many, many more black people can write or relate narrations of a most compelling historical significance. My heroes, and life (not role) models have been many.

My grandfather, a strong man, and a strong willed man, had few.

Looking back, from what I learned from him, and from what others have told me about him, the few people who did have some influence over the way he shaped his life, the type man he became, had an effect so intense, that its strength cannot be measured, by and from so few.]

The slaves on the Brookshire estate had been planning a revolt. Basically, they had had enough. Revolts throughout the plantation system were not unusual. However, they never succeeded. The rule was that any slave who even plotted a revolt, or an escape was beaten to within inches of their very lives. It seems that slave owners always wanted a permanent reminder of what would happen to any who was as much as suspected of wanting to be free, or thinking about freedom through a revolt. At the Brookshire estate in 1861, no one wanted to risk his life at that point because the war, they now hoped and prayed, would solve the problem.

Though the slaves knew what the implications of the war were, they still could not portray their true feelings. In effect, the very fact that they were now working the plantation was to work for the system that maintained them as slaves. Although with no real power to affect change or influence the outcome of the war, the slaves knew that unless the South defeated their adversary quickly, they could not win the war. With the stories of Moses so prominent from Sunday sermons, they believed that their time had come. Deliverance was at hand.

What after Deliverance? Isaiah, Isaiah, Isaiah. It is all recorded, measured and given in the Book of Isaiah. The Book of Isaiah was the favorite of the slaves.

Slaves believed the blessings to be rendered to them, referenced in a classless society were from this book. Their only requirement when the war would be ended was to follow the recommendation of Abraham Lincoln. This president wanted to remove all black people from this country. He favored, initially, a return to Africa. When his advisors, most notably Frederick Douglas, convinced him that this was foolish, he favored a move for all black people to one of the islands in the West Indian lands. This was what the slaves set their minds to. They believed that the lesson of The Holy Bible was setting the course for them. They could not live among these people and therefore, had to leave. This would finalize Deliverance.

Alternatively, whites, throughout the South were just as convinced that their side was righteous. The South, they truly believed would prevail due to their righteousness. There was no doubt throughout the region among the race. If nothing else, the slaves were beginning to believe in the power of prayer. Almost to a person, they prayed for a Union victory in what became for them a more brutal war than it had become for the whites who perished.

Illinois Town in 1861

At the war's beginning, life had not changed so much for freed blacks in Illinois Town. The sun shone through the window in the cobbler's shop on Fourth Street, near the end of Piggot Road. The brown mixed breed collie on the floor simply shifted his head inward to avoid the sun's rays. The dog's owner Pinkard Daniel, marveled how that dog, many of his white friends and relatives, and so many of black people could tolerate the sun so well. His skin, of native European Irish stock, was sure to burn with exposure for just a few minutes. The dog was Pinkard's hunting companion. He was the only animal allowed in his living quarters. Pinkard lived in the back of his shop. Actually he had quit working at his craft, and rented out the work area to other craftsmen who lived across the river in St. Louis. Having reached the point that he fancied himself more the businessman than the artisan, he delved more into the hobbies associated with men of wealth and leisure - hunting, recreation and politics. An ardent opponent of slavery, he had assumed the humanitarian causes championed by his father, a successful attorney during his lifetime. Until his death, his father, Socrates Daniel, had worked on the political campaigns of abolitionists. Scarcely two months before his own death from an assassin's bullet, he had given an inspired , impassioned eulogy at the funeral of Elijah Lovejoy. Although Pinkard was only three years old at that time, family friends and relatives often reminded him of his father's role for the cause. Actually, Attorney Daniel's death was not related to slavery, but to another cause he had endorsed in a court of law. He successfully, and with great compassion, defended a group of Native Nationals (indigenous Red People). Their sacred burial grounds and tribal hunting areas had been claimed by a group of land speculators. They were not only defenseless in waging a semblance of protective warfare in self defense, but until then, had lost court battle after court battle. His had been the first major legal victory for a tribe in the state of Illinois. The entire family of the attorney's was accepted as honorary members of the Cahokia and Chippewa Nations.

Pinkard was one of the men who had accompanied Reverend Omer to rescue the three kidnapped victims, three years prior. He prided himself on his management of a committee that had been formed years earlier by his father. To protect the rights of freedmen and escapees, and Native Nationals, he maintained an ongoing committee to assist these groups in time of need. He maintained an official registry, a list of manumission of former slaves. He added to the list whenever a new arrival was announced, and archived those who left the area for better employment, or who passed away. The census for black folk provided a far more accurate accounting of their numbers, addresses, and means of making a living than for any group in the bi-county area. In fact his accuracy was clearly the highest barometer of exactness in the country. The truth is that whites, by and large, objected to the census takers as an intrusion of their privacy. Often, census takers had to accept as truth, without verification, the information verbally given by whites, even though, for political purposes, their numbers were exaggerated.

Freed blacks dreamed of saving enough money to purchase a plot of land, perhaps as much as fifteen acres. They wanted to become self-sufficient. They could buy some hens and a rooster or two, livestock and horses too. By so doing, they could sell poultry, baked goods, and fresh meats. Of course, they would not have to buy these essentials either. That dream was also Esau's. With the money he earned and saved from his work with Reverend Omer, as well as extra money he earned and saved from accepting details with men like Pinkard Daniel, he had begun to develop quite a sizable savings account. While a very young man, he was becoming astute in learning that large amounts of money didn't simply look good on saving's records. Men with money, including his father, were respected to an extent that approached reverence of royalty. Even black men were treated with greater deference for their ability to demonstrate they were men of means. Esau craved that kind of respect.

He began to accept more extra work from white businessmen. As such, he had less time to spend with his family. However, understanding that he was ambitious, had a lot of energy, and would probably be the great achiever among the bunch, they encouraged him. Black people in the North figured correctly that for the race to succeed in this land, their people would have to learn, and earn a great deal from the white man about business and industry. Blacks believed they would eventually become as successful as whites. Esau pictured himself as the owner of a meat packing establishment where black people could come to find employment, decent housing and schools, and opportunity to build a future. At a young age, he had a vision.

This was the big difference between blacks in the North, and blacks in the South. In the South, black people believed they could and had to get away from white people because that would be the only way to attain God's promise. In the North, black people believed they could exist side by side, build and develop their own institutions and thrive. Esau, at that point personified the black dream.

At the time, in the North, underlying this notion was the ongoing reality that the freedman should be most careful in his interactions with all men. Many lessons were learned from their intellect. Others learned only through much pain and suffering, inflicted simply because blacks, as white men put it, 'stepped out of their place'.

> *[Dear Reader, have you been accused of not staying in your place? Do you know people who cannot stay in their place? Let me share something with you. Do you, like me, really find great annoyance with people who criticize this great race simply because so many of our people cannot stay in*

their places? It is still a sad state of affairs that black people, so the saying goes, cannot remain in our place! Don't they realize that if we had been content to stay in our place, we would still be slaves to this day?]

That Esau was saving more money than he spent did not go unnoticed by whites. First, a bank teller, pledged to maintain confidentiality about the establishment's customers, broke the pledge. He 'let slip' that the young black lad was saving at an alarming rate, for his group. Soon every white person who frequented the main shopping area in Illinois Town and St. Louis knew who Esau was. Word spread that he was a person of modest means. To blacks who learned of his 'modest means', he was rich. Judging by these standards, it was easy to see why they believed this.

The first assault on Esau came on a late Saturday afternoon in late Spring, 1861. He had just finished helping out a hunting party hosted by Pinkard Daniel. His payment had been in cash. The assailants were counting that amount, plus what he already had, having removed all from his pockets. To get to that, they had set upon him as he tried to reach the bank before late closing hours. The rogues, both white men in their late twenties were accustomed to such behavior. One grabbed Esau from behind, while the other man punched him squarely in the mouth. He came to, with his hands bound and the pair looking down on him as he sat in an alley near where he had been accosted. He said nothing, and neither did they. After about ten minutes, the pair was joined by a third person. He appeared to be about thirty-two or thirty-three years old, about half a decade older than the two thugs.

At first, Esau didn't know what to make of this. His initial fear was that he was headed South again. He believed this would be another kidnapping, as had occurred with Paul Montmartre and Charles Rogers a few years earlier. But, these guys seemed more amateurish, more unaware than one so sophisticated as Charles. The younger two said nothing. They let their leader, the older fellow do the talking. He was a tall, blond man. By his accent, Esau knew he was not local. He also surmised quite correctly that he was not a Southerner. With such good command of the language, and with erudite manners, he had to come from the East.

The gang leader knew of Esau's bank account, and concluded that he could exact an exchange, for pledging to spare the boy's life. If Esau were not willing to spare half of his life savings, then he would be killed.

Finally permitted to return home, with face battered and bruised, and his mouth bleeding, Esau didn't want anyone to look upon his face. Mrs. Omer felt it was very odd when, for the first time since he had been there, he declined dinner. That Sunday morning was even more strange. Everyone in the household had washed and scrubbed clean, powdered down, sat to family breakfast and was ready to leave together for church - everyone, that is, except Esau. The entire family became alarmed, none more so than Reverend Omer. “Ya’ll go on outside and wait for me. We go be late for church this Sunday. I needs to talk wi’ my boy.”

Esau looked up because he knew it would be senseless to hide his shame. His dad knew what was going on without looking at the boy. “Pa, now you sees why I cain’t go to church, why I cain’t eat with ya’ll.”

Reverend Omer had figured it out before he went to the boy’s room. But he didn’t know the extent of his son’s fear. He also knew that no matter how they pursued their retribution, this was a matter that could not be shared with the public at large. For now, and maybe forever, Esau wanted to let it be.

“Son, you know your ma and me, we loves you. And we cain’t make you talk to us if you don’t wanna’. But, son, you able to eat. And you able to walk. We saved you some vittles. So you go out there and you git yoself some grub. So now, you go out there and git yoself washed and clean real good. Then you eat some of that food wrapped in that paper. I wants to see yo butt in church before we leave it. Understand?”

“I understands, Pa. I be at church this mornin.”

“Good, now don’t disappoint us, son.”

“I won’t, Pa. And, Pa, thanks.”

Reverend Omer understood what had happened to Esau. The reason was simple. As an ambitious escaped slave, he had suffered a similar accost. Were it not for the ssistance of Pinkard Daniel and two other white men, his cost would have been lost also. He also knew that Esau would not show at church. This was a measure of manhood. The people at the church would have insisted on one response- prayer. Any acts of reprisal would have been characterized as revenge. And, blacks were always told, vengeance was under the purview of the Lord, not of man. However, Reverend Omer was not in the pursuit of vengeance. He was pursuing justice. Vengeance was the Lord’s. Justice, he decided, would be Esau’s.

Chapter XII - The Reckoning

Therefore will I also deal in fury: mine eye shall not spare, neither will I have pity; and though they cry in mine ear with a loud voice, yet will I not hear them. (Ezekiel 8:18)

Since Esau ate no food from Saturday morning and during the entire Sunday, he was famished beyond any measure he could remember, including those awful times as a slave. No matter how he tried to force himself to think of food, he simply could not eat. He wanted to keep busy, to remove from his mind, for the time being, the awful memory of the encounter the prior week. He believed that if he had given the thugs and their leader the amount of money they wanted, they would leave him alone forever. Of course these men had nothing of the sort in mind. What they had decided was that extorting money from weak whites and any blacks could become a profitable and safe pursuit.

Esau worked hard that entire day, and strangely, had no real interaction with family members. Although Monday was the day the banks remained open until 4:15PM, he wanted to be sure that he could withdraw the exact sum demanded, which was one half of his bank holdings. The thieves even knew the amount of interest he had accrued, and included one half that in their demand. As time came for him to leave his family, he became somewhat more cheerful and said pleasant good-byes. Obviously everyone knew his behavior was strange. However, the parents encouraged independence among all family members. For the moment, they knew there would be only frustration in trying to force discussion of the problem.

On duty at the bank that afternoon were three tellers. Although he could have gone to any one of that group, Esau chose the person with whom he had become nefariously familiar. "Why, Esau Omer, are you sure you want to withdraw that amount of money? That is most unusual, boy." Even as he counted out and scooped up the money, he never seriously questioned whether he should withdraw the funds. The other tellers and some bank officers 'overheard' the question. Knowing the Omer family, they saw no need to question the lad.

An hour later, Esau met the same group that had accosted him three days previously. To transact their business, they insisted on a return trip to the very same alley where they had conducted their first meeting. There were, they believed, certain punishments related to the same situation should Esau have decided against complete cooperation. As before, the third fellow spoke. All he did was to thank Esau for being so kind and generous. Just as Esau turned to walk away, the fellow made one more remark and this one tore to the very core of Esau. "We will see you again in three more weeks' time. When we give you the signal, we will tell your scrawny little ass to meet us here again, and we will tell you exactly how much money to bring. You understand."

Saying nothing, Esau proceeded to walk, only to be grabbed in the pit of his arm by the bigger of the thugs. "He said, understand. You acknowledge when your superiors speak to your little stupid ass!" They knew that they had invoked such fear into Esau that he would comply with whatever they demanded.

Still smarting from the whacks they administered only a few days before, Esau would do whatever was necessary to avoid the pain and suffering. His first inclination was to run away. That, he decided, was the only answer that would work. "Yessuh, boss", he answered. "I understands."

"Them darkies sho talks weird", chimed in the other thug. He was still in earshot of Esau as he walked into the street and toward home.
Esau made it no further than the cross street, when he was intercepted again. What a shock! There to greet him were none other than Pinkard Daniel, Reverend Omer and Luke.

"You ain't got nothing to say, son. We knows exactly what went on. Just walk with us. Everything go be alright." his father reassured, patting him on the back.

The quartet had followed Esau from the moment he stepped foot out of that bank. There was a saloon on the corner of Tenth Street at Bond Avenue. Pinkard knew it to be a favorite hangout of the Easterner. Since they believed that would be their destination, they could follow the trio at a safe distance. They were stopped by white people a couple of times in that short one and one-half mile distance, but Pinkard did the talking. He explained that the group accompanied him to a location where they would do some work, for him. Except for Pinkard, the three men waited across the street from the saloon.

Ordering a drink and a sandwich, Pinkard kept an eye on the group to see whether they would approach the gambling area to try and increase their wealth, gained at Esau's expense. Actually they seemed rather to keep to themselves for the most part, never letting on that they were loaded with his money. The trio did assess various patrons, obviously determining their next victim or victims.

After about twenty minutes, a person entered from the swinging doors. Pinkard had a professional acquaintance with the man. He would see him twice every week, always first on Monday, when he deposited his week-end receipts at the bank, and later on a Thursday, or rarely Friday, to transfer funds from one account to another when necessary. This was the very same teller who accepted Esau's weekly deposits in the very same bank. It was also the teller who had released Esau's funds, knowing that they would be removed from him within minutes.

Thieves are an unusual lot. This group had developed what it believed to be a foolproof scheme. They should have known better. Their problem is that they had never heard about the local folklore, or if they had heard, they didn't believe. Word about Illinois Town was that as long as Reverend Omer or members of his family were about, one should not abuse, in any way a member of that family. Years later, the family would protect not just family members, but family friends and business associates too. Truth be told, it wasn't simply the Reverend. Anyone could add the name of Pinkard, and the name of his kin, to those with whom those who took advantage of innocent blacks would have to deal. That is the way it was.

Lusting to divide their extorted money, the thieves were totally unaware that Pinkard Daniel, Reverend Omer, Esau, and Luke followed right behind them as they departed the saloon. They headed for the alley out back. They had no inkling that they were being followed. They had no inkling that they would have to answer to the Reverend. They believed they could have handled any black man. They believed they could have handled any white man who would help a black man in Illinois Town, Reverend Omer, Pinkard Daniel, notwithstanding.

"That be right, you mangy pack o' skeezers. Lay every cent out there, right on the ground. We aim to see the money ya'll stole from my boy, and every cent, down to the last penny in yo' filthy clothes." The Reverend's gun was drawn, and cocked as he caught the cabal by surprise. He talked to the quartet with such a disdain that his voice betrayed his true feelings. Something, perhaps of a spiritual nature, controlled the man, for he might have killed them on the spot.

They looked at Esau, at Luke, then at Pinkard Daniel. Each of the group stared into the barrel of a cocked pistol. Even though the odds were squarely against them, they were not ready to give in, at least not each one. "Just a minute, you niggers. You all ain't got no call to talk to white folks like that." The shorter thug was emphatic in his answer. Absolutely, one would have thought he was in charge. He was incredulous, raising his voice in hopes that someone from the street, or the noisy raucous saloon would hear.

Pinkard's gun was at his nose. He moved the barrel only inches, holding the cartridge round next to the thug's right ear, and he fired. The sound certainly burst an eardrum. He actually helped the man regain his footing, but this time held the gun to the other ear. "Now the next one will be at the other ear. And the next one after that will be through your brains, although you probably have none. Nobody asked you to say a word or anything anyway." Pinkard responded, hiding his anger behind his cool demeanor. Then Pinkard turned to the teller. "Why James Connors, as I live and breathe. I just wonder whether your boss is aware that you use your job to hose down your black depositors. Now you understand, everybody within six blocks heard that shot. Unlike you boys, people around here know how to mind their own business."

The teller said nothing. He appeared to understand the score and the percentages were not in his favor. He saw that he was now in big trouble and that his captors were as angry as anyone; even a white man would be angry in the same circumstances. This was news to him. He needed only to collect himself and regain his wits, to ensure that no real harm could come to him.

"Okay Esau just tell me", asked his dad. "Which one o these mangy skeezers was it who hit you, busted up yo face?"

This was just like the occasion of the kidnapping, all over again. The only difference was that he could not remember who had actually slugged him and this time there were no witnesses, other than the thieves.

"I is sorry Pa. I jis cain't remember. Yo knows, all them boys looks the same when it be near bout dark outside."

"Okay, Esau, we go git to the bottom o' this", his dad answered. Even though he turned his head to address his son, his cocked pistol stayed at the nose of the thief. He turned to the group. In truth, by their behavior he had figured that the bigger of the two initial assailants had delivered the devastating punches to Esau. He believed that the smaller of the original two had kicked him in the shoulder, and face while he was already down. But, the Reverend was the Reverend. He had to teach each member a lesson anyway. "Now which one o' yo mange infested, toad breath, flea bitten, shit brained critters hit this boy!?"

In unison, except for James Connors, the other three answered, "He did". Each named another.

"Okay, Esau", he quietly said to his son, clearly his voice inflecting that it was time for vengeful pain inflicting. "You know what to do."

The first punch landed hard to the left side of the neck of the big fellow. The noise of the blow was like a firecracker shattering the still air. As before, Esau's hand stung, but the rush was fleeting. Whack! He hit the second man, the shorter of the two thugs. He had seen his partner fall. Thus, he had the anticipation of knowing the strength of the young man who would hit him. Then the two bank employees stood and accepted their fate. Surely they must have thought that Esau's blows would be less forceful. They never understood that he was just warming up. He hit them harder than the other two. After a minute, Luke doused the men with water from his canteen, bringing them to. They were stood up, and made to watch as Esau slowly wrapped his oversized handkerchief around the knuckles on his right fist. Each man trembled at his knees, as the other three stood behind them with pistols to the heads of the thieves. Even cushioned by the wrapping, Esau felt the tension as his fist made contact with the smaller thug. He reeled backwards, blood gushing from his mouth and nose like an uncontrollable spigot. His nose was obviously broken and his lips would be swollen for days, even with ice applications.

"Please don't hit me again, please don't. I confess. I was the one who hit you. Please don't hit me." The tall thug pleaded, falling to his knees, begging for mercy.

This was no time for mercy. Everyone in the group knew that he deserved the greatest retribution of all. "Okay, you sissy skeezer", Esau derided. "Git up off yo' knees. Since yo told us the truth, I ain't gonna hit you. I go reserve that job to my brother, when he ready." He helped the man off the ground to the astonishment of everyone. Then he turned to the Easterner. His fist clenched as hard as he could close it, and with the outer wrapping removed, he let loose the most terrific punch he could muster in his long sinewy arm, striking the taller man squarely in the face. At that, Reverend Omer knew his son had come of age. Finally, he was heard to scream Hallelujah! The man's blood splattered all over Esau's face and chest and he felt good. "I think I broke my wrist, Pa. Can somebody else hit these two?"

Luke was taking all this in and he wanted part of it. "I can do that, and mo, Lil Brother. I can hit the nark that you promised not to hit again. But first, jis lemme take care o' these here two skeezers, first. He loosened his handkerchief from his neck and blew his nose into it. Then he wiped his sweaty brow with it, before finally wrapping it around his right fist, just as Esau had done. "I don't see why Esau have to have all the fun!"

Pinkard had to steady the gun behind the heads of the final three culprits to stop their nervous squirming. Though each man bled profusely from the blows, James Connors and the Easterner were somewhat less damaged than the other two men. The fact was that while Luke also delivered a telling punch, his were not so hard as Esau's. But the final humiliation was yet to come.

The Easterner removed the money he had stolen from Esau. It was in his inner pocket. He handed it over to Reverend Omer. Pinkard reminded them that they were to empty their pockets of all their money, to the last penny. When none was forthcoming, the men were ordered to remove their clothing. This included their underwear. James Connors actually wore silk underwear, the kind more befitting a woman of wealth. The smaller of the thugs wore no skivvies. Luke rifled through their clothing and removed a total amount, that while substantial, was somewhat less than what they had taken from Esau. Pinkard looked at the bunch, certainly wanting to punish them more. He would have too, but he wanted to retrieve every cent stolen. "Now Mr. Connors, you have made quite an impression. I am sure that you have no desire for your supervisor, the president of the bank, to learn about what you do to poor black folk. My hope is that I won't have to tell him. And by the way, James Connors. My good friend, Esau here, will appreciate it very much if you see to it that the additional amount which is not here is returned to his account immediately tomorrow morning. Every week thereafter, an additional dollar is to be added to his savings account. I don't want to have to remind you."

"Why, Mr. Daniel, that is extortion, and for a black nigger."

"Tch, tch, tch, Mr. Connors. I am sure you will always remember what happened to you in the spring of 1861, here in Illinois Town as long as you live. Would you rather that memory be short or long?"

He didn't answer. He didn't have to.

There would be many attempts to rob, beat and extort from black people in Illinois Town. As was the case throughout this land, most would succeed. To survive, the black people would have to learn new lessons. Paramount among these was that they had to learn whom to, and whom not to trust. Every city, North and South, had a few men and women like Pinkard Daniel. As long as these men and women knew how to protect themselves, a certain degree of protection could extend to black people and poor white people who lived near them. But the most important lesson for black people was twofold: They needed the help of people like Mr. Daniel, and they also had to learn to fight for themselves. Even for black people who thought they could provide their own protection, this was a lesson worth learning. For most black people, learning this lesson ensured their progeny would live to see another day, another year, another generation. It was key to survival.

The Easterner quietly slipped out of Illinois Town immediately after the incident. James Connors, in mortal fear, quietly returned the additional money to Esau's account. One can imagine his astonishment when he was told to continue adding money to the account. He dared not cross his detractors, who were now sworn enemies. When his fear became too much to bear, he seemed to vanish into thin air. His departure was so sudden that he gave no notice at the bank. The young lady-friend who saw him socially didn't even know he had skipped town. He did make one final gesture of goodwill. He transferred all his savings to the account of Esau Omer. No one could ever understand, really, why he had gone. At length no one really cared.

The two thugs had a different story. They were arrested several times for petty crimes, burglaries and rolling drunks. Their respective families could not afford to hire legal representation or even pay a bail bondsman for the temporary freedom they might have otherwise enjoyed. Their trials by juries (if you could call it that) were done deals before their days in court. They were smart enough to plead guilty. Interestingly, they were given a choice as to their dispositions. They could go to prison, or opt for military service. Even for these two poor excuses for humanity, there was no real choice. Although dimwitted, they knew that their chances for straightening their lives out were better as recruits in the Army of the Union, than as convicts in the brutal Illinois prison system. They were given a one way ticket each, by overland stage to Vandalia, the training site for the Illinois 49th Infantry.

***

The weekend after the encounter with the thieves, Luke, Absalom, and Esau, went hunting with Mr. Daniel and Reverend Omer. Until then, their hunting had been limited to areas about the Omer residence. The boys would bag an occasional hare, squirrel or raccoon. Once in a rare while they would bring home a wild turkey or pheasant. On this trip they were going after something much larger. Deer was the game. Pinkard brought with him a friend whom the boys had never met. His name was Evan Goldsmith. Having heard that he was a fair man in his dealings with all people, the boys knew of him. He owned a metal works corporation just East of the city, and a slaughter house just North. By recent decision, the city had agreed, by statute, that these areas were no longer incorporated parts of the city. Mr. Goldsmith, though he gained financially from these ordinances opposed ratification. He believed them to be detrimental to the city. To make matters worse, the statute included a clause that these newly unincorporated areas could only be reincorporated by decision of each newly incorporated area. He knew this move would doom the ability of Illinois Town to recover quite likely in the short term, but most certainly in the long run.

The boys had heard of his hiring practices, actually providing employment in factories for black men seeking hard work. Furthermore, they knew, he paid black workers the same amount of money that he paid white workers for the same work. Even though no black men could attain management or supervisory ranks, they were happy to be able just to get a job.

While he did have a social conscience, he would not go too far in challenging the political, social and economic realities of the day. Evan knew that were he to move a black person, no matter how intelligent, no matter how bright, into a position of importance at either of his plants, it would surely bring great harm to the worker and spur a boycott of his products. Better, he reasoned, to permit work for all than to promote total justice where nobody could benefit to the extent that they had. For now, he would work to change the climate, and when the time came, he would be the first to make the move.

Their hunting site was a marshy area in Illinois, due East of the Carondolet Pass. Hunters and fishermen particularly preferred this area because there was a great deal of game. The fishing, which took place in a brooked area connecting to the river was plentiful. Primarily, they took Buffalo and Cat.

No sooner were they off their horses than they spotted fresh hoof prints of what appeared to be a rather large buck deer. At a few points, due to the mud underneath the underbrush, the prints of the lone animal were deeper than the first impressions. They gave a clear indication that this was no small buck. Nearing their unsuspecting prey, Absalom spotted the even fresher prints of a male puma. These big cats abounded in the area. At times, female of that species would bond with a lone hunter. Added to the competition were two separate packs of wolves, known to be in the area. Just based on the size of the buck deer, unless the puma attacked from overhead, and was joined by other puma, the lone cat would have no chance. This deer would rout him. The wolves might have posed a different threat. However, many a deer owed its life to the ability to outrun, outmaneuver, or outfight even a pack of hungry wolves. It could require two full packs working in tandem to bring down this guy. Even that cooperation had been witnessed before in the cool valley.

On the hunters trekked. Finally they spotted their unwary prey in a clearing. Lucky for them the wind blew from the deer instead of into the animal. At that time they were about four miles from where they had tied their horses. The big stag was a magnificent animal, well worth the effort to track, and bag. He was so magnificent that Evan Goldsmith, with the best angle to shoot it in the neck, where the blood leads from the major artery, was unable to pull his trigger. He simply froze. Now the other members of the hunting party didn't have the correct angle from their vantage points. But, they showed no signs of deer fever. Their shots rang in quick succession, piercing the air like scalding hot water thrown onto snow. Crack, crack, crack, crack, and then four more cracks, all in rapid succession. The puma, still nearby, was frightened away. The wolves, two packs strong, a good mile away, were alerted and headed into the opposite direction. Hurrying to the clearing, the animal having scampered away, wounded but not mortally so, they espied a bit of fleshy matter on the ground. It was quickly scooped up by Esau, who studied it for a moment, while the others tried to figure from which part of the animal it had fallen.

Puzzled, though not troubled, each erstwhile hunter, examined it closely and then it was back in Esau's hands. He figured it out rather quickly after remembering where he had to aim his rifle if his shot were to hit the animal. With certainty and gusto he proudly proclaimed "It be his left nut. Somebody shot out that buck's left nut".

Of course no one believed him. People around were learning more and more about Esau as he matured. One of the things was that he was really quite an intelligent fellow. Even so, they were not about to allow that he was correct on that score.

They knew they had hit a section of their prey that was vital, because of the obvious signs. His tracks were making a heavier imprint in the soil and the spatial distances between the front and rear hooves were not so long as the earlier imprints. There were also specks of blood along the route.

Now spotting the buck resting in a thicket, they aimed their guns simultaneously. Even Evan Goldsmith participated in this drill. It was a group courtesy, attesting that they all had a stake in the success of the hunt, and that they all believed it incumbent to put a suffering animal out of his misery. The buck attempted to run again, but with four new rounds finding their mark, and the loss of blood, he was doomed.

They were quickly upon him. Reverend Omer took his dagger and mercifully slit the animal's throat. This deer was big. It was even much larger than they had gauged. In a near clearing, they hoisted him upside down. They dug a hole and buried every drop of blood that gushed then trickled out, onto the forest floor. Reverend Omer offered the gutting chore to each of the others, but they all deferred. He knew his boys had never dressed anything of this caliber. He was not about to let them have a go with this game.

After letting the blood, he moved his knife adroitly down the front bottom of the carcass. This man was amazing. His hands and senses were as skilled and as keen as any surgeon's. He disconnected the hide, dissected the chest cavity, and removed the heart, lungs, multi-chambered stomach, liver, pancreas and all the other internal organs save one, the spleen. This he would remove almost at the last. "You all look at this here", he explained, teaching as he proceeded. "This here, this organ here, this be the melt. Now, I knows you white folk refers to this as the spleen, but in our language from Africa, this here be the melt. You all look at this. You have to be so very careful with this organ. Don't that fluid be rushing out, and it taint the meat. The meat get tainted, you cain't eat it."

That explained a great deal to Evan and Pinkard. They had dressed a number of game meat before, and this was the first time they realized they had butchered them incorrectly. They tried to file the method they had just witnessed so as not to ruin the many ducks, geese, guinea fowl, and wild turkey they would bag again.

Finally Reverend Omer was down to the reproductive organs. He disconnected the large, oversized scrotum, leaving the penis intact. Also, maintained intact, still connected to the scrotum was one right testicle, or as they called it, one nut. What a laugh that produced as they congratulated Esau on his earlier call.

They discarded the innards, all save the animals heart, burying them in the forest. For now, Reverend Omer made a spit, pared down the deer heart, and cooked it on the spit. It looked just a like a beef steak, the way he had it trimmed. It made for a good snack, as they continued by foot, deer stag in tow.

Later that day, they brought down a female deer. She was in torpor. As they extravasated her, they found, quite unusually for deer in that region, she was soon to give birth to twins. With puma, bear, wolf, the occasional lost wolverine, other hunters, and the elements, it was a certainty that this ewe would not survive to give birth. In her sickened state, their killing the animal was more kind than nature would have been. They now had more meat to divide among the group. Each man took an equal share. They prepared it and salted it at the Daniel house. Hunting, in those days helped to provide food, camaraderie, education, and a wonderful outdoor experience. If one were so motivated, he could learn to make a living.

* * *

In spite of efforts by men and women of goodwill, and good intentions, Illinois Town could not live down its reputation as a bad place, a deservedly sullied reputation. The 'gentlemen' from St. Louis, the Gateway to the West, retired by ferry or canoe to cross the river, fighting their duels on the levee. The Omer boys, and other young lads found extra employment by retrieving bodies and returning them to the bereaved families in St. Louis.

Illinois Town also had a thriving Red Light District. Saloons with the worst reputations in the country were the primary business and business was good. Hardly a day passed that the remains of a man of prominence was delivered back across the river, the result of duels, suicides due to business losses at the gaming sites, or the result of murder. In spite of inherent dangers, the city remained a popular venue for the adventurous.

On one night in particular, a slave owner and trader from St. Louis crossed over to Illinois Town, ostensibly to have a good time and try his luck at the roulette tables. The club was known as La Vienne Rose. Perhaps as a precursor to the pending war, the place was filled beyond capacity. Those who favored the South were happy for the opportunity to form their own nation. They also reveled at the thought of teaching their more high grounded countrymen of the North some lessons. The looming war and slavery were subjects that most men didn't care to discuss in public. The moral dilemma had already pitted brother against brother, son against father, and all too often friend against friend. Business partners saw benefit and disadvantage on both sides. Ministers of the Gospel used verses from The Good Book to support slavery and the war, while other preachers found Biblical Text to portray slavery as sinful.

This slave owner from St. Louis, usually an affable sort, often brought his slaves with him, to serve as the butt of his jokes, and to give him personal entertainment. He had been losing his welcome mat at the saloon. Even some of the more ardent supporters of slavery did not appreciate the manner he used his bonded servants there. Then too, of late, a number of abolitionists had begun to frequent the saloon in growing numbers. There were so many reasons to create friction and the club owners did little to stop it. As long as they made money, they didn't care. They permitted freedmen and escapees to purchase drink and food. What is more, they could eat and drink inside, at tables and chairs next to bigots from both sides of the river. They didn't even want them to come in and buy food or drink to go. Never one to scoff at a fight, a fight he had started of course, the big fellow never dressed as if he were looking for trouble. That scoundrel dressed like a gentleman in every respect. His friends addressed him as The Major. He insisted that others refer to him as The General. In social and formal circles he answered to his given name, Merrill Laclede. Even though he was losing his money at the gaming tables, he was having a good time, pestering his slaves and by various means, ordering them to make fools of themselves. "A round for everybody on this side of the room", he ordered the bartender, treating the pro-slavery group who tended to fill one side of the room. "This round is on me for all the men who know how to keep things as they should be, for the honest men, the Gospel, and all true brothers who will die to keep this country as it should be. And will kill to uphold our creed."

As the bartender was serving the drinks, Pinkard Daniel walked through the swinging doors. He had heard the boastful salute from the walkway. By his clothes, there was no mistaking who he was. The Major figured rightly that he was an aristocratic member of the abolitionist group, perhaps even a leader. By the same token, Pinkard, from descriptions he had heard, knew that he had come face to face with the leading and most notorious slave trader North of the Mason-Dixon Line. Ordinarily, Pinkard would have been eager to engage in debate. But these were not ordinary times. Due to intense feelings on both sides, arguments, much less discussions, were turning into violence. Illinois Town was not unique in this respect, North and South. "That man, thar", The Major continued, hoping to provoke something. "Why he's the yellowiest, low-life scum round these parts. They says he even got nigger friends."

From deeper in the crowd on that side of the room the insults continued. "They even says that thar white man loves him some niggers." These continued for another minute or so.

At an interval of quiet, Pinkard spoke up. "And a round for everyone in the place, including those who say things about me that they know nothing about." He beamed his eyes again and found the face of the man for whom he would unleash his derision. He totally ignored the loudmouth. He totally ignored Laclede, who was just as happy to be ignored when he noticed the size and musculature of Pinkard's forearms when he removed his jacket and vest. Pinkard appeared to be readying for a fistfight. From his vest, he removed his money pouch and withdrew from there one bill. It was to cover the tab, a rather large bar tab at that. Clearly this was the largest single bar tab, by far, for a round within hundreds of miles of Illinois Town, in all directions.

The music, gaiety, and fanfare resumed as everyone, including those with Laclede crowded the bar to make sure they received their drinks courtesy of Pinkard. As the influence of the alcohol took its toll, that dreaded topic, the very same topic that had the country at the brink of Civil War, caused outbursts among the crowd. Soon the situation was about to deteriorate into a full scale riot when Pinkard jumped atop the upright piano and caught the attention of the assemblage.

The sides were about evenly matched, number wise, with all the men, except Laclede and Pinkard, set to retire to the center for man to man combat. "Could not we, as gentlemen, find some other more socially acceptable means of settling our argument?" Pinkard pleaded, with the faithful belief that cooler heads, even under the influence of the beer and whiskey, would win the day. He was about to deliver his logical suggestion for an alternative (a baseball game or a track meet, or even staged boxing matches) when Laclede, never one to participate in a barroom brawl himself, interrupted.

"What is the problem, cain't you preciate a good fight when you have one?" he shouted above the den at his would be antagonist. "Or, is that nigger lover too much of a mammy's boy to fight?"

The Major didn't understand it immediately but he had spoken out of turn. He just wanted to see a good brawl from his vantage point. He realized he had gone too far when he saw the expression on Pinkard's face. Clearly he had challenged his adversary to a duel, by the choice of words, and just as clearly, he understood that he had bitten off more than he could chew. His only chance lay in insuring that he could cheat at the duel to save his life.

Everyone cleared the middle of the floor, creating a wide space for the two. Pinkard removed his vest again, and his shirt, revealing a high quality cotton undershirt. With that physique, the sturdy build, The Major knew he had no chance against the smaller man. He would be routed quickly by Pinkard. But the Major could not accept the indignity of it all. He caught everyone by surprise. As a gentleman, he demanded a duel, to be conducted the following morning.

All his life Pinkard had believed that any man stupid enough to be negotiated into a duel deserved to lose his life. Although he had never fought a duel, he remained uneasy at the task before him. Sizing up his opponent, he was not unsure of his prospects. And, even though he had been challenged, he was so sure of his ability to excel that he would allow his adversary the choice of weapons.

Every man in La Vienne Rose felt some relief, even those who sympathized with Laclede when he announced, "We will use dueling pistols, at sun up in the morning. The place is the bend in the river where it meets Piggot Way Road."

The two men sat at the table which had been moved to the middle of the large room. There they signed a hastily drawn paper known as L'Article de Combat - The Duel. The Major selected as his second the lieutenant colonel of his state's militia, Horatio Laclede. They were not related. Horatio's reputation was as sordid as The Major's, if not more so. His reputation for ruthlessness was legend. They had used each other as seconds a number of times. They had been so successful that they actually hired out to perform duels and serve as seconds for others. Men had resorted to this form of legalized murder to exact a victory over a foe in business, politics, or matters of the heart.

Pinkard decided not only to make history by this duel, but to use the chance to hurl insults onto his enemies. He selected Esau, as his second. He was a mere boy, to the Laclede duo. The greater insult was the second was an escaped slave. No matter how they would have fared in the duel, The Major ordered Horatio to kill the second, the second Pinkard would be dispatched. Pinkard, not unwisely, felt that due to what he had learned from his misadventures, in his young life, Esau would be best suited to protect him against foul play.

On the other hand Esau knew that Pinkard was in well over his head. He summoned all his brothers, his dad, and key marksmen from the saloon, marksmen who would protect Pinkard to ensure a fair duel. Before they departed from Pinkard's home for the fight, Reverend Omer gave final instructions to all the men.

Now by coincidence, James Butler was in St. Louis. He had been sent to ferret out a spy who had been discretely pilfering secrets from Union Generals. In addition, he had conducted surveys of opinions and attitudes of sentiments for the cause of the South, up North. In his pursuit, Butler had followed the man to this duel. It seems that the Major had enlisted his assistance to tip the fight more to his favor. As far as the visitors from St. Louis were concerned this was not going to be a gunfight. This was going to be a massacre. Knowing the kind of men against whom Pinkard was fighting, Butler wanted to even the odds. About one half hour before the combatants were to meet, Butler was already there. He hoped that Reverend Omer and like minded men would also be there to support Pinkard because with the Major's and Horatio's reputations, this would be anything but a fair duel. When the Reverend asked Mr. Butler whether he wanted to address the men, he simply tipped his hat and smiled. During those early years, when he stopped using his surname Butler, exchanging it for his adopted name, he began to talk much less, preferring that his action speak for him, and his reputation verify it. Knowing Reverend Omer, he also believed that, as usual, he had covered every detail. What more could be said?

The minutes dwindled, but they still seemed an eternity. Pinkard had had little sleep. Esau enjoyed even less. They had a plan too, and if their timing was right, they could not only protect Pinkard, but prove to the people of Illinois Town that black people could be as brave as white men when in battle. As the second, Esau would stand ten paces from Pinkard, rather than the customary twenty. He would maintain the single shot pistol in his belt, but hold the shotgun in one hand and a rifle in the other. Almost five paces behind him, Reverend Omer would emerge and there would be two others, four paces to his right and left. Wild Bill Hickock, the name he used from that point on, would circle around the Major's contingent, but only after the men began their paces.

The principles arrived at the place of combat first. They, and their respective seconds examined each weapon. The weapons were supplied by Horatio. Esau asked for permission to test fire each. As a point of honor, the Laclede duo had to accept. After aiming and firing, he cleaned the barrels, dismantled and reassembled each weapon. Now it truly made no difference which weapon was selected. In firing capability they were no different. In aim, they were all trued by Esau. The other second, witnessing his work, could do nothing else to either weapon. Then Esau placed each weapon back into the case. The second loaded each barrel, and the case was closed.

Now, five minutes before the scheduled combat, there came a tumultuous flare of horses and riders from the ferry, just banked to the West of the dueling site. These were friends of the Major's. Esau, ever cautious and suspicious, turned with a start. He knew what was up. So did Pinkard. He felt most reassured that his and his fighter's cohorts were in place. For the moment, they figured correctly that the horde was a tactic. They wanted to invoke fear into Esau and Pinkard. The tactic simply did not work. Both Horatio and The Major wondered how they could maintain such an air of confidence in the face of the horde.

The time had come. A man of peace was at a setting that he abhorred. Now he was not simply a spectator. He was to be, and actually had become an active, though unwilling and unwitting participant. Even if he won, the aftermath could become just as unfitting to his life as the actual duel. He realized that after having bested The Major there would be one more killing, not just on Piggot Way Road, but by others who would try to prove that his victory was a fluke.

The adversaries looked at each other face to face. A jesting smile appeared on the face of Laclede. Indifference was on the face of his opponent. In the few seconds that their eyes met, Laclede realized that he was looking at an expression, the likes of which, at moments such as this, he had never seen before. Pinkard was fearless, and confident. There was no perspiration. What strange behavior, Laclede thought, for a man to face with the certainty of death looming. Then he figured it out. He was not so stupid as he appeared. Surely, he concluded, the abolitionist must have an ace up his sleeve. This man had to be as ruthless as The Major, or was he not? Certainly he knows about the heavy numbers just up from the levee, and he has to think of the plants I have in the reedy cover.

Laclede was almost correct. Friends of The Major's foe had his back, his sides and his front, even, to ensure the fight would be fair. With the help of Wild Bill, they also believed they were invincible. As the moment of truth neared, a strong sense of unease, of uncertainty, and most uncharacteristic of Laclede, self doubt.

The counting of the twenty paces was over. The men stood still until they were ordered to fire at will, anytime after the count of three. The Major's plan was simple, as always had been the case for him in his duels. He would shoot just a split second before the count of three. Having gauged the height of his foe, he would fire exactly where his throat would be. He wanted to hit him squarely at the jugular. His reasoning was simple. A crack shot, he could have aimed for anywhere on the head, torso or a crippling shot at his knee. The Major liked to see the blood run fast and hard from a fallen foe. He always enjoyed a weird pleasure from its sight. The foe would be disabled, but also feel the extreme pain and wretched despair of his loss. It was very much a sadistic event for The Major and he loved it. He also knew that Pinkard was an expert marksmen and he had engaged his men to finish him off should he miss. In that case, they would dispatch his foe immediately.

There was a slight problem in his reasoning. Pinkard had a stride that belied his height. Then too, Pinkard, suspecting a foul, moved his torso ever so slightly to change the angle, making of himself a smaller appearing target. The Major's shot, therefore, went awry. It caught Pinkard in the upper right shoulder, the impact of the bullet knocking him to the ground.

Suddenly one brave man from the rear sprang to his feet and trained both his six-shooters on the horde. At once they recognized the steely eyed gun fighter. They didn't dare think of doing anything, though they had him outnumbered forty-eight to one. The odds, they felt, were not in their favor. In truth, Wild Bill was taking a gamble so significant that he truly believed he would lose. Like all his gambles and gambits to date, this one paid off. It's not that some of those men feared death. It was more a matter that not a single man craved the distinction of falling to Bill Hickock. One by one the men dropped their guns, turned and ran tailcoat to the ferry.

Returning to his feet, Pinkard raised his gun to take aim. At that, two gunmen from the brush to the South, raised to their knees , took aim and quickly cocked their weapons. Just before they could fire, Esau let loose with the shotgun. He fired both barrels in quick succession at the men who readied to kill Pinkard. The firing was so quick that it seemed as one loud blast. They didn't know what had hit them. Neither did the eight others in that area with them. In quick succession, his dad, and his two brothers fired their rifles. The bullets coursed through their torsos before they hit the ground.

Evans and his group took aim at the bushes at the tree stand to the North. "Please don't shoot, please don't shoot. We give up!" the voices rang out as if in terror from the cover there. Guns were hurled toward the clearing, and men followed. In total number, there were twenty-three. It all happened so quickly that Pinkard was stunned. Now with the upper hand, and by fair means, he quickly accepted that dueling was no gentlemanly pursuit. Like everything else that had been elevated to a level of sophistication in this country, it was a shameful sham. By definition, a duel could not be fair because one fellow was always better than the other. Pinkard, though disdaining the method, wanted to leave that impression stamped firmly in The Major's mind. He would now prove it. Lowering his gun, he transferred it from his right hand to his left. "The duel is a pursuit for fools, Major", he proclaimed. "I regret that I allowed an imbecile like yourself to lure me into this tawdry exercise. You, I shall not kill, though killing is what you deserve a thousand times over. I shall be happy to relieve you of your right ear. Now simply do me, and yourself the honor of standing still, or your very own second, Monsieur Laclede, will be required to kill you. If he does not kill you when I give the signal, then my second will be required to so do. Do you understand these rules previously agreed to, Monsieur Laclede? Nod your head and gesture to your friend, if you understand."

Horatio Laclede nodded. Then he aimed his weapon at the face of his friend. In that brief moment he decided he would not lose his life for the sake of his fellow scoundrel. The Major stood still then closed his eyes. "Only a coward would shut his eyes, Major, Mon Ami." Laclede scolded his friend, in Laclede's preferred, and ethnic language.

The Major was not out of tricks and he clearly was not a man of honor. Although he had been searched, somehow, someone had slipped him a derringer. The only man who could have done that was the official who carried the agreement signed by both men for the conduct of the duel. Though the weapon was small, it was high powered. This time his aim was true. He caught Pinkard squarely in the chest. The missile, a ball rather than a bullet, lodged in his heart. If Pinkard would seek medical attention he would survive. But medical attention by a competent physician had to be provided immediately. For him, the duel was not over, he had a decision to make. The Major could not understand why Pinkard had not died. Now desperate, he pleaded for his life. He offered money, freedom for his own slaves, any price Pinkard would accept. "Surely, as a man of honor", The Major begged, "you will live up to your word and not kill me."

"Your deceit and treachery change nothing, Laclede. Prepare to lose an ear." The last act of his life was one of honor. His aim was true, and the right ear of The Major was blown cleanly off.

"He was a man of honor, and the terms of the duel have been met", Reverend Omer shouted from just the right side of the clearing. "But I am not so honorable. Die, snake, die!"

One bullet to The Major's skull and his life was over. Pinkard turned to Reverend Omer and with his last words admonished him for killing the Major. Then, Horatio added his opinion, while he gathered his friend's body to return across the river. "What kind of man are you, to take ze life of a decent God-fearing white man like that? What eez more, you should be ashamed of yourzelf, a Reverend, a preacher of zee Gozpel, and you behave like these. Just what kind of man are you anyway?"

Reverend Omer walked to Horatio in quick step. He wanted to kill that rascal too and would have, but that might have been considered murder. Then the thought of a duel by guns or knives was considered. But then he reconsidered because that would be the easy way out for the cutthroat. The best way to deal with him was to let him live, so that every day for the rest of his life would be kept alive with the memory of how his boss fell, and they were overwhelmed by men who, though vastly outnumbered, got the better of them.

"Just remember one thing, you evil, beady eyed Frenchman. I ain't no minister o' no Gospel. I ain't even no preacher. I just likes to read that Good Book, and I knows a lot about it. People think I am a preacher because they can think what they want to think. They call me Reverend because my first name is 'Reverend'. That be what my momma and papa named me when I was born. I am mighty proud of my name and my color too. I ain't got no excuses."

Reverend Omer wanted to kill Horatio, but he just could not bring himself to do so in cold blood. Walking away from the man, Reverend Omer had not realized that Horatio had raised his gun and taken careful aim. But,

Esau saw it. With one shot from his pistol, the life of Horatio Laclede was ended. The bullet entered equidistant his eyes. It was a perfect shot.

***

For a brief period after the duel, the cause that Pinkard championed enjoyed attention, but not adherents. Even some who were aligned with him for the duel were pro-slavery. As time passed, some of these men began to look upon the Omer family with disdain. The problem was that they were beginning to think of themselves as important, and as competent as white people. The Omer family had been notified to be present at the reading of Pinkard Daniel's will. Pinkard had maintained the children's bookkeeping records, their numbered passbook accounts, and was registered as their financial advisor. His estate or his executor would have to formally release the funds to the care of the Omer children to their direct care, or to the control of another trustee. Of course this would also require permission of each child. If they could not agree on a single trustee, each could select whomever he or she wanted, or they could manage their own accounts. The initial plan from Pinkard was unmistakably clear. His will called for the prompt transfer of their funds directly to a separate account for each, totally unrelated to any of his personal matters. Disbursement was to occur immediately upon his death. His executor, Samuel Mathers, an attorney, promised that "The full length and integrity of Dear Brother Daniel's estate will be executed as he wanted". However, everyone within earshot knew that he had no intention of disbursing one cent to a black person, even though the money was theirs, not Mr. Daniel's to control in the first place.

Unfortunately, the people in power in Illinois Town had the same disposition of the family's money in mind. Just so long as the Omer family could not touch their own money was what they wanted. They didn't really care whether Mathers feathered his own nest.

After two weeks of broken appointments and promises not kept, the young Omer people realized that the tone set was a united one by the bank and the authorities, to prevent them from receiving their money. They made inquiry after inquiry and when unable to hire an attorney to represent them, simply gave up trying.

In the city, tempers had been rising feverishly high and tension was tight. Finally the bell tolled and the war was begun. In Illinois Town, before volunteers were accepted, the city fathers issued a unanimous resolution calling for the government of this nation to return all former slaves and all freed blacks to Africa. This resolution, also enacted by the State of Illinois was the final solution that had been suggested a number of times in private conversation, and championed by the President of the United States of America, Abraham Lincoln.

Any solutions about slavery quickly became of no immediate interest in the North, especially the Northeast. The war effort was underway in earnest with many men enlisting. They truly wanted to teach the Confederacy a lesson. There was, Northerners and Southerners believed, a simple need for some serious bloodletting. Native peoples had learned to beware of white men. Freedmen, were just as leery in the North and South. Most men alive at the time, on both sides, had never fought in a war, long term or short. Nevertheless they were excited now about having new, live targets. The Omer boys, to a one, wanted to join the Union army. But, to a one, they knew that as things stood, there was no chance of acceptance. After reassessing their status, they decided that this would not be a war for black people. This was odd because there was not a black person in the country at the time who didn't have a relative who had fought and died in every war for this country. Just based on the performance of their forebears in war for the United States, slaves believed there should not be an issue of slavery. Therefore, when the war began slaves believed, with good cause, that they were slaves when the war began, they would be slaves at war's end. As the war would continue, that view would change.

However strong their disdain for the treatment of blacks, slave or 'free', they pined for justice. The Omer boys were determined to regain their money, the fruit of labor, long hard work, and honestly earned. They also wanted to take 'a little extra' for their troubles. The time for a well planned, and well executed bank robbery was now. The time was perfect.

Chapter XIII - Fighting a Personal War: A Slave's Point of View

The Underground Railroad had practically ceased to exist in the sub-Delta. Throughout the South, there were fewer and fewer attempts to systematically free slaves after the Confederate attack on Fort Sumter. At this point, in a effort to weaken the defensive capability of the South, slaves secretly organized revolts. To ensure freedom for greater numbers, a small number of young black men and women were only too eager to sacrifice their own lives. It did not matter that these rebellions had been quashed almost as quickly as they began. The very sight of their fellow slaves' lynching had the opposite effect of the hangmen's intent. Eventually the Southern aristocracy and military's fear of the Union Army would be surpassed by their fear of a slave revolt. Their fear was borne out of the freedmen's power. With arms, followers, and the ability to free himself and herself, the escaped slave was now eager to exact revenge, rather than to flee to the North. He or she could also provide logistical and military information to the Union. At all costs, and initially greater than providing resources to the Army of the Confederacy, the South wanted to invest more money and effort in preventing the bonded man's escape. Freedmen still in the South, were now unlikely to remain. The South, due therefore to this great fear, would essentially deny them permission to leave.

Unofficially, freedmen in the South were under house arrest, restricted to move no more than a quarter mile from their living quarters, when the war began. This had a horrible impact on freedmen. They had not been permitted to farm their own land. Those who worked, often worked on slave plantations where they worked side by side with slaves. Others had found work in the towns that permitted service work. Hardly a freedman had a job within a quarter mile of his home. As a result, during the first two years of the war, they were as apt to participate in rebellions as slaves, and just as apt to die. Their only saving grace was that some were finding new roles in the South, due to the war. For a few, these roles could either mean a better opportunity for freedom, or being drawn more deeply into the pain and suffering of slavery, felt more by family members than the slave in the new role.

Through Plumpsie, the slaves on the Brookshire Plantation had learned that Isaac was to be volunteered by Master Brookshire to participate in the war effort for the Confederacy. The elder slaves had decided that it was time to teach their master a lesson of life. The lesson would be harsh. The lesson would certainly result in the death or deaths of slaves. The master, after all was done, may not understand, or refuse to accept the lesson. That was all too bad. The time was upon them. If not now, it would probably never be, they decided.

Everything hinged around Isaac. If he didn't cooperate with them, or of he divulged their plans to any white person, they would have to kill him.

Isaac's life would hang in the balance.

In spite of all his efforts to curry favor from the master, Will knew that he had been used. His exploitation had been almost total. He had been thrown onto the scrap heap. Only pride was left. As far as any white person was concerned, and a number of blacks, Will was just another filthy, nasty, stupid, dumb slave. Maybe that is the reason Will assumed leadership of the freedom movement on the plantation. Although Isaac had no real knowledge that his father was Will, this news would have to be announced. Isaac, just as many slaves did, simply looked upon the master as his father figure. Will's role required harsh enforcement. To ensure success, at times this meant the ultimate test for the leader. Will's reasoning as far as his son was concerned was stated simply:

"I brung him into dis world. I kin take him out!"

Will, his brothers and sisters, and other children of his, those whom he knew could be trusted, met with Isaac down by the quarry. It was beyond the back road, about two hundred yards from the smoke house. There they explained to Isaac that he would be expected to play a role for the Confederacy in the war. He would become the service attendant for the militia unit representing the Northern part of the state. His job would be to take care of the horses, ensuring that their nutritional, and exercise needs were met. He would have to test the equipment of the cavalry's horsemen, to make sure it was always in order. Their instructions to Isaac would have to unfold over time. What they wanted, over time, was for him to become a person who would supply secret information to the spies from the North. Some would approach him even in his camp.

Unlike most slaves, Isaac remained deeply loyal to his master, and his master's family. His devotion was sincere. The other slaves only feigned such devotion. To that extent, they were very good actors. He would have to become a long study in the slaves' efforts to sabotage the Confederacy. Their initial discussions with the boy did not concern sabotage whatsoever. They simply explained in very simple terms what an implication of a victory for the North would mean. Then they compared and contrasted those to the meaning of a victory for the South. This meeting ended rather quickly, and they set the next meeting for two nights later. "I sho duz preciates ya'll tellin me bout my duties to my army and all", Isaac rolled his letters over the smooth velvety articulation of his voice. His voice was low, and he seldom raised it, though he could have with ease. He had the type voice that was made for singing, for he could modulate sounds, tones, and rich whistles with the ease of the birds in the trees. "The thang, the one thang I jis cain't unnerstands is why massah cain't tells me hisself."

Still young, immature, and most impressionable, Isaac was unaware of the implications of his role in the favored position as the master's primary jockey and horseman. It was at this point that Amos, a cousin of Will's and about the same age as Will, spoke up. "Isaac, we dudn't know if you remembers your brother", he took his time trying to attain the correct perspective. Since they had been forbidden to so much as utter Esau's name, this effort would require great care, and great trauma. The success would depend upon their ability to decrease the psychological trauma. Isaac nodded as Amos continued. The slaves believed they were getting through to the boy. They felt they were getting him to believe they would convince him to accept their rationale. This, they hoped, would lead to his cooperation. "You wuz jis a little one when he had to be taken from us."

"I has a vague recollection o' him' I sho duz. Hear tell he up and run away. Folk here don't talk about it too much no mo."

The truth was that anyone, white or black was forbidden from making mention of the twin. To infer that he had succeeded in his run to freedom was a worse thing to do, for it brought serious, if not grave consequences. Isaac had been made to believe that his brother had forsaken him and his people. His act, according to that way of thinking was callous, selfish, and disrespectful to his own people and to his master and his master's family. "Anyways, I dudn't rightly sees how he gots anythang to do wid whut massah want me to do wid. I's mighty proud to be o service to my massah."

Isaac's delivering his point of view only served to help the slaves understand how difficult their task would be. To get Isaac to understand that Master Brookshire was an enemy, not a friend was impossible. Up to then, he had received what he perceived as favorable attention, and minor privileges, such as better food and good attire, due to his skills as a horseman. He had even been permitted to travel far and wide, having displaced Nathaniel and Thomas in their former roles. Isaac simply believed that they were jealous of his new found favor, and growing favor, from their master. Now they had no choice but to tell him the full truth. They prayed the truth would free the boy. "Listen, you lil bastard", irritated, perplexed, and angered, Thomas finally yelled. Isaac had never ever heard this tone, or seen such rage directed at one black person from another. You gots to know the truth!"

Thomas remembered years earlier when a slave named Prissy reported to the master of a pending attempt to run. Two slaves had been involved. The slaves were beaten to death by Buck King, the overseer. About a month later Prissy was lured into the fields where the cotton was high. She was hog tied and her mouth was filled with cotton, unrefined, painful, and a perfect muzzle. There they beat her, just as the slaves had been beaten. By the following morning, the buzzards had done their work. Only mere bones were left, all flesh picked clean. "The massah, he wuz go sell your brother. He didn't run away. He was saved to freedom", Thomas continued, removing the anger from his voice, now addressing him with sincerity and patience. "If you had half a brain in that thick skull, you wanna do the same thang. The truth is the massah, he cuddn't git a dime fo yo lil scrawny ass that time. He could git a lot mo, a whole lot mo fo yo bro. Yep, sho nuff, a whole lot mo fo him. Why, I bet he be jis up North, organizin a group that go come back here jis to save all o' us, incLudin yo undeserving lil black ass."

If Isaac were older, Amos and Nathaniel would have killed him right there, and Will would have done nothing to stop them. He couldn't have, even if he had wanted to. A few, very few, knew that is how Will felt, but what they didn't know, and could not understand was why. They wondered. Will, Amos and Nathaniel understood that they didn't understand, and they understood why. They would have explained but they decided that if they had to explain, those few didn't really need to know.

"They toll me ya'll be sayin such bout the massah. They toll me ya'll come round to spread that filth. Massah and Old Buck King, they wuz right."

At that, they let him go, but concluded they could not 'let go'. Isaac presented too much of a threat. He represented the type of problem which required positive redirection, rather than physical pain. The latter, they knew, would only reinforce his misconception about the white race. There were basic lessons he had to learn. At length, if they failed in their teaching, the ultimate price would be paid by Isaac. Their punishments would be more immediate.

***

The group never expected that Isaac would go immediately to Buck King and Master Brookshire. But that is exactly what he did. Amos, Nathaniel and Will were aroused from their sleep, one hour before dawn. Three hired hands, all white startled them, guns drawn, barrels on their noses. Not a word was spoken. They were met behind the main barn by Master Brookshire, Buck King and twenty-three citizen council white men from the town. Saying nary a word, the three men stripped off all their clothing. The slaves gave no resistance as they were tied to separate axles and wheels, taken from buckboards not in use, and staked to iron bars. Immediately after, all the slaves from the plantation, house and field slaves alike, were roused and directed to the area behind the barn. No matter how young, they all had to be there. Newborns had no reprieve from this experience either. The only question was whether they would lose only their skin, or their lives too. In many ways, the men preferred the latter.

Master Brookshire walked quickly to the wheels, freshly oiled leather bull whip in hand. His stride appeared that of a military officer performing official duties.

CRACK!! The first lash pierced the fresh early morning air, then hair and skin on Will's head.

CRACK!! The second strike lashed the back of Thomas. It opened a gash just at his spine.

CRACK!! CRACK!! Two strikes in succession found the right shoulder of Amos, then the left.

CRACK!! CRACK!! Two more strokes went into Will's back.

CRACK!! CRACK!! Now it was Buck King, lashing Amos.

CRACK!! CRACK!! CRACK!! CRACK!! The two men were lashing out at all three, methodically beating them as if surely no mercy could be in order. "Will, you all above all the others. Ah nevuh would have thought you all would do this to yo Masta. Afta all Ah have done fo yo and yo boys. Ah just don't understand." Crack! Crack!

Again Master Brookshire hit harder. CRACK!! CRACK!! and harder again. Now Buck King and a third attacker, his top assistant, were beating the three men. They said nothing as they continued their execution with a passionate fury. "Ah ask yo black carcass again, Will," the irritated voice of the master bellowed. His anger became more pronounced because, as had become the practice, not one of the men cried out in pain. As they inflicted strike after strike after strike, the well oiled, and sharp iron reinforced leather, infused with coal oil, tore into their open wounds, burning their flesh as they suffered. "What have ye to say fo you alls selves?"

Again they cracked their lariats deep into the slaves' backs. They were impatient for a response. It was as if they would be the first executioners in a long time to make slaves show that the physical torture was too much for even them to bear.

Will would keep quiet no more. He was finally, at this stage of his soon to be few minutes of life, understanding that he could do by dying what he could not do in life. He had been smart all his life. It was just that now he realized it. He knew he was doomed. However, he could make an attempt to save the lives of the other two. When the beatings commenced, Master Brookshire had decided that all three men would die. It would take a great deal of convincing to persuade this blood thirsty cabal to spare two lives. "I is powerful sorry, massah. I really, sho nuff is. And yo been so good an every thang."

"Then you all admit it, you all did talk to Isaac, your own son?"

"Yessuh, yessuh, massah. I talks to de boy. Ain't nobody else say nothing. I be de only one."

"So you all admit it; you all admit you all tried to turn him agin me?" CRACK!! Another lash. CRACK! CRACK! More lashes for the other two as well.

"Massah, I knows I got no rights to talk wid dat boy. Dat be where I wents wrong, massah. But I ain't put no idees in his head. I's guilty cause I jis talks to him. So, massah, jis beat my black ugly carcass as yo sees fit. I be as guilty as sin."

"Now Ah don't understand. Your boy, Isaac, says you all and Amos and Thomas told him some nonsense bout his twin brother, me and Buck King."

"Now massah, dat whut I be tellin. I toll him don't be disrespectin dis here plantation, like yo brother. Don't be gittin no idees bout runnin. Dat be de God's honest truth, Massah Brookshire. But I knows I ain't got no right to say dat to de boy. Massah, I believes dat boy bin round dem hosses and jackasses too long. I dun toll dat boy to live up to massah's espectations."

Buck King figured that Will was trying to pull a fast one. Due to the master's arrogance, the master didn't believe that Will would cross him, let alone tell a manipulative lie. The story began to make sense to Master Brookshire. Until that moment Buck had been silent. Seeing that his employer was buying the story, he had to interject some sense back into the process. "Boss, them niggers is lyin. Why did it take three o' you all to talk some so called sense into that boy? We thanks he knows how to be a good nigger. You all, and these here two low lifes ain't got no call to butt in."

"As usual, you is right, Mr. Buck King, suh", Will continued to try and talk himself more quickly into the death that was coming, and Amos and Thomas out of a sure death. "Lak I always says, I knowed I wuz wrong. Dat be why de massah gots to do whut he gots to do. Ole Fedderson, before he up and die, he use to say dat in de Good Book dat we should help our brethren. Dat be why Ole Amos, and Ole Thomas be wi me. I also toll dem boys I go beat they carcass good, they don't come wi me. They be knowing how I beat dem so bad, they comes along. I be tryin to save they souls too. I says, if we goes agin our massas, we goin straight to hell, we does. Dat whut Ole Fedderson be sayin; he still be alive, he be sayin dat. Massah, I knows I gots to die. If I be lyin now, when yo gots to send my carcass to glory, I cain't go to heaven. So jis do whut yo gots to do. Show us all dat by doin de right thang, yo be de man o' honor dat you natcherly is."

Although they were in great pain, Amos and Thomas were laughing under their breath when they heard that presentation. Had they not been able to make their laughter sound like moans, they would have been killed instantly. In his way, Will was teaching a valuable lesson to the slaves. Always, always, no matter what, save your friends and those you love when you may be doomed. If necessary, be convincing enough to die in such a manner that others will know you have given them a chance to survive.

Based on the message Will was giving, Buck King and all the other white people there, except Master Brookshire, understood just how smart and cunning Will was. The slaves, and certainly the white folk, had underestimated his intellect. The slaves and the white folk knew that Master Brookshire was a smart man too. Now the intent of Will's message became clearer and clearer as the master engaged him in conversation. Will knew he was getting the better of the man, and though also in pain, he was enjoying the discussion. Every time he opened his mouth, for every word, for every breath, he hurt. In his mind, Will told himself, this is a good pain. I have to go on. The master was matching wits with a man who was smarter. No matter the price it would exact, his life, Will was determined to illustrate a clear and precise lesson to the slaves. Likewise, he was sending subtle messages to his son, while he advised the slaves of the manner they should respond to his son when this would be all over.

"You all are so right, Will. Now Ah understand. You all are doing the work of the Lawd. You all are doing the work Ah taught you all how to do. But, you all admitted you all did wrong, because you all spoke to yo son without my permission. Release Amos and Thomas! Let those two niggers go!" Master Brookshire ordered Buck King. The stern visage on his face, the forcefulness of his voice, were all that was needed. Even Buck King knew when he had to obey. "Now as fo you all, Will, you all admitted you all violated my rules."

"I duz, massah."

"As fo yo black carcass, I aim to finish beating that devil out of you all."

The following morning Will was buried in the common burial ground for slaves. Every plantation, every slave owner, had one. They stretched from Virginia to Texas. To make use of space, the pit in the back of the Brookshire estate didn't take up a lot of room. It was, on the whole, very deep. Burial was simple. Corpses of those recently deceased were simply dropped onto the rotting flesh and decaying bones of those previously interred. Then new dirt was thrown onto them.

[*When I look back over my life, I am putting so many things into perspective. I have always believed in The Bible. Everyday I read The Bible, The Journal, The Crusader or Citizen, or The Globe, in sequence. I read every article in the newspapers and a set of full context from The Bible. At my funeral, I want the choir to sing the song Be an Overcomer, and the verse from Second Timothy, Chapter 2, verse 12, to serve as the theme of my life. "I know whom I have believed, and am persuaded that He is able, to keep that which I've committed unto Him against that day."*
I do believe every thing that is in The Book, and I accept every word. I rarely spared the rod. Even if I did spare the rod, my children were not spoiled. So, that does not trouble me. But I am not a preacher. I am not a simple man either. One day someone will come along to put all this in the right perspective. The single regret I will have is that I won't live long enough to see that person do so. (William J. Moore)]

[I find it somewhat odd that my grandfather seemed to make eye contact with me when he made statements about the need for an interpreter. He had heard of men and women who cautioned that the precepts of The Holy Bible were, at times, read knowingly with or from the wrong meaning. Like no one else in our group, I believed that the readers with the 'right' meaning had made the 'right' interpretations known. Perhaps this was what he wanted me to do. For me, just as for my grandfather, that was too akin to being a preacher. Men and women with the gift and calling should do that. I never had that calling. Suffice it to say, I learn so much about the right reading and the right interpretation when I listen to his son, a man who I believed, did receive God's call. Like Big Daddy, the consternation due to a number of verses has left me concerned about interpretation. I believe that men and women who are truly called to interpret, not so much to preach, are best gifted to explain the real meaning of The Bible. In our search for greater experience with the truth, greater fulfillment, these are the people best able to help us attain that fulfillment. I don't have that gift, or the calling. My grandfather, I am convinced, fathered a man, and a daughter, who do.]

> I won't need my guitar for the rest of this Narration. I have done enough singing. You boys want to hear me sing and strum at this guitar, be here when that mood hits. (William J. Moore)

(We were puzzled by so many aspects of the War Between the States. Our history books, and the lessons we had learned in school simply didn't give the time and attention that we needed. The summer activities back then included two weeks of Vacation Bible School at the church as the only formalization we received. From what I recall, the lessons concerned stories from The Bible, of course, the heroes and heroines among the children of Israel, and how the ethnic group, God's chosen people, always survived. They were always triumphant over their enemies. When Bible verse was quoted about God's chosen, some of the text cited their conquests of peoples who had no quarrel with them. They were simply in the way and had to be annihilated. Then there was always attention to Christ. The one aspect I recall most emphatically about Vacation Bible School during those youthful summers, was that we should pray and pray and pray. This country, our lessons declared, was founded on the search for truth, the establishment of faith, the belief in one God, and justice, equality and the pursuit of happiness for all. These goals were attained, our lessons maintained, through the perseverance in prayer by all early Americans.

The real history lessons were the brief narrations from my father and uncles, who were real treasures; fathers, uncles, grandparents and family friends of my friends; and the many public school teachers (all black) who didn't take a back seat when the truth required that they step forward. Most importantly were my friends, who lived in the Housing Projects where I was reared. Most notably I remember Frank Bender who opened a lot of eyes to the value of black men and women to our race. He knew of the true contributions. However, the foremost single lesson in history came from my grandfather in this Narration. My only regret is that I don't remember half the names and roles of the people who were significant to the Race Riot of 1917, and the Honky Tonk blues wars a decade later.

Like so many of my peers, friends, my sisters and brothers, I also have vivid memories of the Sunday School classes. Interspersed with Biblical teachings were modern accounts of historical people, to whom 'we owed gratitude'. The books for our lessons came from the church affiliated headquarters in Anderson, Indiana. As far as I am concerned, this was a horrid attempt by that organization to 'brainwash' us. It grew even worse. I don't recall one single hero who was a black person, a red person, or a brown or yellow hued person. Let the headquarters have it their way (and they did). Crispus Attucks, a black man, the first American to give his life in the fight for freedom against Great Britain, never existed. There were no Red hued people to help establish the first Thanksgiving for the Pilgrims. The black man who served as the navigator for Columbus, and advised him that he was not in India, but on a new continent, never existed. The Chinese immigrants played no role in the construction of the first transcontinental railway. The truth is that phenomenal accounts of bravery, heroism, and faithfulness to the success of this country were contributions of people of color as much, if not more so than others. Our history books never provided this information. We are all grateful to our forebears who kept these memories alive through so many narrations.

My grandfather told us the stories, these narrations, but he never instilled his own interpretation of whether the outcomes were right or wrong. Nor did he try to instill any values. He simply wanted us to know about these things and we could decide on the moral or ethical value there from.)

In truth there is learning, and it is the learning that shall set you free.
(William J. Moore)

Let me give you a word of the philosophy of reforms. The whole history of the progress of human liberty shows that all concessions, yet made against their claims, have been born of earnest struggle. The conflict has been exciting, agitating, all absorbing, and for the time being putting all other tumults to silence. It must do this or it does nothing. If there is no struggle, there is no progress. Those who profess to favor freedom, and yet depreciate agitation, are men who want crops without plowing up the ground. They want rain without thunder and lightning. They want the ocean without the awful roar of its many waters. This struggle may be a moral one; or it may be a physical one; or it may be both moral and physical; but it must be a struggle. Power concedes nothing without a demand. Frederick Douglas

Chapter XIV - Trust No One

As the highest ranking member of the State Militia in Illinois, Samuel Mathers had assumed the role of leading recruiter for the Union Army. When the war began, there were 2,037 members of the standing Union Army throughout the state. The total number in the state militia was 4,794. (A number of members of the standing army were also in the militia but there was no accurate count.) Since times were bad economically, Mathers had no trouble in his recruitment. Volunteer numbers throughout the Western fringe states ran particularly high. This made for an interesting situation, one that Mathers could exploit temporarily. There were two ingenuous methods. The first simply involved the sale of deferments. Mathers recommended deferments to the local draft board. The fee paid was three times more than the actual amount authorized by Congress. Mathers simply referred to the overage as a processing fee for one of the overcharges. For the other, he referred to it as a simple surcharge. He kept the processing fee and gave the other fee to the Draft Board.

The second means was more involved, in that negotiations were underway with neighboring states. These were Iowa - the state from which the greatest number of soldiers lost their lives; Wisconsin - the state whose soldiers were reputed to be the most ferocious on the field of battle; and Michigan - the state which provided the greatest financial support for the war on a per capita basis. The problem is that Illinois, due to its economic recession, saw many of its young men enlisting, far more than other states. The land of Lincoln had to deny entry to a number of these men because it could easily have become 'Lincoln's war'. Mathers simply enlisted these men and gave as their official residences homes in the other states. This ensured that their draft quotas would be lower. In turn, these states paid Mathers a fee, by act of their state legislatures. For the men who lived in those states and could pay for a deferment, Mathers was given a small percentage of that fee. Within six months he had become a very rich man just from this process. Since the State of Missouri was technically a Southern state, committing its militia to the Confederacy, young men who were sympathetic to the Union crossed over into Illinois and sought out Mathers. They joined the Army of the Union as though they were Illinoisans. Of course, Mathers could enlist from other states also, particularly those whose young men avoided the war.

Esau, Luke, Absalom and other young black men, whose savings were denied them, continued thinking about how to reclaim what was rightfully theirs. Time was on their side. Reverend Omer had explained to them that contrary to what white folk believed, this war would last for years. Their best time to regain their money, and retrieve much more from the bank would be during the darkest of days of the war for both sides. They simply needed to exercise patience. To ensure that Mathers would not interfere in their lives, they simply ignored him. He was so powerful that he could easily accuse them, or have someone else accuse them of a crime, and banish them to prison for life. Just as they held their peace in slavery, their peace would hold them while free.

Mathers was into image. He wanted to change the city's image too. On the city council, he pushed through an ordinance changing the name of the city from Illinois Town to East St. Louis. His hope was that by that simple gesture of name change, the city would garner some of the trade, manufacturing and reputation that was going to St. Louis. All was going well for Mathers. He brought his four sons into business with him, teaching them how to wheel and deal and gain the support of the rich and powerful. In so doing, he befriended many of the little people who believed he wanted to help them. The awful truth was that he did want to help them. He wanted to help them let go of their money and he was there to claim it. At the end of every scheme of investing, handling, management, borrowing and lending of money was Mathers. The war provided profiteering for many and foremost among this group was the Mathers family.

At one point an emissary from President Lincoln was dispatched to the Regional Union Headquarters outside Illinois Town. Lt. General Morton P.S. Gruber, originally from Tennessee, had settled in Chicago. An ardent supporter of Lincoln, he had made the military his career since his days at West Point. Scarcely six months into his presidency, Lincoln found himself in a major war. With advice from his senior staff in the War Department, Lincoln accepted a limited 'unofficial' role for black men. When atrocities began he wanted and saw no purpose in using black men to fight alongside, or in concert with white men. The role for the freedmen was a simple one, and men like General Gruber were charged with executing it. Lincoln clearly intended that only Freedmen who had escaped should be used for these purposes. Men who were born of free parents, disassociated from bondage before birth, were not acceptable. Even slaves born to free parents, whose efforts would buy the freedom of their children before they could suffer the pain of slavery were unacceptable. Mathers, and other recruiters from the area were invited to the tented bivouac of General Gruber just North of Illinois Town, near the Granite City. There was also a push to involve the resources of black farmers as contractors.

Mathers was for any idea that came from above. But this idea also held greater potential for him to attain more wealth. The profit potential was enormous for the agent of these enterprises. As a bank officer, he had a hunch that Reverend Omer and the other black farmers throughout Southern Illinois were making much more money than they deposited in local banks. Now, through negotiating a portion of their goods for purchase by the Army of the Union, he could assess their relative wealth, and begin to scheme for some of that. He envisioned forming partnerships, ostensibly to endure only through the war. In truth, he intended to take over their entire farms. By the end of the war, if it lasted long, not one black man in Southern Illinois would own land. He would take it, unless other white men had beaten him to it.

Two Mondays later, Reverend Omer, John J. Brown, J. W. Worthington, and Lewis J. Cummings, owners of the four most productive farms (in that order) met with Mathers and general Gruber at his bivouac. Each was given a document that contained terms for the supply of fresh meat, to include pork, beef, limited amounts of poultry, and lamb to the Army. They were also to supply an amount of vegetables, in season. These were corn, wheat, oats, tomatoes, onions, beans, cucumbers, okra, potatoes and greens.

General Gruber suggested that they should not sign the Agreements right away. In fact they could refuse. However the terms were generous, far more generous than anything they had ever realized in the past dealing with the likes of Mathers, in whom they had no trust. Even though the agent for the deal was identified as Mathers' oldest son, to receive ten percent, not from them but from the government they felt comfortable in signing. The sight of the amount to be paid was just too large for them to turn away, Mathers as agent or not. When General Gruber suggested that they take extra time to have their attorneys review the contracts, before signing, they found it all the more hard to say no.

Black people knew about Mathers. No black person trusted the man. They made no secret to General Gruber that they felt Mathers and his son could not be trusted. But their deal was with the government, not with Mathers. The government would have to take their chances with Mathers. Since he was a key player, they would take the contract to their attorney for review. The four men agreed to watch out for each other, and to keep a wary eye on Mathers, his family, and his friends.

Evan Goldsmith was the first to look at the contract. He too believed the terms were very generous. He also believed that the inclusion of the Mathers boy as agent would require ongoing scrutiny by the black farmers. Still reticent, he took the document to his personal attorney, in Alton, Illinois, a day's ride, roundtrip, by horseback.

After the various attorneys and friends had reviewed the contracts, each farmer agreed to sign. Multiple copies were drawn up, each an exact duplicate of the other, prepared in calligraphic script by the General's staff. As a gift, a show of good faith, each farmer made a personal gift to General Gruber.

John J. Brown, a specialist in hogs, presented four complete sides of his most succulent hogs (salted to preserve); five smoked hams, twenty smoked shanks, thirty slabs of smoked and cured bacon (sliced); thirty pounds of cured premium sausage; and eight slabs of smoked ribs, ready for eating. To enhance the gift, he presented the general with two, live Chester Whites.

J. W. Worthington, a specialist in sheep, presented him with eight racks of rib; eight legs of lamb; eight sheep shanks; 100 pounds of ground lamb meat; and thirty pounds of cured and smoked sheep sausage, ready to eat. As a special gift, he used the lining of the intestines to shape sixty-nine prophylactics for the personal use of the general and his aide de camp.

Lewis J. Cummings was an expert in beef. He delivered 200 pounds of ground beef burger steak; 100 pounds of short ribs; 300 pounds of round steaks, 400 pounds of smoked beef sausage, ready to eat; and 500 pounds of roasts.

Reverend Omer presented two gifts. The General was provided two of his most magnificent horses, with blankets with these words stitched in the corners:

General Gruber: Army of the Union

Of all these gifts, each obligingly accepted by the General, he prized the two stallions, one dark black, the other a splendid roan, most of all.

Mathers must have felt like he was biting nails. He couldn't understand why these men brought him nary a gift, even a token one.

The next morning, General Gruber visited the properties of the four black farmers. It was an expected call. He asked whether they could meet that night at his quarters in the Granite City. He also requested that they bring the young men of their families. They agreed to be there. When that was done, he stopped at the Mathers home also. His was the last invitation extended.

General Gruber was not simply being hospitable. Everything he had ever done since just reporting to the Point was calculated. He had used such behavior to attain his rank in the military. There was a hidden purpose in this matter as well. The evening, on study, was uneventful. Mathers acted as though he accepted the company of the black farmers as social equals. He only did so because he understood that General Gruber respected them as relevant and honored participants in the Union's cause.

At dinner's end, the four were asked to join the General behind his bivouac. Mathers was not included. In fact, just before they joined the general, he told Mathers he would see him later on in the week, when his customary report was due. Reverend Omer understood immediately. Mathers was on notice that he had to treat the four with respect. Shady dealing would not be tolerated. He left that night fully believing that the four black men were in the confidence of the general. He was so very right, for once. Fair deals not withstanding, the black men trusted only themselves.

CHAPTER XV - Revenge is Mine; Thus Saith The Lord

Mathers, by now, had control over every facet of business in Southern Illinois. The only farmers who were able to thwart his interference were the four who did business directly with the government. Small farmers, black and white were squeezed. Their profit margins had to be shared with Mathers or he would simply eliminate them through competition. As the lead recruiting officer he also controlled the draft. When men could not come up with their tax assessments, he simply exacted a deferment at a cost, for their children. It was very strange how a man, without argument let money go to the government for one purpose but would not part with it for another.

To continue to conduct their independent business, as they always had, Esau and Absalom moved from the Omer home. They reported for work just as they always did, and continued to enjoy meals with the family. As in the past, Reverend Omer continued to pay them for their work. The boys did not obsess over it, but they had decided to get every penny, and then some back from Mathers for his thievery, and to rob the bank, for their help to the man. The idea was Esau's but Absalom, after some thought, decided this was a mission that had to be accomplished. Time was their ally, and they would use it to devise a good plan.

On their own, the boys hunted, fished, trapped, and furnished logs for construction and firewood. They covered a wide area to make the most of their effort. They were doing so well, that they could have left their father's employ. But, that was unthinkable, and they never missed a day. During this time, black people enjoyed a sharecropper system with the county governments in Illinois. Esau and Absalom considered going into this phase of farming but again, decided that was unfair. They reasoned that although black farmers were earning good money, they could never own the land. Land ownership, like their father and the other successful black farmers had demonstrated, was their goal. They believed that they could not in good conscience make money from the sweat of their brow for a county government that permitted men like Mathers, and banks to rob them of their money.

Occasionally, in their travels, they came across Mathers. At times, they would sell him dressed deer, duck, quail, pheasant, or wild boar. As time went by, and their paths crossed, Mathers would not pay the boys. Accompanied by a formal platoon, he would simply suggest that he would pay them when the Army paid him. To avoid him, they simply altered their trade routes, adjusting their schedules so that he never knew where they would be next. For the boys, this worked wonderfully. Their goods were now finding their way to market, and Mathers only found out well afterwards.

Just as they became adept at avoiding Mathers, he became all the more determined to find them. The word had gone out that he wanted to talk with them about a certain debt that he owed them. He claimed that he wanted to set matters right with the Omer family. Of course they didn't trust him. Though skeptical, they agreed that since they wanted to remain in the area, because of his power and reach, it would probably be better to meet with him. Due to their resourcefulness, they did not want to jeopardize the substantial amount of money they took in. Since he also had influence over the law enforcement function, they didn't want to risk accusation of a trumped up charge. As they saw it, they had to meet with the man. However, they were determined to outsmart him this time.

For his part, Mathers had a hunch the boys were making money and salting it away. Through his informants in every area bank, he knew their money was not deposited in the banks. To allay the fears of the lads, Mathers decided to meet them at Army headquarters. What Mathers had in mind was extending a commission to Esau and Absalom, to supply a certain amount of food to the Army. For their own pay, they would be permitted to keep a certain amount of their products to sell as they pleased. No mention was made of the fact that Mathers had been granted a budget, which included a goodly amount for food. This budget was to supply food from freelance contractors like Esau and Absalom. For every bit or morsel provided in free states, and slave states not in rebellion the government had enacted a law to pay. Mathers, through his efforts in this regard, demonstrated profiteering at its highest level of deceit.

Mathers would never have thought of exacting these terms from a white independent. The boys knew it too. At the meeting, the boys gave him a veiled promise to cooperate.

Three days later, on a Sunday morning, the boys made a modest delivery to the troops stationed on the Carondolet Levee. This was their first step in getting even with Mathers. Mathers, as they knew he would be, was on hand. They insisted on his signing a receipt that the goods were delivered. He not only gave them a receipt, but also itemized everything they had supplied. The was the second step in Esau's plan to regain what was truly theirs.

That night, they extracted from their secret hiding place, a slight portion of their savings from their work. They placed this amount neatly into an envelope. In turn, they placed this into a leather pouch that Absalom had modeled from the skins he had tanned. The leather grain was of remarkably high quality, a testament to his skills as a tanner. His leather goods were beginning to fetch greater profits than their fresh meats and wild vegetables. They also enjoyed a healthy market from selling apples, pears and wild grapes.

The following morning, they called upon the Mathers home, ready to put their plan into practice. "Good mornin' Commander, your honor, suh. Good mornin' to you, and yo good family", Esau flattered him, smiling shyly as he continued. "My friend, Absalom, and me, we is here to offer you to participate in a opportunity that wuz jis made available to us yestiddy." He had never called upon Mathers before and he prayed that his adversary would not become suspicious of his intentions. The success of operations to fleece those who fleece are based on the motivation of thieves. That motivating force, Absalom and Esau knew, was greed. They knew Mathers would listen to any proposition that could gain him more money.

The boys even ignored the social custom of visiting the homes of white people at the back door. The reason Esau broke the custom was that he wanted a sign of receptivity. When Mathers did not object, they believed their plan would succeed. "All right, all right, what have you boys got to show me, waking me up so early in the morning? And this had better be good." Yawning and stretching, Mathers tied his robe with the sash, revealing a rumpled nightshirt at his chest.

Esau deliberately displayed a fear of suspicion. He looked all about him, into, then round about the house before he would enter. He checked his inner vest, to ensure he had the leather pouch, then repeated the scanning of the house and the area about them. "They ain't nobody roun heah, Esau", Absalom mumbled. Once in action, he began to fear that the scheme was not such a good idea, and feared detection. If he failed, they would surely land in jail. He wondered whether exacting revenge against a tyrant was worth it. He began to regret that he had permitted his younger brother to convince him to pursue this stand. He wondered why they had not simply chalked it up to experience. The learning would provide resource to overcome the evil of men like Mathers. He also realized he was deeply into the plan now. Had he thought it out clearly, feeling as he now did, he would have said no. Now they were beyond the point of no return. He could not desert Esau.

Esau showed the pouch to Mathers, then asked whether they could come inside to explain why they had it. Mathers permitted them as far as his foyer, and demanded that they keep their voices low. Esau continued the suspicious ruse. Then, as Mathers turned away to light a candle, he saw exactly what he wanted to see. The Mathers bank book, with withdrawal and deposit slips was on the credenza under the stairwell leading to the second floor. "Mr. Mathers, I knows you be a truthful man, and everything, but my friend Absalom here and me, we be sworn to secrecy. We promised that we be talking to nobody but you, suh. So, if you doesn't mind, suh." Again Esau looked at the back of the foyer, and up the stairwell. He even peered back through the kitchen.

Mathers realized this was serious, and it involved the pouch, or rather its contents. "There is nobody back there, but just to satisfy your leery nature, I'll check it out for you. Mathers was growing more impatient now, but he was more than curious. While he searched about the downstairs area, Esau tore from his bank books two deposit slips and two bank withdrawal slips. Then he removed three of the bank envelopes which were furnished only to their major accounts. They were identical to the envelopes that Pinkard had maintained for their money and accounts. Those envelopes were not personalized. Absalom's eyes were as wide as silver dollars. He had no idea that Esau would have done that. Esau, for now, had tabled the matter of robbing the bank. But he had not forsaken the idea of using the bank to teach Mathers a lesson.

When Mathers returned, Esau began his story. "This is the situation, Commander Mathers", Esau whispered in a hushed tone, opening the pouch, then removing an envelope from a pocket to show him. He then removed another envelope from his other vest pocket and placed it onto the table. This was one of the same envelopes he had removed from the credenza only seconds earlier. This was the final bit of bait. The trap now was set. They just had to pull everything off. "Absalom and me, we met this gentleman who come down here from Chicago way. He plan to build a big marketplace to process meats for sale and for feeding our army in the war. He offer my friend and brother Absalom here a opportunity to go in with him. We toll him how you be such a good man, Commander Mathers, and we said that we would not mind setting up with him, only if he would bring you in also. We gives him a whole heap o' money. Then he say, I am sending this pouch to Commander Mathers, I has heard o' the man, and the President hisself say, get that man too. So he offers you this here chance. He sent this money in his own pouch. He want to leave this with you. He say it be showing good faith. I don't know what that mean. Anyway, he say that if you want to go in with him, then you spose to meet with him at sundown, this very day. He say he be at the Collinsville Mound, right where the road got them twin forks, a mile from the clearing. He say that if you don't meet with him there then it be just as good, cause he go get somebody else to take yo place. He say you be the loser."

It seemed believable, even plausible to him. The ingredients to bear out the story were accurate. Then too, there were always people from Chicago, and elsewhere exploring business deals here. Quite often, innocent couriers like these two were used. "What about the money? Do you mean that if I don't meet with him tonight, that I can keep the money?"

Esau nodded, then looked to Absalom whose nod backed him up.

"Well, I think I just have to think about it, and give it some thought. Will you see him before tonight?"

"No Commander, suh. He already have our money. The only way we know you done struck a deal, be if when we sees you tomorrow at the encampment. Oh, one mo thang. He say he want you to bring a sum of money that be four times what be in that pouch, if you want to go in with him. He promise that in three months time, you go double or even triple that every week."

Back at their shack, Esau wasted no time in the second phase of the operation. He was so focused that he didn't realize how Absalom perspired profusely and shook like a leaf until they were miles away from the Mathers home. The plan gained impetus because he had pilfered the bank slips. These would offer added insurance in the confidence game against the commander. With continued good luck, everything should fall into place. He had no worries. Esau removed the recorded listings and receipt from his private box. These were the items Mathers had given him only days before, unwittingly. He studied carefully the penmanship of the commander, particularly his signature. Now he felt ready to try his hand at something he had never done. He practiced forging the details of Mathers' handwriting, capturing nuances, strokes, and characters. When he was assured he had everything in order, he then transferred the transaction to the withdrawal slip. That accomplished, he altered the un-cashed check that Mathers had provided for the goods the boys delivered a week earlier. (For black people to cash checks written by white depositors, a full description of the circumstances of the transaction was required. Then the amount was to be recorded on the transaction or withdrawal slip, signed by the check writer.) The amount on the check was the sum of the deposits of all the Omer children; the interest that should have accrued; a fair amount for the goods provided one week prior; the amount that the pouch would have cost, and the amount of money that was in the pouch. All the work, the plan so far, and of course the forgery were letter perfect.

That afternoon, Esau never even batted an eye as he lined up at the bank to cash the check. When he reached the front, the teller looked it over, questioned him about it, then excused himself, to request guidance from the bank president. After reviewing Mathers' signature, on file, and other documents bearing his handwriting, they concluded it appropriate to honor the check. They also knew Esau, and didn't think he was capable of any kind of charade. To make sure, however, the bank president wanted a word with Esau. He scrutinized the receipt, solely for the purpose of ensuring that Mathers had written it. He didn't really understand whether the items were worth the highly inflated amount on the check. Now, all doubt was erased. The big grin on the bank officer's face was all the proof that was needed. Absalom had been with him, but he had retired to the lobby. Considering his condition, he didn't need to be within miles. For the rest of the day they had planned relax, going over the steps for the next phase of the plan. More importantly for now, they had to get out of the bank safely.

This money they were now taking, Esau decided, would represent a simple down payment on the bank's eventual loss. Their suffering, considering the full extent, would be much, much higher.

When Mathers appeared in line, four spaces behind Esau, the teller nodded and the business was completed. Esau never even flinched, even at the sight of his nemesis. The boys returned to their shack. For them the business just conducted was certainly more dangerous than what they would undertake that evening. At least they believed it so. This was due to their being out of their element. Certainly they would be more comfortable, more capable of using the wide open space of the landing near Collinsville Road, to control the situation, including their escape if things didn't unfold as planned.

As sundown fell, they proceeded to move the second phase of their plan into action. Even if it failed and the Mathers group did not appear, they were already ahead. The money they had moved from both accounts was more than had been stolen by Mathers. When considering the amount in the leather bag, they still came out ahead. The boys agreed that Luke, who though he could not read, should be the leader of the band that night. He was the most efficient at effecting the quiet refined drawl of a Southern gentleman. Therefore, he would do most of the talking when the Mathers group would be confronted.

The boys fashioned six dummies, and tied them onto six horses that they had actually rustled from the livery stables on Broadway Street. They knew that would be easy. Since horse theft had been all but non-existent in Illinois Town, nobody paid much attention to their horses. They simply walked in with other men, and surveyed the stables. When they had identified the horses they wanted, they simply walked them out the front. The attendant, Jed Ebsen, was doing what he usually does - sleep, after too much whisky. And he does that well. The dummies were strapped atop each mount, and led by Luke to the spot where they were to meet the Mathers group. This was nothing more than highway robbery. The dummies were hidden behind a stand of trees, just where the road formed a fork, one heading North, and the other going East, to the county seat.

Mathers had three men with him. They were his son, Francis, a hunting partner, Jules Josephs, and Francis O'Flaherty, an employee from the bank. Just as the Omer boys had expected, he had an auxiliary group of five locals trail him by two minutes. Since they knew he would not take a real chance, they were ready for this eventuality.

Esau, Absalom, and two more of the brothers accosted them with a rope tied from one tree to another. Before the second party knew what hit them they were on the ground.

"Raise your hands to the sky, raise them Ah say", Absalom fashioned a Southern accent too. One fellow was slow raising his hands. He was promptly dispatched by a blow to the back of his head with the butt of Esau's gun. "Now if you boys don't want that same treatment, Ah advise you all to do likewise."

In a second each gun was gathered, and the men were tied. The bindings were so secure that it would take hours for them to obtain release.

Meanwhile, two miles up the road, Mathers and the others were accosted by the boys, a mile ahead of their destination. If they had a group of cohorts there, the boys would have done their work before they would have known. Luke confronted the men by himself. Behind him by the trees stood one brother, and the six dummies on horseback.

Luke said not a single word, dashing out just as they reached the intermediate clearing. His gun pulled, he gestured for the trio to alight from their horses and remove their weapons. He could tell that they were about to make a move because he believed they thought he was alone.

"Alright, boys, now let us just take off them waist coats too. You all be quick about it, now", Luke drawled in his best Dixie verbalization. His brother had to struggle to hold back his laughter. "Damn Yankees. Cain't you all move no fastah than that? Git to gittin, befoah Ah put a hole in yo big nuff to ride mah hoss through."

Then they saw his brother approach from the thicket, and the horses, with dummies on back, moved to the undergrowth. They appeared as six men, accompanying the two highwaymen. In tandem the three decided to obey. After all, they would have reinforcements from the South (their rear) and from the North (just ahead). Feeling they would gain the upper hand soon, if not quickly, the group, emptied their pockets, exposing money, and other valuables. Elijah searched their bags, and found what he wanted. Francis Mathers carried the pouch. It contained the money they had presented to his father early that morning, and included an amount greater than six times what had been requested. Their greed had cost them dearly. Their money taken, their pride besmirched, Luke then ordered them to walk back into town, leaving their horses.

"Damn, stupid Yankees. How they expect to win a war if they cain't hold on to they belongins!" Luke got in a parting insult as they walked away. The Mathers crowd would have never believed they had been set up, and bilked not once, but twice in one day by young Black men, still in their teens.

Boys grew up fast. In their short life span, every boy and girl in the Omer family had learned so much, that they were wise well beyond their years. Esau had become the wisest, and most daring of all.

The boys hid their money they had taken that day, and returned home. They went about their work, never anticipating that Mathers would call to 'investigate' what had happened. They were right. He never would. His arrogance is what prevented him from pursuing the one person truly responsible for his misfortune. The motive of his adversary was obvious - revenge. The boys then took the dummies south east of the city, where they burned them. Then they released the horses. Finally, at day's end, they buried their money in a place where nobody would ever find it. It was in the middle of a wooded area, two miles behind their house. That area was bordered in all directions by quicksand. The boys knew exactly where it began and ended. A young man, a native national, was a good and close friend of the Omer family. Quentin Two-Bears, of the Comanche/Chippewa Tribe had taught them. They had learned much from him and now were finding it all very useful. Essentially, they used a high powered bow, shooting an arrow with rope attached into a tree. The other end was tied to a tree on the land side. Moving the distance was easy.

The boys changed nothing about their lifestyle. They continued to work hard and obey their father. As they worked, so they learned. As they learned, so they prospered. Eventually all that would change. The war grew in intensity and they would be asked to give more, earn less, and make greater sacrifices.

Chapter XVI - Whose Side Are You On, Boy?

The War between the States was entering its third year. The Brookshire Plantation, just as with all farms, businesses and establishments throughout the Confederacy, had endured a rather high loss of income. As the most productive farming business in the country when atrocities began, it would fall upon Master Brookshire to contribute more to the cause of that war. A friend and confidant of Jefferson Davis, he vowed to do more than his fair share to support the war effort. He exhorted others throughout the region to make food, cotton, and livestock available to the Army of the Confederacy. Although the war was costly in terms of the loss of human lives, initially it had not weighed heavily on the ability of the Confederate States of America to wage war. They continued to negotiate favorable trade agreements with other nations, most notably France and Great Britain. Until then, the North had decided to ignore this very fact, that the effectiveness in waging war was due to favorable trading on an international sphere.

Conversely, the North was able to maintain the war effort also due to the same factor. Though they might have attacked Rebel business interests, to do so would have created a greater disadvantage for them due to the free travel of rebel saboteurs in the North. It was a matter of 'quid pro quo' - if you don't attack my factories, farms and mercantile pursuits, then I won't attack yours. All that changed with the issuance of Lincoln's Executive Order known as the Emancipation Proclamation. While it did not free one slave, in truth, it gave the appearance of attacking the most precious commodity owned and perpetuated by the South - slaves, and the institution of slavery. In one fell motion, Lincoln had changed the rules of engagement. Not only had he changed the rules but he had done so in a manner that would create a grave escalation in the behavior of rebel conduct of the war. This escalation would create such immediate hardship for blacks, that it would prove so devastating that their survival would be at risk. Many blacks maintained alive the vivid memory, related through narrations of the lives lost in the transportation of black people from Africa to America. With Lincoln's pulling them into the forefront of this war, they would relive an experience that could make slavery appear but a sad experience by comparison. North and South, free and bonded, Blacks wanted to enter the fray for one reason. There could be one and only one reason. Black people wanted to be at peace.

The painful, worthless life of the slave in the South echoed the sentiments of Nat Turner who had led what was considered the most spectacular of all slave revolts. Every slave from Virginia to Missouri to Texas pursed their lips to quote this favorite of the slaves' heroes. 'Nigger life ain't worth dog shit, horse shit or pig shit.' Nat Turner also gave another admonition to the slaves. He told them that heaven did not exist. If black people 'want to see heaven, then they have to create their own heaven here on earth'.

The furthest thing from the life of a slave was peace. Lincoln's pronouncement simply made life more miserable for the slave than it had ever been before. What was worse was that slaves had believed it could get no worse.

On most plantations in the South, training quarters were provided for rebel infantry. While the number of slaves was on the rise sharply, their living quarters were decreasing. Estates like the Brookshire simply ordered their slaves to upgrade their quarters and then to move out. The new digs became the temporary lodging to house rebel troops in training.

Due to Isaac's ability to handle horses, Master Brookshire had permitted his assignment to the Mississippi Militia. Under the command of General Beauregard, his assignment was with the Nineteenth Calvary headquartered in Vicksburg. In truth, he was one of a large number of blacks who had been assigned support duties in the Army of the Confederacy. To signify his task as a support person, rather than a military one, he always wore white. That was the nearest he would come to wearing a uniform.

During that period of the War, Isaac saw his family back at Brookshire at irregular intervals. Sometimes it would be after five months. Usually, his stays were shorter, although he rarely saw them within five weeks of a return home. On those visits, he glorified the role of the rebel soldier, extolling their bravery against the weak kneed, sniveling Yankees. Isaac had only one disappointment. He wished he could don the Rebel uniform and fight for the South, along side the people he loved.

To the black men on the farm, he was considered a traitor. They never could forget how his love for his owner had caused him to betray his own father and uncles and cousin. They looked upon him as the very reason his father had to dic. The very sight of him caused such rancor that a few wanted to kill him on sight. But for the young ladies among his relatives, they would have set upon him at night and slit his throat. They alone held out hope that he would see the light, understand that what he was doing was the work of the Devil, as they put it, and change. They asked him to simply consider that for all he was doing to perpetuate slavery, working for a Confederate victory, his services should be rewarded with money. After all, they reasoned, many others give much less and gain so much more. There were free white men, they offered, who performed the same services as he did. While not members of the Confederate Armed Forces, they were paid a good wage. Word had filtered back how they all did less than Isaac. The girls could not grasp the hold that this concept held on him. It was simple when you look at it. He could not accept that Blacks were destined, or should be destined to be free. He felt very comfortable working for the 'good master'.

Near the Northeastern perimeter of the Brookshire property, a makeshift hospital had been constructed by slaves, under the watchful eye and exact plans of Ebenezer Horatio Irons. A military man, he had finished third in his class at West Point, only ten years prior. At its completion, a number of physicians from all over the South and North established practice there to treat Confederate wounded. They even attracted medical doctors from Europe and Bolivia. In addition to their duties in the fields, a number of slaves were assigned to work in the hospital.

The war was now taking its toll more and more on the families that supported the Confederate Army. The predictions, from both sides, of victory in two years gave way to the reality of this war. At first, it was thought that the North would tire of this and capitulate, permitting secession. Many people tried to determine when the positions became juxtaposed. No matter how they studied the trends and all the factors weighing on the conduct and behavior of the course, no single factor or set of factors has ever been delineated as the reason their positions became juxtaposed. It simply happened. By the middle of September in the year 1863, it simply became apparent that with only minor victories in limited arenas, the North needed but to hold on, demonstrate staying power. Even if the Southern white man and the Confederacy were too filled with pride to understand it, every slave could see it coming. There was no way the South could win the war. The slave was catching hell, a hell even worse than that which befell the unfortunate Yankee infantryman captured alive in the field.

What every slave could see by that point in time was that there was no way Lincoln would permit the Union to fall to the Confederacy. The force of his will was to maintain the Union at all cost. By issuing a meaningless, unenforceable proclamation that slaves in the states of rebellion were free, Lincoln had placed the slaves in grave harm's way. By shoring up the Union forces, selecting generals with a will to win, slaves understood it better than white Southerners. As the war continued, Lincoln's edict became increasingly one that removed the slave from harms way through no intentional effort on his own part. At that point, and for that reason and that reason only - the firm resolve to win the war - the slave viewpoint to accept rather than disdain the Sixteenth President of the United States of America began to gain acceptance. Except for a few black educated, it had never been so theretofore.

From the observed battlefield accounts, as reported by slaves, both sides exacted grievous tolls on each other. For each rebel soldier brought down, a Union fighter also fell. For each rebel taken prisoner, a Union soldier was taken. This is why the Southerners believed that a stalemate would favor them. Sheer mathematics, the slave believed, would be the order of the day. The North simply had more people and more fighting men. They could afford to lose men on an equal basis. This thinking alluded to the last man standing theory. Even worse was that more battles, even skirmishes, were fought on Rebel soil. As such, they had much more to lose. They had to fight not only an enemy on their land, but too many other forces were against them. The most telling, in the eyes of the slave, was the North's employment of the slaves and freedmen as intelligence officers. Prior to then, intelligence roles had been the restricted province of the elite men and women of both armies. Owing to the resourcefulness of their spies, the Rebel war machine soon learned about Yankee efforts to gain vital information on Confederate encampments, manpower and war materiel. They decided to fight fire with fire. When told of these new plans, Master Brookshire was asked whether he had any slaves who could operate in a counterintelligence mode. Without hesitation he nominated Isaac. He discussed the matter with Reverend Rogers, and he nominated Plumpsie, his own granddaughter.

At that point, no two people were more unalike. Only a few slaves had been aware of Plumpsie's role in the Underground Railroad's successful run to freedom of Isaac's twin, Esau. Every slave throughout the State of Mississippi had heard of the role Isaac had played in the death of his father and the beating of the others. Even though slaves did not know of Plumpsie's role, they knew the type person she was. If anyone could dissuade Isaac from his harm to the race, it could be Plumpsie. She had no choice but to go along with the plan. However, she had decided that she would take every chance to use this opportunity to defeat the Confederacy.

The biggest worry of the Rebel leadership was that Lincoln's proclamation would confuse slaves. The offer for slaves to run to freedom and join the Union Army was a singular cause for alarm, because the offer was so attractive. Some plantation owners even asked their slaves whether they would be willing to go to war against the families that owned them, particularly since so many shared the same blood.

Slaves who served the Rebel cause were outfitted with phony papers of manumission. They were instructed to travel through the border states. They were clued in on certain passwords which fellow spies would use for identification. Their primary job was to seek work in places of Union Army strongholds, keeping their eyes and ears open, listening for any tidbits of information they could get to help the cause of the South. They were given no money and no letters of credit. Their ability, as 'former slaves', whose freedom had been purchased by 'friends from the North' would be put to the test.

The community of whites, the slaves, their owners, and the South had come to rely on both Plumpsie and Isaac. Their owners' hearts were indeed heavy to have them go. In spite of their enthusiasm in undertaking the mission, albeit for very different reasons, their trainers and masters never told them the price to pay if they were discovered. They would be put to death. Somehow, they understood that without having been told.

The pair was escorted to the port city of Memphis, Tennessee on the Mississippi River. From there, they were on their own. Interestingly, no one on the Brookshire Plantation, other than his sons, knew of Isaac's mission. Regarding Plumpsie, Reverend Rogers told his son, Charles, who expressed no feeling, one way or the other about her assignment. If she took to it naturally and succeeded, they would know why. Her father, by now was the most accomplished secret agent from the South. He was first among a most accomplished cadre of undercover agents.

Memphis was different from anything either had seen before. It did remind Isaac of the larger cities where he had raced horses but it had so many differences. There were the Union soldiers and officers. Then he saw so many white men and women who simply ignored him, whether he got out of their way or not. They found temporary lodging in a holding pen which only two days prior housed cattle to be slaughtered for the army. Even yet, the smell of death, with which he was all too familiar, permeated the air. A battle for the garrison had been fought only four days previous, with the Union forces overtaking an out manned Rebel force. There were rumors of executions behind the town dump. In truth, retreating Confederate military left their wounded there to die as they saved themselves.

After three days Plumpsie secured work as a cook in the Union Fort in West Memphis, just to the other side of Memphis. Each day brought dangers, not so much from the young soldiers who would stop at nothing to have a good time with any available female. In her job, Plumpsie dressed as a boy, developed the manners of a boy, and pulled off the disguise with no problem. Her major fear was that she would be exposed as a Southern spy. Her second greatest fear was that she would lose her life in a sudden attack, attracting a stray bullet or mortar intended for an infantry, cavalry or even an officer.

Isaac, similarly, found work as a barracks crewman, but not in food preparation. He worked closely with the barracks orderlies, assisting at whatever task was requested. They marveled at how willingly he accepted duty, no matter how distasteful. One day he would be found in the dispensary, assisting the nurses clean up after surgery. Other days he would be in the makeshift morgue, icing bodies to preserve them for return to hometowns. When war dead were shattered beyond recognition, he had to clean them up as best as could be, matching bone against bone, body type against body type to come as close to a match as the human eye could conceive. By the end of his first month, he would have hoped that a loose tongue would reveal troop movement or Yankee strategy in the border states.

Neither he nor Plumpsie had much free time. Their duties, though not so backbreaking as slavery, demanded just as much of their time. For him, their were two aspects that would make it all pay off. The first was that the money he earned from the Union was deposited into a bank account of his own, in Memphis. The second was that he was on a mission for the Confederacy and he hoped to make his owner proud.

Plumpsie, likewise, saw two valuable assets for her undertaking. The first, like Esau's, was that she had opened a bank account and was earning money. At the end of each two week period, she deposited her earnings and looked at the amount that grew from interest. Since Isaac hadn't learned to read, the first thing she did was teach him how to understand the entries for deposits. Her second goal from the undertaking was to be able to relate to the North information that could help her with the their war effort. Like most slaves, she hated her masters. Even though she was blood kin, she would have done anything in her power, including risking death to insure the defeat of the Confederacy. She had resolved to seek the opportunity to work against them.

After their third payday, it suddenly befell Isaac that she was an accomplished reader. Other than black preachers on the plantations, he never knew of slaves who could read. If they did know how, it was not something that they could show. For him, in his twisted way of thinking, that a slave knew how to read was sinful. It represented the worst sort of evil, approved by the devil himself. For blacks to aspire to attain this gift, and to use it, a gift reserved for whites only, was one of the most dreadful sins that could be committed. The concept of heaven and hell was strong among slaves. It rarely had anything to do with their personal desire to remain a slave, or become free. Due to the hell the slave caught everyday just being a slave, no one wanted to enter the after life where conditions would be far worse. For Isaac, even though he was learning valuable lessons from his cousin, he didn't want to learn too much for fear that his soul would be tainted.

He had to perform a number of tasks within the barracks of the enlisted men. The task he loved most was shining the boots of the infantrymen. Like anything he ever attempted, he took exceptional pride in this as well. After a few weeks, he was assigned duty to shine the boots of the sergeants and lieutenants of his company. He wondered whether this would be the opportunity for which he had waited. For a scheduled social function, he and Plumpsie were assigned to the General's quarters at the Mansion at Buttermilk Street intersecting West Clyde Road. The residence had been the living quarters of the Ryan family, who owned the largest cotton processing mill in the border states. Milton Ryan, the family head, and his wife and children had been permitted to come and go as they pleased. However, they were restricted to an assigned area in their own home, the major portion taken over by General Gregory Morton Trowbridge and his immediate Union staff. They felt no compulsion not to take it since the previous Army 'guests' were General Stanton T. Margulis and his staff of the Confederate Army. Twice during that year, that very home had been visited by Jefferson Davis. At his last visit there he met with General Robert E. Lee.

By act of Congress, as a strategic planning site for military purposes, the Union Army could have burned it to the ground. To General Trowbridge it seemed such a waste to destroy it. He decided that he and other officers could use it as they saw fit. Use of the mansion would continue for but another two years. Eventually, General Pershing, under the command of Major General Phil Sheridan, leveled it to support Sherman's march to the sea.

How Milton Ryan felt about the war was no mystery. As a member of the state legislature, a successful cotton processor, slave owner and entrepreneur, he not only voted for secession, he was the leading advocate in the border states. He vowed to fight to his death for the South, even if Tennessee remained a non-belligerent. He offered money and full use of his property, his wealth and his slaves to support the cause. After the vote of Tennessee, he traveled to Frankfort, Kentucky to lobby the legislature there.

Atrocities had begun and the buildup was underway before Kentucky would decide. A slave state, they were lobbied heavily by proponents for both sides. At length, the politicians here were motivated not by whether slavery was evil or whether the South could win or lose. Like most Southerners, practically every Kentuckian believed that the South would emerge a strong victor in the War. Their sentiments were strongly pro-Confederacy. However, their politicians knew that after the war, the South would return to its pre-war values. As a border state, Kentucky would absorb too much of the war's ravages. To survive, it would officially take no sides. The young men from that state, however, left their homes in droves to join Rebel forces in Tennessee, Mississippi, and Georgia. A larger number enlisted in the North. Those most ardent, exalting General Lee, trekked by foot all the way to Virginia to join its Army. State contingents in the South were actually known as the Armies of specific States, while in the North, the concept of the Union Army as central entity was taking hold.

For the function, General Trowbridge was meeting in the parlor with Maximilian Maxwell, a mill owner from Ohio. Through Yankee intelligence networks, literally millions of bales of cotton and hay, collected in the South, destined for London and other ports in Europe had been confiscated. These goods were to be exchanged for guns, cannon, ammunition, and smelted iron. The iron was designed, by agreement, to meet specific specifications known only to the Confederate Military establishment. General Trowbridge and Mr. Maxwell were negotiating for the delivery of half of this cotton crop to be delivered to Memphis. There, in a Confederate city, the cotton would be processed into fabric for use by the Union Army. One half of the shipment would be delivered to its original destination. The difference was that the North, not the South would receive the war materiel.

Isaac knocked at the door at the appointed hour. The guard on duty peered outside the curtain and recognized him as the bootblack. They let him enter. Thirty minutes later Plumpsie arrived. After a similar ritual, she was allowed to enter. Since no one from the Union trusted the slaves who lived at Ryan Mansion, only freed blacks were permitted to work in a food preparation function. The General and Mr. Maxwell continued their conversation, just beyond the foyer, while Isaac waited for his orders. He listened attentively to every word they said. The cotton, it was related, was still under guard in Lexington. It had been confiscated in Knoxville, and brought through Sandusky, in a circle route to Chattanooga. From there it was to arrive, by rail, in Memphis in two days. It was actually being delivered through Rebel strongholds and they didn't know a thing about it. With his kit in tow, Isaac shined the General's boots while they talked. After finishing the job, he stood erect, waiting for an order to leave. "You may go", General Trowbridge smiled, totally satisfied with the spit shine applied to his boots. From what he could see, Isaac had done a better job than when they were new.

When one thinks of the application of saliva to wearing apparel, one could easily become rebuffed. However, shoe shine boys, never really needed to apply expectorant to create a well shined shoe. They were always sure to get some of it onto the trousers of their patron. Truth be known, spit could be applied in a number of ways to ensure that the vilest of substances was transmitted, not by accident, to whites, North and South. Just as blacks didn't have to be taught not to cry out in pain when horsewhipped, food preparers of color didn't have to be taught to spit into every meal, even sandwiches, they cooked for white people. The worse the malady of cold, or tuberculosis, the more they released into the dishes to be eaten by whites. Not even ice water or lemonade were spared this treatment.

As Isaac turned to leave, he was stopped by Maximilian. He had learned enough about their plans and wanted to get out of there as quickly as he could. To earn another nickel by shining the shoes of this patron would be welcomed though. "Wait a minute, wait just a minute," growled Maxwell. He was sure he had seen Isaac somewhere before, but he could not remember exactly where. "I think I know this boy from somewhere, General. I just can't remember exactly where."

"Why, Max", General Trowbridge chimed. "You are beginning to act just like all my men. See one darky, then you see another one. They look similar. After you see a few, they all look alike to you."

"No, General, this is different. I'm sure I've seen this boy before. Where are you from, Nigger?" he asked, turning to Isaac. "Are you local?"

At once Isaac was afraid, fearful that he could say something that would surely get him into deep trouble. "Ah doesn't knows zactly what yo mean when ya'll says local. Ah knows Ah ain't crazy, Sir. Dat do mean crazy, don't it?"

"No, no damn it. I don't mean to say you are crazy," Maxwell grew exasperated. What he perceived as the naive dumbness of blacks and poor whites was simply an inability to converse in the common vernacular. "Never mind. I am sure no nigger as stupid and as dumb as you are has been anywhere. Just never mind."

"You may go now, boy," the General ordered and this time he left hurriedly. Isaac's heart beat rapidly. He sweated profusely from this near brush with exposure. "I tell you now, Max, you see one darky you see them all. They all look alike."

In his travels, conducting his business, Maximilian Maxwell had been throughout the South, in all States, and as far North as Iowa. In spite of the General's viewpoint, he was sure he had seen that face and that it was in more than one place. The men agreed that the cotton would be processed in a factory in Cairo, Illinois, known as Carter Mills.

* * *

The train carrying the cotton was equipped with additional goods. This was a large load of cotton, more than had ever been assembled in one place at one time. Even though half had already been shipped to Europe, it was still the largest amount ever assembled. Those bales stretched for miles on all sides, even before they were loaded. Union soldiers were assigned to protect the cargo. However, they were not in uniform, posing as travelers headed West to avoid the war. Four locomotives were used to haul the heavy load. At times, they didn't seem to carry enough power. There were mountain passes and steep down slopes to traverse. It would take power to climb and extreme power to control the acceleration on descent. At various points along the route, especially where ambush could be attempted, Union soldiers in full dress guarded the track beds. They, and their comrades on board the train made contact by courier. The cotton that they carried was significant enough. But this was well beyond the normal security involved with such commerce. Common sense dictated that there was more at stake. The convoy did have other bounty. They had raided the vaults at banks in Louisville, Knoxville, Perryville, Chattanooga, and Frankfort, relieving these towns of their gold bullion, silver, and silver certificates. To these would be added the gold of the banks in Memphis.

As the convoy of trains headed West, with military escorts along the way, everything was smooth. Along the route, just West of Frankfort, they encountered a group of five men in civilian garb. Immediately one would have assumed they were tenderfeet, having lost their mode of transportation to thieves. They hardly appeared the types to put up much resistance when bullied. Just the same the army officers were cautious, extra cautious. Two officers and five cavalry approached them. Half the others waited there and the rest retreated back toward the track to send a message for the engineer to increase his speed. For any encounter that might have cast even minor suspicion the order to increase speed of the convoy was paramount.

The group of five showed papers of identification. They indicated they were cattle buyers from the new State of West Virginia. Their mission, and they had papers to prove it, was to organize men not involved in the war to round up loose cattle, boars and fowl, for the Union Army at Fort Littleton. They confided that the round up would commence in Evansville, head due East to the West Virginia-Ohio border, then North from there. The rest of the route would be through the Pennsylvania Mountain Pass in the Alleghenies. Finally they would end in Fort Littleton. The group, to a man, claimed they were horseless because they were set upon by Confederate troops the day earlier. They took their food, money, extra clothing, and headed South toward Birmingham. The Union group was convinced they were telling the truth. They fed the men from their own mess kits but told them that for security reasons they could not offer them transportation. This information was dispatched immediately to the officers on board the train.

On hearing about this, the officer on board the train became incensed. He had received intelligence that no one would be permitted anywhere along the line the train was to traverse. The payload was too important to risk. He ordered the train to stop immediately, and the messenger to return to his platoon. The five strangers were to be brought to the train at once. A message was wired to General Grant in St. Louis. They would follow up this message with another within the hour, after a full interrogation of the five.

The men detained by the military had served their mission well. Theirs was to delay the convoy long enough for the dynamite laden track bed to be fused and detonated. When that fuse was detonated the sound could have been heard more than one hundred miles away. The explosion totally destroyed the entire train, its engines, boxcars, and track bed too. All its contents were ablaze. The entire crew, and company of men, including the Confederate spies were killed.

As the convoy of Union soldiers looked on in amazement, they were not aware of the Rebel military, hundreds scurrying, it seemed from thin air, to attack. They were everywhere. The Union men never had a chance. Only four were spared the ultimate price. It was small consolation to them that they were captured by the enemy.

As the news of the successful Confederate victory was wired back, the Union was intercepting the cable, reading it as the wire was transmitted to the South, simultaneously.

On the Brookshire Plantation there was great celebration as well. That is for the whites, and one black young man. Isaac's information had led to the greatest Confederate victory to that point. They seemed to know of it before their masters.

* * *

The triumphant news in fact preceded Isaac's return. Even before he was back with his owner, the celebration was fully underway. Master Brookshire and his entire family whooped it up with the town mayor, members of the state legislature, county officials, and all the ministers of the local Baptist Churches. All whites in the region rejoiced.

The only people who were totally unhappy were the slaves. Now almost every slave hoped for a victory for the North. However, even the few who favored the South, felt that blacks should not have a role for either side. In their minds, it was best to stay out of it. It was a mess, they reasoned, that white folk had created. Let them take care of it. They had grown tired of cleaning up white folk's messes. For that very reason they were in concert with their majority brethren in expressing a singular disdain for the role of a slave in securing a victory that had created overwhelming loss of life and destruction of property for those who would free them. It had become apparent that someone would have to kill the boy, even if Master Brookshire would exact death to the man who delivered the death stroke. In truth, he would also kill family members also.

Before Isaac's return, Master Brookshire convened a meeting among all the male slaves age thirteen and over. It lasted exactly fifteen seconds. He made one statement:

"If any harm should come to Young Isaac, the savior for the Confederacy, I shall personally beat to death every man here assembled."

Then he turned and left.

Now they could not kill the boy. They knew that there would be two, three, four or five, whose lives would have to be sacrificed for killing the boy. They could not risk the lives of so many. It was a risk they could not take, because whenever Master Brookshire made a threat, he carried it through.

Amos, one of the older slaves on the plantation, had thought it all through. A brave man, and a stout of build fellow, he was also strong of purpose. He had seen the twins when they were infants, taught them about the ways of the farm, animals, plants and husbandry in general. He truly loved all his brothers, sisters, aunts, uncles, cousins and fellow slaves about the plantation. A free thinker, he had now reached the point that he could not let the others decide what was best for him or for the others. Acting alone, he would sneak upon the boy while he slept, awaken him and then choke him to death slowly to make sure he would suffer. He would also present himself to his master immediately after, admit that he acted alone and accept his fate. His plan might have gone as he wanted had he not come upon a misfortunate incident.

Julida was a slave for whom the plantation had traded from a farm two counties North. An octoroon, as blacks with her percentage of white ancestry were known, she had been particularly attractive to the handsomely darker white men in the area, as well as the black men, with perfectly smooth and dark skin, slave and freed. Master Brookshire had obtained her simply for her ability to breed.

Simon Fitzpatrick, brother-in law to Master Brookshire, was a merchant in town. Though he was married, still with wife, six daughters and seven sons, he preferred the sexual company of female and male slaves who were of mixed ancestry. He was particularly fond of pre-teen boys and girls. Occasionally, especially when Master Brookshire was away on business, he and his wife stayed overnight at the estate. Rumor had it that due to an oozing discharge from his genitals, he had infected a number of female and male slaves throughout the area. Usually using the pretense of hiring slaves out to help in his mercantile and retail businesses, he would seduce them in exchange for money. After awhile, when word spread about the disease he had spread, slaves knew better than to permit him to have their way. The problem with Julida was that she had not been warned to use other methods rather than full sexual intercourse to satisfy him. Just the same, she was not the type of young woman to permit just any man to have her. Simon Fitzpatrick was the very type man that she despised.

This was a time, when with the slave master's permission, any white man of means could have his way as he chose in the slave quarters. Anyone he did not select had to act as though he was not there, and keep their mouths shut in the community. Contrarily, about the plantation, the goings on the night before were the talk of the plantation.

The moon lit through the ceiling and open windows. A candle glistened at the opposite end of the crowded quarters. That candle had been requested by Amos so that he could see exactly where Isaac lay.

When Julida saw Fitzpatrick, she had no idea he had come for her. Pot bellied, bland of color, short and balding, he bore no resemblance to her idea of what a real man looked like, and could be like in bed. She fantasized about men like Will, of whom she had heard, and men like Amos, the tall, dark, husky and muscular men who were at every plantation throughout the South. Having also cared for young white men when they were sick, she wondered how they could ever please a woman. She had seen them when erect, and swore that she would never ever permit one to use her as her mother, a 'mulatto', had been used. Since none of the other slave men and women stirred at the sight of Fitzpatrick, she figured it out. Though she had no fear of the man, she was uneasy as soon as she knew the reason he was there. He had come for her. The whole situation was strange. She knew that there were always a few slave girls who desired the chance to have a baby by a white man. Why was no one eager now? Why did they all make room for him to move freely, as long as his movement was away from them? This man was after her, and she would have none of that.

His approach was not threatening. His manner was calm. His voice was quite quiet as he asked her to be with him, to lie with him, to let him have his way with her. The more he touched her, the more unbearable his closeness grew until she could take no more. She felt dirty, disgusting, and felt that she would rather die, than to let him touch her again, as he ran his hand under her skirt and petticoats. Fitzpatrick was a strange man with his sexual behavior. When he had a man, he always wanted to see the man's penis as if to examine it. Likewise, when he had a woman whom he wanted, he even insisted on looking at, almost examining her entire vaginal area. He actually put his nose very close every time. Some of the women exclaimed that he actually used his mouth and tongue in that area on them as a prelude to having sex. Julida didn't have to be told. She knew from this brief encounter he was that type of man. As his face neared her parted legs, where his finger played, she let out the loudest scream that had ever been heard by anyone on that, or any, plantation in the South, in prelude to sexual intercourse, whether consensual or forced. One might have thought she was being tortured. To her, physical torture would have been preferred.

The yelling was so intense and so strong that it woke everybody who was sleep, including Isaac. He jumped with a start, barely eluding the tines of a pitchfork that Amos would have landed deep into his shoulder. That scream saved her from a rape, while at the same time it saved Isaac's life. "Stop, stop it now", Fitzpatrick yelled at Amos. Isaac ran behind him for safety, shivering in fear. "Don't you dast harm a nap on this boy's kinky head!" he ordered, shielding the boy from the angry Amos. Amos knew one thing now. He knew that his life was over.

Briefly, he thought of killing Fitzpatrick and the boy. However, he knew right away that that would bring the collective anger of many whites all around. They would be sure to exact revenge on many slaves. The slave shacks at Brookshire would have turned into bloodbaths. He was wont to go that far. He understood quite clearly that to kill Isaac, he would have had to go through Fitzpatrick. At length, he decided as horrible a person as Fitzpatrick was, he was not worth getting many of his family and friends killed.

The next morning began with that incident. Amos was taken across the plantation where new recruits for the Confederate Army were in training. The slaves were ordered to gather firewood. The foreman of the plantation, Buck King, took barbed wire and tied it around the neck, face and legs of Amos. They poured kerosene and coal-oil around it, then ignited it, burning that man alive. Through it all, he never screamed or yelled. He didn't even flinch. He simply closed his eyes and entered peace.

"Let that be a lesson to all you all", shouted Master Brookshire, his voice gruff with anger, his words slurred from drinking too much whisky. "Anybody else among all you all niggers wanna go against the will of God in heaven? Ah'm here to help yo asses with a one way ticket to hell."

A few times before Isaac had thought he was facing death Never in his short life did he think it would come from the hands of another slave, another black man. This was all the more strange because he lived under the same roof as this man. Poor Isaac, he never connected that due to his mission of espionage, he had had a hand in the perpetuation of slavery. Isaac never understood that it was his gullibility and love for the oppressors of his people that had led to the beating death of his father, and the harsh beating of innocent black men. However, he still believed that Will's death, Amos' death, and the deaths of all those on the train, were the will of Jesus. Those wretched souls, he was convinced, were going to hell. The white people, and blacks who served them well, were bound for heaven. He could not feel any sorrow for the losers. But now he was confused. Now he was frightened. He was more afraid, than anything else, and therefore, asked Master Brookshire could he sleep in another place that night. He was provided quarters in the storage area, just off the kitchen, as he had been provided before. That was the day his father was beaten to death.

There would never be another attempt on Isaac's life after that. He didn't sleep anymore that night. Hardly anybody did, except the white folk.

Later that day, The Major in Charge, Buck King, and Rudolph Williams, another local merchant joined Master Brookshire and his house guest, Charles Vander Groot, a slave owner from a large plantation in Alabama for a game of horseshoes. The clanging of the iron bars against the poles was not an unusual sound. Many a slave had actually become very skillful in the game. White folk would never join them, or let blacks join with them, because they knew that was just another skill that the slaves could perform better. That morning, the whisky and the horseshoes flew wildly. When men become inebriated, they often make statements that they wished they had never made. When the truth is discovered, they often try to cover their truisms by explaining that one cannot take as face value what one says when in a drunken state. It was Vander Groot who provided the opening as he pitched his horseshoe.

"Why, Cousin Brookshire", he blurted out, the term he had come to use in address many a time when he had had too much to drink. "To think, you had made a deal to trade that little runt of a slave to my nephew's plantation in Alabama. Cousin, if you had sold that boy to us like we decided, then Ah would be the hero for the South, Not you all."

"Now that is where you all are wrong", Brookshire blurted back. Now it was his turn to take a swig from his bottle directly, and then pitch his shoe, its finding a spot nowhere near the target. "If Ah had sold his ass then like Ah wanted to, then I just would've sent another one of my slaves. Ah got me some smart slaves, and as you all can see by the example ah set this morning, Ah know how to make all my slaves love me. Where else can you all find a slave who would get his own papa killed just to please his owner? Ah tell you all. They love me."

Isaac heard every word.

Chapter XVII - Forty Acres, and a Mule, and a Plow

Proud of their continuing business accomplishments, the Omer boys, led by Esau, grew more successful. They actually provided employment for other black and white youths from the area, on both sides of the river. The family enjoyed what could be described as a virtual monopoly on the supply of meat, wild and domesticated to the Union Army. Lately, they had taken to raising and dressing more hogs on their land. In a short while they had captured wild boar and introduced this to their tame animals. They found that the pigs grew faster, attaining the ideal slaughter weight of 168 pounds, approximately 38 days faster than the domestic breed. The resultant cooked meat was more lean. When smoked just one day longer, the meat was just as tender.

The War effort for the North became an entrenched struggle to maintain the territory it had captured, while forcing the Confederacy to burn up greater natural resources just to fend off their advances. The destruction of the train, the crew and the Union Army in Kentucky had created a new problem for the South. Instead of attempts to take processed and unprocessed cotton by force, the Union simply decided to use Confederate efforts to produce and market cotton, against them. They would not lay a finger on the goods. They wouldn't even try to do so. The new strategy called for an ocean blockade. It stretched from the Chesapeake Bay in Delaware all the way South around Florida, to Texas. Then the Union made deals with Native Nationals to harass Rebel efforts to find new routes through the West. With the success of that blockade, it would be just a matter of time before the South would have to give up. Or so it was thought.

But, President Lincoln and his new man in charge, Grant, took nothing for granted. They knew that for a brief period, maybe one year, two at the outside most, the blockade would infuriate the Confederacy. It was like the quintessential wounded animal. The more in danger, the more dangerous it becomes. So it was with the South.

Lincoln and Grant needed more foot soldiers. With the stepped up enemy activity, they would need to truly place more men in harms way. To have more men give their lives for this cause was the only way to shorten the length of this dreadful, hellish war.

Although Lincoln's proclamation had announced the end of slavery in the states that had seceded, not the slave states that remained in the Union, it suggested that those slaves needed to join Union forces. Like the slaves in the border states, the slaves in the deep South had no real faith in Lincoln's desire to free them. Most all believed that after the war, things would return to normal. One man changed that. That man was Frederick Douglas. His recruiting trips throughout the North, and his messages to Union spies of color, found their ways to the ears of free and enslaved black men. Douglas promised more than freedom. He promised them a stake in building a life for their future. For every man who fought in the war, and gave his life, each of his surviving offspring would receive forty acres, a mule and a plow. If he had a wife, she would receive a pension. Every black soldier who enlisted and survived, would receive twenty acres, a plow and a mule. All the land to be provided to slaves, would be absorbed from the land they worked as slaves. He also promised that every slave who could not participate in the war effort, of fifteen years of age or older, would receive twenty acres and a mule.

Mathers had maintained his role as the chief recruiter in all of downstate Illinois. Since the number of men who joined was decreasing, taking nothing for granted, Grant appointed an assistant. His job was to seek out Natives and blacks, to try to get them to volunteer. For obvious reasons, blacks still were not drafted into military service at that point. The assistant was a man named Benton Twiggs. Originally from Boston, he was on his way as far West as he could travel when Fort Sumter fell. His commitment to the Union, and his adoration of Lincoln caused him to stop where he was. His pledge was to do whatever he could as a civilian to support the Union. He had traveled as far as East St. Louis when he made that pledge. Now Twiggs had a most favorable reception from black men in town. He never tried to hide his disdain for his nemesis, Mathers. Though they championed the same cause, neither trusted the other. Local Blacks, led by Reverend Omer, seemed to favor Twiggs. Local whites, fell behind Mathers. General Grant, headquartered about thirty miles away, had no hesitancy in building a good, friendly relationship with Twiggs. For whatever the reasons, he simply didn't trust Mathers. Later he would explain he never knew just quite what it was, but that Mathers fellow was just one of only two men on earth he simply hated. He described it as a simple gut feeling. The other fellow he chose to hate - Jefferson Davis. This was a man that Grant had never met. He swore to his cook that if he ever saw him, he would run through a volley of musket and cannon balls to wring the man's skinny neck with his bare hands.

[One of my grandfather's cousins, a woman by the name of Sadie Victoria Moore, was the cook for General Grant. At that time she was a slave in St. Louis. She was owned by a family in St. Louis living then on the street known as Van Deventer. When Grant and his boys overran that farm, she made every last one of his men go out back, wash their hands, and come in and sit down like gentlemen at the dining room table. She fed them the best meal they had had in days. By the time the General ate (His men were always taken care of first), there was scarcely anything left. That woman simply went out back, took two live chickens, wrung their necks, cleaned their carcasses, and cooked them out back over hickory and oak wood. Then she rubbed a special concoction on the birds. She fixed a cobbler, corn bread and made fresh cold lemonade with water from the deepest well. After that, she had a paying job for the rest of her life. My aunts used to say that that little General loved that woman like she was part of his family. William J. Moore]

Twiggs had talked with the Omer boys and at length, Esau and Absalom agreed to be inducted into the Union Army. They only agreed to use this measure to show that they supported the war effort due to their trust in Twiggs. He promised them in the presence of Grant, that their duty would require no frontline assignment. However, they were on their duty to kill any Rebel soldier they could, when they had the chance. Due to the political reality, much could be gained from permitting Mathers, rather than Twiggs, to officiate at their induction, and actually swear them in.

Still using the ruse that he was unable to read or write, Esau gave his vital information to the recorder verbally, just as Absalom had done minutes earlier. Everything seemed to run smoothly until their ages had been recorded. Each lad gave the age of fifteen. At that the registrar stopped abruptly and asked them to step down. He then went over to discuss the situation with Twiggs, who didn't know what to do either. By law, the boys should have been denied acceptance into the Armed Forces of the United States of America.

Immediately aware of the problem, Reverend Omer intervened. He whispered to his boys. "Don't you knuckle heads realize that you gots to be eighteen years old to join the Army?" he scolded. "Now git to gittin back up there and tell the man how old you is. You is eighteen years old, the both of you. And one thing mo. Your actual last name is Reed. I changed it to Omer, on account of I like the name. I saw it first in the Book of Genesis in the Bible. I liked it so much, I named me after that name. So from now on, you can use Reed or Omer. They both is legal"

That brought resoundingly good news to the recruiters and good news, but confusion about their father's name, to the boys. Both black and white men cheered. Quinten Two Bears who already had two sons in the Army was the only one who didn't whoop and shout. He had been involved in activities to menace Confederate trade shipments of cotton, lumber, and raw ores for transfer to Europe. Quniten's fear was the lust for blood he saw among Southerners and Northerners alike. He warned Reverend Omer, his good friend, that the white men would reunite after the war. He feared for blacks, but he feared for his own people even more.

The next day, all the men who had enlisted reported at city hall on Main Street. Every one in the group left, led off by a sergeant. Two miles up the road they were swashed with clean water, shaved and had their hair cut.

Absalom and Esau, however, went West with Twiggs. They were taken to General Grant's headquarters, twenty miles or so West, where they were given their orders. They were met at the front gate by a familiar face. There before them dressed in full Union attire was there good friend Golden Bear Walking, Quinten Two Bears' eldest son. The boys beamed wide smiles when they saw him. Though he recognized them he maintained the strictest formality. He was now in the Army, on duty, and he had a job to do. Holding his rifle extended out, in front of him hc hoped they understood the gesture.

At first they did not. “State your purpose, Sirs” he ordered, with a stern, more serious countenance than they had ever believed him capable of expressing. He was more of a trusted fellow of Grant’s than anyone, and would stay with him until his eventual ascendancy to the Presidency.

“Golden Bear, it’s me, Absalom. And this is yo boy, yo best friend, Esau”, he explained in response. “We has come to join up with you. We is on the same sides now.”

“Please state your purpose, Sir”, Golden Bear ordered again, this time with more force and strength to his command.

Twiggs, now joined by Jeremy French, the Officer of the Day, grinned at the boys’ novel approach to formality. He would have broken out in abject laughter had not Golden Bears Walking been replaced, on schedule, by another guard. Now officially off duty, he grabbed each of the boys and gave them hugs, admonishing them how to behave when they encountered a soldier on duty.

Twiggs interrupted and introduced the boys formally to Captain French. Their impromptu reunion with their Native friend was short-lived. Inside the tent, the Captain would explain their mission. “Even though you boys are in the Army, I want you to understand that neither of you are obligated, in any way, to accept this mission. You are both under age. We believe, my good man Twiggs, and I, that you both will become excellent soldiers. This mission is very important. We know that without you, it doesn’t have a chance to succeed.”

It was so odd that for blacks like Isaac, and his twin brother Esau, the Army, whether for the North or the South, saw their value in espionage. Though Esau believed what he heard, he wondered whether he would ever encounter any frontline action. That is what he craved.

They made it plain to both that Esau was the man in charge. They simply wanted them to go wherever they could find work behind enemy lines, find out whatever they could about troop movements, and Southern strategy, and find a means to get back to the North with that information. That the two could stay together was cause for singular rejoicing. French talked to them briefly, then gave them direct orders. “This project will take you boys to Tennessee, the Chattanooga area to be exact. This will be an area where the borders of the three states approach.” French was very exact in his presentation. His enunciation was slow, deliberate, and very clear. He used a map to explain the area, and to tell them what to expect in resources for their movement. They could not use horses, unless they could rustle them away at night. Of course they could always hop trains and travel on the back of travelers’ wagons going in their direction. They were to always ask permission first, and offer to perform work in exchange for a ride. “Now in the area you are to work, our reports indicate that a certain young black man is operating as an intelligence officer for the Confederacy. Your job is to find a way to sniff him out. All of our white soldiers have been unable to find him. We do know that he is operating out of this area. To date he has single handedly been responsible for the destruction of a whole battalion, one infantry, and a third of a cavalry. You two are at your own resources to flush him out. We believe it takes two very good black men, to find one good black man of the enemy. Find out how he obtains his information. Give our boys a chance to bring this man to justice."

Esau and Absalom had heard a great deal about Frederick Douglas. From his new family in the former Illinois Town, he had learned that Douglas had had a great deal to do with the success of the Underground Railroad. It had not only served as his means of escape to freedom, but so too for many others in the North. It was due to his faith in his knowledge of and awareness of Douglas that convinced Esau to join the Army. When his father, Reverend Omer championed his enlistment, he simply couldn't say no. Their cause had to be a just one, and for that cause, he was willing to lay down his life.

That commitment to a cause was a trait he shared with his twin. The cause for the one was the perpetuation of slavery and victory for the Confederacy. That of the other was for an end to slavery and a victory for the Union.

Esau had heard much about the black spy. He and Absalom wanted nothing more than to attain the honor of killing him. Responsibility for his death was a badge they were sworn to attain. To stop him had become the singular dream of every black man in the North. Strangely, by now, there was not a black man in the South who didn't want that honor as well. Even more eerie, the few black men and women who owned slaves too, didn't trust him. Esau and Absalom wanted to kill him too. They felt confident that they would succeed. With their exploits of the past, they knew they had the mettle to do the job. Their only question was whether the black Southern spy would elude them. Somehow, they felt a kindred spirit, the spirit that would cause something to click, the moment they set their eyes on him. They would know. There was no doubt in their minds either. They would surely know.

That night they had a good reunion with Two Bears Walking. He introduced them to life in the military and explained what they were likely to expect. The Omer family referred to all Native peoples as N.N.s. Many people dismissed this as a mispronunciation of the word 'Indians'. Reverend Omer's point of view was that they were not Indians because they did not come from India, the country, the nation in Asia. As Pinkard Daniel had insisted, they were members of tribes, or nations, and they were native to this hemisphere. Hence, he referred to them as members of Native Nations and simply abbreviated the designation. During that time, the designation actually caught on in the Missouri Valley. Two Bears, his family and all the nations in the area preferred the term also. Proudly they disdained references of American Indians or Native Americans. These terms, mandated by the white man, were unacceptable to NNs with self respect.

What a surprise Two Bears observed the next morning. The boys were jostled, and taken directly to the Bivouac. There they were briefed by Twiggs and French one last time. The meeting was short and to the point. What was so surprising to Two Bears Walking was that they were not in uniform. For their work, they would have no formal connection to the Army of the Union. French allowed them to say their goodbyes to Two Bears. Horses were provided them there, for passage back through St. Louis via the Post Road.

Their first stop was the bank. Their accounts were reviewed, and their pay for the first three months of duty was deposited in advance. Thereafter, Twiggs would deposit and sign for their pay into the account. To ensure that the accounts would be protected from the likes of Mathers, the boys' father was listed as the only trustee who could handle the money should they become unable to do so. Both Twiggs and French were listed as guarantors, supported in writing by the Branch of the Treasury. When it was all accounted for, all the Omer children had their correct moneys credited to their files. This included the same money Mathers had believed he controlled. Therefore, the boys got every penny back. The money they had taken from Mathers in confidence game remained with them, buried deep on their property, protected by quicksand. One thing didn't matter. The boys still did not forgive the bank for their duplicity with Mathers. Their resolve to rob that bank was as strong as before. That would simply have to be tabled until a later date.

From there, they met their father, their brothers and sisters and Mrs. Omer at the area of the levee. No more fitting location for their sweet goodbyes could have been found. They left the horses there, and embarked downstream in a canoe. Mrs. Omer cried fitfully, as did each of the others, after she could not control her tears. This was the very first time anyone had seen Reverend Omer shed even one little tear. They promised to do what they could to get the war over fast. They would be back in East. St. Louis before anybody knew it. They promised.

The boys were provided with no money, no other resources, no other means of transportation than themselves, and no maps or navigational tools. All blacks were able to understand direction and topography without formal training. They were taught about the various stars, the constellations, and phases of the moon. They were taught about the sun and how to use that as the basic navigational tool it represented.

In their briefing, they were given code words to be used in the performance of their duty. These words, when requested and/or replied to correctly, would gain them safe passage. They were to utilize them in only the direst of circumstances, to save their own lives or the lives of a comrade.

Their journey carried them as far South on the river as Columbus, Kentucky. From there they headed East on the Daniel Boone Trail. They had barely reached the outskirts of Columbus when they realized they could go no further. Fighting the currents and the rugged waters of the Mississippi had taken their toll. They had met a number of travelers but they were all going West. The two boys forged a clearing in a glen for their first night's resting spot. Building a fire there, they were kept warm by the burning embers of dried oak, birch and wild grasses. The next morning, feeling the full pangs of hunger, they formed a make-shift trap. They hoped for the element of surprise to overtake a wild boar, pheasant or quail. As luck would have it, the first game they spotted was rabbit. There must have been hundreds or thousands just beyond that clearing. In just a few minutes that had trapped six. They tried as best they could to determine whether any were obviously pregnant. Those that were not, would be slaughtered to provide breakfast. Whatever scientific or unscientific measures they used did not work. Both of the rodents killed were pregnant, they found, though in the early stages. They skinned and gutted them immediately, burying the innards, their paws and the blood about sixty yards away. Rabbit had been among their regular menu items at home. Though they enjoyed it, they wondered whether they would find other fare in their travels. They surely hoped for more variety.

The boys were on their way by seven. They felt good. They expected that this day, something good would befall them. Eager, excited, and even more thrilled than they had been, they set out. Their route took them South East, following the trail know as the Bayou de Chien, just East of Clinton. Along the way they passed small villages. A few settlements, and houses which they came upon seemed to give two messages. The first message was if you are not from these parts, keep moving. The second message was as if they were saying to strangers this: if you are from around here, but not exactly here, then go home, don't stop here. Nothing seemed warm. Nobody was friendly. In that area of Kentucky, nobody could ever wear out a welcome. There was none to wear out. By the end of their second night, they had reached the Kentucky Lake. They would spend the night there. Nighttime in the moonlit low country accorded a friendly scene. Fishing was good. The night was unusually warm. They had removed willow leaves and made a soft sleeping palette. By the sound of the shallows, they could hear that Lake Kentucky teemed with fish. Absalom had a wonderful idea. He took his shirt and undershirt, and Esau's as well. These he tied together and made a net. He had Esau to herd the fish toward him, just as they had done for cattle, leading them into a corral, or toward a train. It worked. Within a minute they were cleaning two silver perch, four pollock and one jack salmon.

In that area on the lake, there were a number of camping spots. They had been told about the lake, especially in the low lying areas. Here was where bear, mountain lion, and an occasional wildcat would ambush deer. That night, no such encounter befell them. They had the lake area to themselves and they rested contentedly.

The next morning the boys had a choice to make. Remembering the geography, they had options on how to continue their journey. The first route they could go was to continue South to where the lake turned into the

Tennessee River. Crossing, and reentry to Kentucky would take longer, but it would be easier, and the trek to Chattanooga would be a lot safer. The other route would take them due East, fording the lake at its widest point, and taking the Rosetta Pass through the heavily forested Land Between Two Lakes. For them this was not that difficult. The shortest distance between two points is a straight line. There would be no easy way out for these two. In no time at all, they had fashioned a raft and make shift oars. They headed due East across the Lake, reaching the other side by nightfall. That night was a repeat of the night before. The only difference is that they enjoyed a number of different kinds of fish. This night would find the boys dining on bass, both silver and striped. They fell asleep to a virtual symphony of owls, various fowl, crows, ravens, turkey vultures, buzzards and other birds howling, singing and cackling. At length it sounded like an overture, a sweet blend of harmonies which were controlled by a central theme, lending order to the wildness of nature.

That following morning they set out somewhat earlier than they had the day before. This is what happens to travelers when in the company of no one else. They don't understand deliberately what is happening to themselves. They just seem to be pushed to be on their way. They simply need to see different faces, to interact with different people. Soon they finished off the last of their bass. By 5:30, they were on their way. The land they traveled was beautiful. They saw wildlife, even wild horses. They bypassed hills, ridges, mountains, and swam through small bodies of water. Going through largely uninhabited area, they saw no humans. By now, by choice, they avoided settlements. Though they wanted to see people, the boys had decided to stop nowhere until they came upon obviously outwardly friendly people. For them that could only be members of the Union Army. Just North of a place called Fairview, they were met on a trail by a group of fifteen white men, all on horses.

The man who appeared the leader sized them up and down, wondering their purpose in that part of the South. Were they runaways? Usually this was the first notion that crossed the minds of white people when blacks were encountered. They seemed very suspicious of the boys. For their part, Esau and Absalom simply stood their ground, although to Esau, there was something very familiar about them. At first he couldn't put his finger on it exactly. The staring continued for just another minute until he broke the ice.

"Ugh, we bees comin from Memps, boss", he decided to flatter the man, still recognizing something familiar about the leader, but unable to explain exactly what it was. "Me and my brother here, we bees lookin for work. Cain't git no job in Memps. They ain't gots no work at all fo a po boy."

"So you niggers lookin for work. What you all able to do, boy?" the leader answered, with yet a question. That twang, that pitch rising higher and higher on each word from the first to the end of the sentence. That was familiar, but Esau needed more.

The men circled their horses around the boys, a training maneuver that had become standard incorporation for small bands of Rebels. Appearing to look away, Esau maintained a veer from the corner of his eye on the leader. The man actually seemed to have a knowledge, an awareness of him. While Absalom cringed and started to tremble, Esau decided it was time to exploit the situation. "We be good cookin vittles, Suh. Yes, suh. We cook up some mighty good vittles."

"You all do anything else, niggers?" another of the riders chimed in. His eyes were moving from an examination of Absalom, then to Esau's, then back, again and again. He had hoped to invoke fear. With Absalom he succeeded, but on Esau, his seering, beedy eyes had no effect.

"Yassuh, boss, we does lots of good things", Absalom answered, a strong quiver in his voice. "We wash yall's clothes, and take good care of ya'lls horses."

"Never you niggers mind", the leader growled. He was surly. He was the type that if he perceived that you had crossed him, you'd better not turn your back on. His men knew it, and the boys could see they had read him right. "We don't need no niggers slowing us down. You niggers see anything back there on the trail?"

"We seed lots of things, boss", replied Esau, looking toward the man, focusing on the brand on his horse as the horses turned a full circle and back, in place. "We seed varmints, critters, and fowl of the air. That bees zactly what we seed."

For a number of reasons they believed the boys. Primarily they thought they told the truth simply because they were too afraid to tell a lie. The reason that the leader knew they were telling the truth is that he was convinced he recognized Esau. He knew the boy was a spy. Since Esau surely knew who he was, he would have told them had they been in danger from Union patrols. Those patrols had engaged rebel groups in skirmishes. This band was on the hunt for such patrols. At the leader's signal, they were off at a full gallop, having to make up for the few minutes they had spent with Esau and Absalom.

Then it clicked in Esau's mind. That speech pattern he had heard. That particular color of horse he had seen many times. The training in recognition of physical characteristics at the Omer place had paid off. That brand on the horse a letter B, superimposed over an A, and a small P. It had a bar running vertically through the center. This was a symbol he had remembered from his youth. That man had to come from the area of Collinsville, Mississippi. That horse, with that brand, could come from one place. That place was the Uriah Agrippa Brookshire Plantation. That man seemed to not only know him, but to believe that he was a friend. His discovery created more confusion. Why, he wondered did they not give him more questions? Why did they allow the two of them to proceed? He could only wonder, pondering the reasons.

Soon their minds were off the encounter. They talked about it, and how they seemed to have luck on their sides. Those men were Rebels, they understood. Yet those men seemed to feel reassured, or at least, the leader did, that the two meant no harm. After thinking on the matter more, Absalom was very, very puzzled too. Why didn't they either take the pair on, or detain them for reward as runaways? Certainly they could not have been so convinced solely by their explanation. There had to be a reason. To put his mind at rest, he decided it was due simply to their innocence. Black people had a naive innocence about them. White people, to a person, believed that the black man who would deliberately lie, and pull it off successfully on whites had not been born.

The leader, however, knew something. He worked at Brookshire Farms prior to his enlistment. He was assigned to a group of guerillas, rather than a regular unit. The South would need men like this to wage war in a field that complemented normal warfare. This leader thought he was up to the task. He also thought he had recognized Esau as the crack spy from the farm where he worked. He figured that was the reason the boy so convincingly refused to blow his cover. That guerilla really believed he had provided a strong act to support the war effort. In fact, he had let two northern spies fall through his hands.

At that point, the boys had had enough of Kentucky. Although it was considered a safe state, they knew they had survived to that point because they were lucky. They hoped not to have any encounters in Tennessee. As they turned South, they could hardly wait until they were engaged in battle. They knew the battlefield for them would never be level. However, they had no fear of encountering the enemy. They welcomed it.

Soon their wishes would be answered, and on their terms.

Chapter XVIII - Plumpsie, Absalom and Esau

Immediately after that encounter the boys changed their plans. Since their orders described a high degree of urgency they wanted to cut the time for reaching Chattanooga. They would have wanted to get there quickly anyway because there had to be some fighting going on somewhere. That surely would be a likely spot. From the map, Absalom remembered that Schachah, a settlement was no more than ten miles away. There they would find a tributary. Since the area had seen more than its share of rain earlier that month, it certainly should provide enough water for them to continue in the southeastwardly direction toward their destination. Though tired, they really wanted to cover those ten miles. Based on the time of day, noon, they figured to get there just before nightfall. There they would fashion a raft, and if the currents were right, they could hook up with the Forks Lakes by morning. Sleeping through the night on the raft, then reaching Forks Lakes by mid morning, then building yet another raft, they would take the Cumberland River directly into Nashville. Their best arrival time, they believed, would be by nightfall the day after. It was ambitious but attainable in their situation. For them it had to be attainable.

They did reach Schachah with about an hour to spare before darkness would fall. As expected, the waters of the narrow river were running high. There were a number of water craft in the area, including canoes for one, and larger canoes for varying numbers. They would simply take one that fit their purpose and number. The boys had traveled down river no more than two miles when they heard a loud noise, motors chugging, iron on iron, just off their Eastern perimeter. It was the East bound Birmingham Express. If they could catch that train that would be a dream come true. They didn't need to catch that train in their mind's eye. They had to catch that train.

They ditched the canoe in that spot, and ran as fast as their legs could carry them to catch that train. There were three engines and at least eighty box cars. Absalom, with longer legs, and a smoother running style got there first. The uneven rocks along the path gave him no problem. As Esau ran, he began to lose pace. If something didn't happen soon, Absalom would be riding to Nashville by himself. "Come on, come on boy", he pleaded with his younger foster brother. "Come on, Esau, cain't nothing out run you, boy. Hurry up."

His pleadings and cries helped for a brief moment. It appeared that Esau was about to grasp Absalom's outstretched hand. But the train appeared to pick up speed and hurry along at a faster pace. "You go ahead, Brother. When you get there you know what to do. And save me some of them Johnny Rebs to kill, boy." Esau yelled between pants and gasps for air. "You just save me somebody to kill."

Absalom was not about to leave him. They started out together, they would stay together. Nor was he about to forsake this chance for fast transportation to Nashville. Without thinking ,he jumped off that fast moving train, beyond the rock bed, onto the tall grass forming a nice cushion. Up to his feet he jumped to his feet to find Esau, trotting toward him. He looked up and yelled to his traveling companion. "Come on ,boy, this is it. We got us a train to catch and we ain't go be late."

By now they were both panting, struggling for air. He grabbed Esau's hand, holding on tightly as if his very life depended on it. From there they ran, now faster than before. First, on overtaking the third car from the back, Esau leapt, dragging himself onto the side step ladder. He made it. Then Absalom made his dive, barely missing the ladder, but maintaining his balance. For his next leap, his timing was perfect. He was at the back of the box car. They climbed to the top and just sat back, then lay back, and slept. By the time they reached Nashville, they were still asleep. On top of that train, traveling at speeds approaching sixty-five miles per hour at some points, amid bells clanging, train tracks cracking, wolves howling, owls cowling, wild dogs barking, even with the rustling cascade of white water as the falls and the Cumberland met forming a rising peak on its sharp turn Northward just Northwest of Nashville. After a steady rain that point would roar like the thunder, with currents so treacherous that the river fish had serious problems maintaining their equilibrium and strength. Through all that the boys slept.

Nashville was not the type place to hunt for food or catch fish for that matter. The boys were hungry and without a cent to their names. The first place they visited was a restaurant on Hickory Road, about a quarter mile from the train station. They agreed to work for food and a place to spend the night. They knew to go around back.

"Last boys I had here to keep the place clean left me and went up town to work", the manager explained as he considered whether to hire them. "I could use some help, but I only need one boy to keep my kitchen clean."

That was the last thing they wanted to hear. In the few days they had lived, fished, hunted and struggled together, they had no intention of splitting up. As before, Absalom was quick with the response.

"Well, suh, Ah thanks ya jis the same. But me and my brotha here, we cain't be splitting up. Ah promised our dying Pa, we go be together to the end. Yes suh, Ah sho nuff did."

Nashville was an active place. It seemed to be crawling with all kinds of activity. There were no signs of Rebel military, but just the same, they had no illusions about where they were. In no time at all their cover could be blown. Right away Esau knew that Absalom's gambit was the right move. They were learning as they worked, gambles' paying off. Another realization became clear to them about themselves. They had nerves of steel. They hadn't understood it before but they knew it now. They could add it all together. That trait, common to each, is why their father nominated them for this work. That is what Twiggs knew too, that if any two could succeed, it would be none other than these two.

"Well wait up you black niggers", the manager reconsidered. "I do suppose I can find enough work for the both of you. You can wash the dishes, and stack them up real nice. Then you can do whatever the cooks and the waiting staff tell your black asses to do. If I hear one word that you all ain't doing your job as you all should, then I will personally kick both of your black, sawed off puny asses back to Mississippi. Ya'll understand?"

"Them's good terms, suh. Ah always says, if'n a man cain't work fo a good white man like you is, then he ain't got no business wif a job. Them terms is good, sho nuff."

Each of those boys had sworn they would never eat from the same plate that a white man used. That also meant they would never even think of eating food that whites had bitten off but left for discard. Hunger has a way of making one reconsider all the 'ain't go never do(s)'. They couldn't remember when. Added to this was that the food was good. The steaks were a bit rare, though tasty. The pork was rather dry, but filling. The potato salad was a mite spicy. But the lemonade, oh that Nashville lemonade, there was nothing like it. Folk used to talk about it. Its distinctive taste, it had been learned, was due to the sugar mill on Lafayette Street, across from the Church of The Nazarene. All the other sarsaparillas, tonics and flavored milks were imported from other areas, serviced by different sugar plants. Nasvillians knew there was something special about their sugar. Many locals believed that it had a great deal to do with the church across the street. The truth was a lot different, but they couldn't really let the truth get out about that sugar, why it imparted much more than sweetness to cakes, pies, breads and lemonade. They never told it either.

By noon, the boys had stuffed themselves so full of scraps and leftovers they had no need for food. They were showed to their sleeping quarters, a shed out back where the owner housed his horses, wagons and a great deal of food and storage items for the restaurant. There were also stalls for eight horses. Somehow, the boys knew that they had slept for exactly one half hour. The manager didn't have to come and rouse them. He didn't bat an eye when they proceeded right to their work. The food that had been prepared for them was left there. They nibbled on the ears of corn, biscuits, ham and green beans with okra until their work shift was over.

The manager had a keen eye, and he really liked what he saw in Esau and Absalom. He believed them when they said they would remain on the job with him. He offered a favor, something he had never done before. He gave them directions to the livery. He advised them they could make real money when the men came in to leave their horses there for the night. The horses needed to be fed, washed down, and to have their saddlery removed. Their stalls needed shoveling, as needed. Just up from there was a place that the boys could pay for a wash basin rental, fresh clean water and soap. He asked whether they wanted to use it and they both nodded yes. That man actually gave the boys a pair of clean underwear each. He told them that the following morning he would have clean clothing available for them as well. The church ladies auxiliary collected these for blacks and poor whites who performed the menial labor in Nashville.

Their earnings that first night were not bad. By ten o'clock, they had about thirty-five cents each. More importantly, they had a better place to sleep than the barn in back of the restaurant. That hay was much softer than the thin mat on the wooden floor in the stables. They were so tired that the smell of horse droppings didn't bother them either. Besides, they were accustomed to much worse, having to live and sleep amidst pigs, goats, turkeys, geese, ducks, dogs, and outhouses, with cisterns dug barely five feet deep.

This existence continued for the boys over the next few days. They would overhear a word, a sentence or two in the livery, about rebel troop movement, but they never could understand a total message. Their fourth night there changed all that. They saw no faces, but feigned sleep, to overhear gentlemen discussing battle plans. From the gist of what they could understand, a Yankee unit was transporting coal, cotton and soybeans up the Newsom Trail. These goods had been confiscated from a small Rebel detachment. The standing militia, now incorporated into the Confederate Infantry, had orders to overtake the convoy and seek and destroy every Yankee in the unit. The rebels had learned that the Union planned to arrive at the Duck River, just west of Murphreesboro, early the next evening, and ship the goods by barges westward using various waterways. The militia was the perfect detachment to attack the Yankees. This was due to their effective deployment of half of their company to assist Lee in the East, and the other half to assist Downs in the West. They planned to attack the Yankees so quickly that they wouldn't know what hit them.

This was the kind of news the boys wanted to hear. Now they hoped their assigned role would begin to pay a healthy dividend for the Union. They listened attentively and pretended to be roused when the men asked for their horses. The boys, still mindful, ever mindful of their goals, dutifully prepared the horses of the men who talked so freely. Their tips were very generous considering the amounts they had received prior to this night. They watched as the men slowly made their way out of town. Their route took them southeast, on Central Street. It was clear they were headed toward Chattanooga, with an intended slaughter in Murphreesboro, along the way.

In their short careers as agents for the Union Army, the boys had stolen a canoe. They had been lucky in finding materials to fashion homemade rafts. Now they had a stable filled with horses, coaches and buckboards. They thought about it and considered all the ramifications. If they took the horses, then that could invite the ire of townspeople. They would surely track them down, perhaps overtaking the boys before they reached Murphreesboro. The boys had hoped to reach the convoy well before Murphreesboro. To intercept that group further south, before they reached the spot where the militia planned its ambush, would be ideal. So even had they taken the horses, to reach their destination before the attack would have required traveling at a full gallop for most of that day. They would have needed to steal more horses along the way. They had no reason to believe that more horses would be available. Undaunted, they left the stable anyway. Their hope was that that would be their last time in Nashville for a very long time.

Though it was prior to dawn, the harbor on the Duck was abuzz with activity. There were farmers loading goods already sold. There were fishermen bringing loads of channel cat and mud trout into the city. Trappers with pelts clogged one side of the harbor. Stream ships with well dressed ladies and gentlemen off loaded, with many rebel troops and baggage filled with war materiel. Amidst this chaos, the boys hoped no one notice them as they scoured the basin for what could be the swiftest transportation to Shelbyville, via Murphreesboro. Their luck, still good, in no time at all, they stole out of the harbor, literally, following the river due South. They were on their way, not really knowing what lay ahead, but neither with fear as they rowed into the wide area of the river, hugging the coast moving fast. In their haste, they had forgotten about eating. As soon as they were in the open they could find something, they hoped, downriver.

Using the sun as their timepiece, the boys figured the hour was approximately two in the afternoon when they arrived on the perimeter of Murphreesboro. The apples, pears and plums they found along the way, growing in gardens, groves and the wild provided great food. As far as either could remember, this was the first time they had not eaten meat during the course of a day. They made no attempt to enter the town of Murphreesboro. It had gained a reputation as unfriendly to freed blacks. This was bourn from the town's history as the major slave trading center in Tennessee. They had heard a great deal about a number of slaves who had purchased their freedom and attempted relocation in the North. While traveling by rail to Ohio, they were set upon by a group of slave traders. Here they were 'captured', actually branded, and shipped to Mississippi. For this reason the boys were also hesitant to hop the train headed in their direction. They were too near their destination to risk any kind if detection. They also feared that even with their 'papers' they were not totally safe as freedmen. They would take no chances.

Their travel, in stolen canoe, proceeded. Within in an hour they were well south of Murphreesboro, on the way to their destination, as fast as their arms could row, and the tail wind could push their craft. A birch wood boat with buffalo gut twine fastening the hull and aft, the boat's strength belied its weight. It was constructed in a manner such that its weather beaten appearance and its faded bearing misrepresented its true value and worth. In normal use, this little water craft would last well over one-hundred years. With constant use, easily it would last fifty. It had been made by a Cherokee group that had been driven away from Nashville, forced to leave behind their canoes, weapons, utensils, horses, ponies and pelts. The boys had no idea but the canoe they stole had been previously forcibly stolen from Native Americans. No doubt, had they known to what purpose it was used then they would have been most proud.

Recalling the direction of the river, they ditched the canoe just South of Murphreesboro. Further South of that point, the river would bend, changing their route to north by northwest, fighting an angry river flow with strong currents. The afternoon was yet young, but they wanted to be sure to reach Shelbyville about the very same moment that the Union detachment would be there. By foot, they needed to cover an additional forty five miles. They knew they could make that distance by dusk. That might have been too late, in this endeavor because you never really know. They needed to take risks if they were to succeed. They didn't have to wait long for an opportunity to take that risk. There in an unincorporated fishing and travel village they found a number of buckboards, carriages and coaches with horses. They also saw a number of horses unattended. It appeared that everyone in the village was taking a break in the local tavern. They knew, with no hesitancy that this was the best opportunity they would have. They kept walking, in the path along the area, just behind the businesses and houses, the school and the two churches. Their plan was to stealthily creep up the stanch, loosen the reins, and make off quietly with four of them. They would ride two, then alternate with the other two. Their impromptu plan worked to perfection. Without overworking the horses, they would cut their travel time to Shelbyville by more than a third. With luck, they should arrive no later than seven, though they figured that six would not be out of the question. By so doing, they would warn them in time to forestall the Confederate ambush.

The beaten path to Shelbyville seemed innocent, and free of hazard. However, they knew they would be in deep trouble if they were accosted. No explanation would suffice for two blacks taking four horses on a road known for its use as a ferrying point for both enemies. They had surveyed possible escape routes along the way. They anted to ensure success. Therefore, the decided, if danger lurched, one would flee for his freedom and the other would take whatever means were necessary to fight their attackers, giving up his life for the safety of the other. The fleeing partner, they agreed, would be the one who was in a better situation to flee. If the plan had to be used, the moment would determine which would flee. Things seemed too easy. Why would such safe passage attend them when atrocities were sure to follow?

As luck would have it, the saddle bags on those horses were well equipped. The boys found corn bread, bacon, and salted turkey. The canteens even contained sarsaparilla, in one, with still cooled water in each of the other three. With four horses, they wouldn't want for food or drink.

The key for them had been their moving through that town on the back path, rather than up the main road. The lookouts would have discovered them. The boys weren't lucky. Luck had nothing to do with their success. They were smart. Living for most of their short lives as slaves, then as freedmen in East t. Louis taught them how to survive. They had learned that lesson well.

Their fear, however, escalated as they moved onward. That evening, about 5:30 PM, on their final approach up the slope to Shelbyville from its east, they heard gunshot. It was loud and constant, unrelenting barrages off to their north. Although their approach became more rapid, it was also more cautious. There was a full scale battle ahead, and they didn't want to be early casualties though they both wanted to join. When they reached the top of the slope, two full miles from where they heard the gunfire, they dismounted. The survey of the scene, the realization that they were too late to warn their side, the full sight before them of blue-coats, surrounded on all sides by gray coats, gave vent to their emotions. If that Union unit was going down, they would go down with it. Before they would become martyrs, they wondered whether anything could be done to save the day. What was clear was that the rebels were maintaining a holding pattern. They were not ready to rush their quarry. Perhaps they wanted to wait for nightfall. Perhaps they had reinforcements coming. Perhaps they wanted to establish a siege. None of that really mattered. Now it was a do or die situation. Absalom and Esau decided that for them something was about to be done, because they were not about to die.

The rebels had delayed their attack for one reason. They wanted the materiel that the Yankee caravan carried. It had been stolen from the Confederates and they wanted it back. They knew that if the Yankees were going down, they would take all of that with them. That delay would prove detrimental to the Rebels.

On the field of battle, the Rebels deployed about sixty men behind shields on the north flank, about forty to the South, and sixty more behind shields to the West. They had scattered infantry, their best marksmen, directly along their route to the woods, where, if they broke through, they would be largely ineffective as soldiers. Even outnumbered, the Rebels held the strategic advantage.

At the back of the clearing the rebels had left wagons with their canons, extra weapons, and food. Off to the right they left their extra horses for officers and cavalry. They had left one man guarding the front of this area, and one more at the rear. The boys knew what they had to do. With no weapons save their bare hands, they had to subdue these two men. On their stomachs, they crawled, slowly, purposefully toward the men. In a few minutes from one hundred feet away, they reached their quarry. At the back of the wagon, Esau sprang quickly to his feet. Looking across the field, he saw Absalom spring to his. The boys knew exactly what to do. It was as if the visions of the lessons Reverend Omer had taught about how to hit a man, to strike him in such a way that the pain was so devastating that he thought he was about to die. The pain was so intense and inflicted in such a manner that the man could not even arrange his vocal chord to utter a single word. Those Rebels couldn't even cry out in pain.

About that same time the gunfire from Rebel musket, rifle and shotgun raked the Union positions, wounding some, killing four. These were the first casualties. With dusk approaching, the rebels raised the stakes and the Union was at a distinct disadvantage. There was no way to fight effectively. They could hold out for awhile. But their positions were untenable. Their leader, a major lieutenant who was from Chicago, wanted to fight. His second course was flight. But the woods, their only way out, were an alternative worse than frontal charge into the jaws of death. He consulted the other officers. To a man they opted to move into formation to charge. They had already lost four men. At least, if they attacked, they had the chance of taking some Confederates with them. They would also burn their bounty, preventing the Rebels from reclaiming their own property. Not one single soldier among that contingent wanted to give in.

The rebels held their fire when they saw the Union men moving into attack formation. This would be like shooting sitting ducks, and they were ready for the hunt. Though they were ordered to hold their fire, they didn't have to be so ordered. They knew when it would be time to fire.

Now well armed, and sitting in covered wagons filled with explosives, ammunition and gun powder, Esau and Absalom were ready to spring into action. They whipped the horses into immediate full gallop, one group coming from the West, the other from the East. It was a flanking motion attacking the Rebels on two sides. The marksmen were left at their discretion. The plan worked to perfection. The gray coats scattered, but not before the gunpowder and dynamite exploded, killing a third of the men on the left from Esau's wagon. Then Absalom's wagons exploded, killing more than half of the men on the right. The men broke loose from the cover of their bunkers. They were so throttled by the suddenness of the rear attack that they lost their sense of direction, running into harms way. They provided easy targets for the Union.

The marksmen ran after Esau and Absalom, who scurried to their horses that had been tethered to the wagons. They made of themselves small targets, skillfully dropping down so that they could not be killed unless the Rebel marksmen killed the horses first. They would have done that too had not the Union marksmen taken dead aim. Now they were mowed down like sitting ducks. The Union provided all the cover that was necessary for the two to reach their site unscathed.

This was a resounding victory for the North. Soon word would be disseminated of the role that two black boys had played in it. This was a message that the South would rather not entertain. Until that point, they had held the upper hand in using resourceful black agents. Now the North had deftly proved that they could use this resource even better than its enemy.

The few Rebels not killed, wounded or captured scurried to horses and escaped safely. Their enemy regrouped, counted their four dead, and hastily prepared them for burial. They were interred at that battle site, outside Shelbyville.

The established code of conduct required the victors to accord the same respect to the bodies of the Confederate Grays. Perhaps it was really due to the time factor. Perhaps it was really due to the urgency of their mission. Certainly the Rebel wounded, unable to shoot a gun ever again might have been left behind to take care of this responsibility. On the other hand, the Union regiment didn't want anyone from the group accepting even a non-fighting role against the North. Perhaps it was even due to that. On the other hand, it might have been due to the emerging code of behavior becoming so prevalent. The enemy, on both sides, could not be provided any comfort, even in death.

The leader of the Union group, the Major Lieutenant from Chicago was all business. His name was Mark Lathan. When the war broke out he had been one of the few physicians in the country with degrees from a medical school and from a university, having majored in Zoology at the University of Chicago. Even though he was a physician by education, training and oath, he showed no hesitation in ordering his men to kill every fleeing Rebel. He ordered their support workers to break camp immediately. Then he summoned his second in command to bring to him the two men responsible for their victory.

Esau and Absalom, summoned to the front wagon, were very cautious as well as relieved as they trod to the Lieutenant. Actually they were upset that there had been no blacks in the battle on the side of the Confederacy. Their reasons were very obvious and the disappointment shonc in their faces.

"I want you boys to know we appreciate what you did today. You boys are heroes" he congratulated them shaking the hands of each stiffly and firmly. His grip was absolutely the strongest they had ever felt. "Where you boys from, what brought you here at this time?"

"Well, Cap'n Suh, this be what happen", Absalom answered. "Ah sho nuff hopes we can talk, Cap'n Suh."

"You boys should feel comfortable talking with my staff, and me. We mean you boys no harm."

Something in his manner set them both at ease. Both Absalom and Esau had developed that knack of reading people, often when they never even uttered a single word. It was their look, their appearance, their countenance. They knew people. They easily knew about the Lieutenant. But they also knew about the second in command, the man who ushered them over to see his commanding officer. That man looked like he would rather have died on that battlefield than to owe his continuing life to two black men. The man also thought he knew Fsau from some other place, but could not remember where.

"We recognizes that Cap'n Suh. We wuz sent out o Saint Louis, Sir. We wuz brought in by Mr. Twiggs."

"I know Twiggs", the Lieutenant interrupted. He relaxed a bit at the mention of a man he had met also in St. Louis. Twiggs was with Grant's aide de camp when Lathan was commissioned. "If Twiggs brought you boys in that speaks for itself. Now I want to know how you came to save the day."

"Well, me and brother wuz sent here on a mission. This wuz not that mission. Last night, we wuz sleeping, and we overhear some Rebs say they plans to attack. So, therefore, me and my brotha, we forsakes our mission. We hightails it down here to tell you. Onliest problem is, we be too late. We gits here after the shootin commence."

"You boys got here in just the nick of time. This entire regiment owes everything to you. I shall see Twiggs tomorrow and I will be sure to tell him about you two. Lieutenant, take down these boys' names."

"Aye, aye, Sir", he answered. He withdrew his tablet and marker to record their names. The few seconds the boys were with this fellow an uneasy feeling came over them. It was as if their whole countenance had turned suddenly cold. His eyes almost seared. His unwavering eye contact was like a knife. Then he remembered. "Memphis, it was Memphis, I knew I knew this boy, Sir."

"I don't understand," responded the Lieutenant. "What is the meaning of this?"

"This is what this means, Sir. This boy here, this Absalom, might be one of our boys. But this boy, this Esau. He ain't nothing but a Flaming Gray Coat. He is a murderer. Why I am sure the only reason he is here now is to kill all of us sooner or later. I know for a fact that everywhere this boy goes, we lose a great battle."

The Lieutenant was shocked. He couldn't believe what he had heard. In his mind he simply could not believe it was the truth. This news was disturbing. How could a person so bravely risk his life? How could a person assist in killing and capturing so many of the enemy? He refused to believe what he had heard. Yet he didn't feel assured to let the boys go to continue on their mission.

"Cap'n Suh, Ah means no disrespect to the General, here, but he mistaken, Suh. This boy here, he been wi' me fo the past few years. He my brotha, Suh. Ah swears, he be my brotha."

At that point, it hit Esau like a thunderbolt from heaven. He knew then who the Confederate spy was. It had to be no other person than his twin brother, Isaac.

"Cap'n, Suh. Whut this here General say he done see, he be right, Suh. He did see me, but he ain't seen me. That be the truth, Suh."

At that, they all looked dumbfounded, first at each other, then at the sky, then at each other again. Even Absalom didn't know what to make of this 'confession'.

"Boy, now you is talking touched in the head. Is you all right boy?" he asked Esau. Then they all figured the stress of whatever he was about had gotten to him. No matter what, they were not about to let them proceed.

From the work group traveling with the regiment, one of the cooks approached. This person appeared to be a slightly built man, about twenty years of age. With hands outstretched to show there was no hidden weapon, permission was granted by the Lieutenant to approach.

"These boys are telling the truth, Sir. This shorter one here, ain't never killed a Yankee. I have known this boy since he was a baby."

"And how do you know so much about this situation? What have you to do with this, anyway? I hired you," explained the Lieutenant. "You know nothing about this. Why you are just a cook out of Ohio."

What a shock they saw appearing right before their very eyes. The cook was not a man. It was a woman. It was Plumpsie. She removed her wide brimmed hat, and the pins from her hair. The beautiful tresses fell into springy curls down the middle of her back, and beyond her shoulders. Then she said not another word, but looked directly at the Lieutenant.

"Well, young lady, we are waiting for an explanation."

She looked at Esau with pride and at Absalom with admiration. Then she turned to the Lieutenant and he nodded. She felt relieved, finally, to give the full story. She explained the complete story, as much as time would permit, to the group. This included the escape of one of the twins, and the success in race horse riding of the other twin. Fifteen minutes after she began, the Union had buried their dead and were ready to reassemble to resume their mission. The Lieutenant knew that time was of the essence but he wanted to make sure the trio would be taken care of, before leaving them. "You Miss Plumpsie, you may either stay with us, or go with these two heroes."

"These boys are my cousins, Sir. This is the happiest reunion I could have dreamed about. I be staying with these boys. Besides, it be time for me to get back to my people. It be time to make some changes on that plantation."

"Well, you may do whatever you please. With this group of men, and everybody knowing you are not a man, but really a beautiful young woman, I can't protect you. You would be better off with these boys."

They gathered a few items that they wanted to bring with them. These included guns, extra ammunition, horses and food. Then the Commander turned to the boys.

"I know the fate of the Union is in good hands with soldiers like my boys here, and agents like you young people. God be with you, and may we meet again."

"We thanks you, Suh. We be goin soon. But fuhst, we go do the right thang bout these here dead boys. We aims to bury every one of these varmints. They ain't bad boys, Suh. They just be on the wrong side. Too bad they is all wrong, dead wrong."

Lieutenant Lathan might have argued with them. While he knew that they were not inherently bad, he knew they had a very different opinion about slaves in particular, and black people in general than he. But this was a Northern Black man. Certainly his slant would be very much different than a Black man from the South. He bade them goodbye and noted in his journal all that happened on the main trail from Tullahoma to Shelbyville that day late in the summer of 1863.

He knew, without any acknowledgement, that Esau, Absalom and Plumpsie had a date with destiny. As such, they were in no hurry. They were on a journey to meet, and deal with a young man whose every waking moment, whose life and whose purpose were the complete antithesis of theirs. He could only hope that they would succeed on that endeavor as they had succeeded here.

The trio examined each fallen Rebel soldier. Their final tally of men who had fallen was ninety-three. Of that number, seventeen still showed various aspects of breathing. This created their first real dilemma. Theirs was a mission that required secrecy. Mercy was not a consideration. Although they had a degree of time they could not afford to jeopardize the mission. Certainly, they considered some of the Rebel group had escaped. However, the Union contingent had scattered them, and none could move toward the East. Running for their lives, they had all moved North, South and West. For them to double back Eastward would keep them at least a full day behind. More than likely, the best they could make up would be two days, tops. Plumpsie had never personally involved herself in the infliction of pain and suffering on another human being. She had been whipped by her owner and grandfather. She had seen black men and women suffer corporal punishment, some costing their lives. Still she didn't have the stomach to do what the boys decided had to be done. They chose not to use the guns lest others, traveling anew through the area, come to investigate. They couldn't bury them alive either. They simply were not that cold. There were Bowie knives, hunting knives and cooking knives among the equipment and items they had taken. With the precision that their father had used in the slaughter of animals the boys went to work.

Then there was a new problem. There were a few among the young Rebels who actually begged that their lives be spared. When the boys ignored their pleas, the Rebels cursed at them, uttering with their last breath curses upon all the slaves. They showed no emotion as they went about the task. It was a job that had to be done. And they did it.

One particular officer, whose age they estimated at twenty-seven or so, accepted his fate calmly. He made one last request to Absalom. "Please, nigger, bury me with my uniform on", he asked, muttering a prayer as if to invite death. "My family will find me eventually, and I would be so happy, and they would be so proud, to find my remains in my uniform."

"We ain't got no time to conversate, General Suh", Esau responded. "But Ah sho is glad you is acceptin your fate like a man."

"I understand, nigger. But even you cannot deny the last dying request of a gentleman. Now can you boy?"

The boys were workmanlike and efficient. Of all the men that they buried that day, that confederate officer was the only soldier permitted to remain in uniform. On parchment paper, using the officer's plume and scented bottle of ink, Plumpsie recorded the vital information of all those men. She noted a description of the place of burial, the exact location of the graves and where they had fallen.

A plan was sprouting in Esau's mind. He took the clothing and placed it into a number of piles. Some of the smaller piles he ignited. The others were then rubbed into the ashes and folded neatly. These he placed onto the backs of four horses.

The group was dead tired by then, but knew they could not take anymore time. They had to be on their way. Plumpsie figured what to do. They would tether as many horse as they could, including those with the clothing, use a covered wagon, and head due Southeast, toward Chattanooga. They would alternate two hours sleeping while one drove. As they made ready, Plumpsie and Absalom listened attentively as Esau explained the reasons for burning some of the clothing. Plumpsie volunteered to drive first, but she was overruled by Absalom. In turn he was overruled by Esau. Plumpsie and Absalom were just about asleep before their heads hit the floor of that wagon.

During different times of the night, they seemed to understand the lesson etched on the mind of the Lieutenant. They were headed for a date with destiny. For the first time since they left East St. Louis, and since Plumpsie left Collinsville, Mississippi, they knew the meaning of fear.

In their lives they had seen the part of life, and lived lives that, at times, were pure hell. Now they had seen war that was pure hell. Then they all seemed to realize one characteristic that each shared with each other. They understood this characteristic to be one they shared with every other black person in this country. t mattered not whether that person was slave or freedman. It was that the living hell they experience in everyday life was no different from the everyday hell of war. There was only one reason that Abasalom, Plumpsie, Esau and his twin brother Isaac were perfect choices for the work they were chosen to do. That is why they, like any Black man, woman or child whether slave or free, no matter which side any one favored, was well suited for this kind of work.

Life was easier for the rest of the trip to Chattanooga. They had high country to traverse, but now they didn't have to use back roads or rush to avoid detection. The well worn paths proved easy to manipulate. With ample food, and cooking utensils, to find and gather food, and to find a means to prepare it was not difficult either. No matter who they encountered, Yankees, Rebels, or civilians, they were able to produce evidence that could convince either side. Safe passage, they concluded would be guaranteed. Victory would be within their grasps soon.

The first test was their first real test. Their plan was to approach Chattanooga from due North. This would require their taking a mountain pass through low country, following the Sequatchie River-Stream just North of the Naylor Pass. There, approaching nightfall they stopped to prepare dinner. Just as they began to eat a group of approximately sixty or seventy men, ages ranging from fifteen to fifty-five, entered their camp. Right away, they had no illusions. These men were Southerners. They were not enlisted, or even part of a State militia. They were not agents either. Absalom was the first to figure who they were. These men played dirty, and didn't abide by any rules. They rode into a formation surrounding the three. Evcery fourth man in the group carried a well illuminated torch. The leader surveyed their horses, their wagon and their attire. He spoke first to Absalom, who stood up to greet them.

"Well if we ain't come up on the most stupid bunch of black niggers in the whole wide world. These here coons done stole horses and rifles, and food and a wagon from the Confederate Army of the South. We go string us up some fresh niggers tonight", he drawled, spitting tobacco from the side of his mouth as he talked. Then, turning to his men, he gave six quick orders in rat-a-tat succession, forsaking the drawl. "Bobby John, Silas Jim, Robert Jesse, git rope, noose hangin' rope. Paul William, Luke Walter, Richard Wilkes, you boys git me some hosses, We go git to hangin."

This was not unexpected. Even though the boys knew they could encounter this type of mob and even though they believed they could prevail, they were not unafraid. They practically trembled in their boots. So did Plumpsie. She prayed that Absalom's explanation would suffice. Though these boys were obviously slow witted, they still were dangerous. They were out for blood and they wanted to take all of theirs.

"You is a mighty angry man, Cap'n Suh. I can sho nuff tells, you a mighty angry man. And I would be as angry as you is, if them damn Yankees keep up that killin. In fact suh, the way them damn Yankees done killed them boys last night, that be a shame."

"Come on, Boss. We ain't got no time to talk to these here damn niggers. Let's string um up!" countered another of the men. The others joined in. However, their leader wanted to hear everything. He had heard of no killings, no victory by Yankees.

"Wait a minute. Wait just a God Danged minute. I'm the head honcho in charge here. I want to hear what these here niggers got to say", he replied in strident, authoritative tones. He didn't try to hide his anger from his men at that point. They had seen him angry before, many times. However, they had never seen him like this. They knew to shut up. He turned to Absalom. "Okay, nigger. Your black ass better tell me the whole story and don't even think of lying. You tell me a lie, and I'll beat your black ass to death, hear with my bare hands."

"Beat his ass, Captain. Beat that nigger's ass to death. That way we only have us to hang two." The cries urging the leader to kill Absalom right there continued, only stopping when the leader raised his hand, and alit from his horse.

"Yow's mad, Cap'n Suh. Ah knows yowl be mad. That be why Ole Absalom here, he ain't go lie to yowl. He go tell the God's honest truth and that be a fact. Don't ah prays the Good Lord, he smack me down dead right now."

"Go on, tell us what happened and take your time, nigger."

"Well, we is all from Collinsville, Mississippi, Cap'n Suh. We belongs to Master Brookshire. He be the best lord and master in the whole state." Absalom swallowed hard, the spit stopping at a lump in his throat. "My throat gittin mighty dry, Cap'n Suh. Can Ah haves a drink from my canteen here?"

The captain nodded, but then turned to his men to send for a young man from Meridian. "Bartholomew Henry, bring your stupid ass up here." The men roused the youngster and he came running. "I want you all to look at these three. Now be careful and don't tell no lie. These boys say they from Collinsville. They say they belong to Master Brookshire. You know anything about that?"

He looked at each against the tall flames of their fire. First he studied Absalom. Then he fixed his gaze on Esau. Finally, he gawked at Plumpsie up and down, even having her to turn around. She recognized the boy. Actually she used to play with his sisters until she was nine years old. Then she had to do their aunt's bidding. Their aunt was her grandmother.

"Well, boy speak up. You live around that area. You know these boys?"

"Why Captain, I know them. This little one here, he is Isaac. He is a good nigger. He is the one who spied on them damn Yankees and was single handedly responsible for that great victory."

"Are you all sure, boy?"

"I ain't got no reason to lie. Old Master Brookshire would be most pleased to know that you gave this here boy, and his friends safe passage. He will make it most worth your while when this dang war is all over and we done defeated them damn Yankees."

It had worked. They were free. That boy knew Plumpsie but he didn't know Plumpsie. He wouldn't figure out until the next night, when they would be miles away from each other that it was she. As for Absalom, he just figured that he looked like any other slave from the area. Even when he realized about Plumpsie, he simply figured she had been selected as an agent to gain intelligence too. In fact she had, and in greater fact she would.

That night they cooked for the rebel band and showed them the uniforms, some charred, some burned, and others intact. They shared with the leaders the record of the burial place and gave them identifying information. Never would they have thought that Plumpsie had made another copy. The copy and the names, with identifying marks of wounds was a phony. When they sought to recover remains for removal to their homes, they might come upon graves. However they certainly would not be those of the men killed and buried near Shelbyville.

The leader of that group of men was not very bright. He accepted everything that Absalom and Esau told him. Then he took them into his confidence. He warned them to be careful in Chattanooga. The place was crawling with Yankee spies, and agents from foreign countries. He estimated uniformed Confederate military at about one hundred thousand strong, with the ability to detach thirty thousand more in an emergency. He estimated that there were another twenty thousand military, including experts in explosives and poison gasses, who would join the Rebels if combat occurred. He also gave them the names of the two places most likely to house Southern Blacks, most slave, a few freedmen, who worked as agents, like them, for the Confederacy. He even gave them names and descriptions. As he led his men off, the leader made one request of Esau.

"Now boy, you know how good I treated you and your friends out here tonight. Ya'll go be sure to remember well to Master Brookshire. Now don't ya'll forget."

Esau simply nodded as the group rode off. He had lied very well. Absalom had done even better. Those Rebels really believed they would overtake the Union regiment by morning. They all wanted to be heroes. This would clinch it. They would have caught them too, if the event had really happened one night, instead of two nights earlier.

Chapter XIX- In Prison, Out of Prison

For a late summer's night in Southeastern/Central Tennessee the weather was somewhat cool. This night was not like any night that Chattanoogians had seen in many a year. Unfortunately, due to the danger about the town, every one was suspicious of everybody else. After their meeting the night before, Plumpsie, Esau and Absalom saw no other faces until they arrived at the main road leading into town. It was just as the Rebels had described. Every building, every establishment was ready to change from its usual activity and become a fort, with armed men and women at the ready to defend it. By then, every white person they saw believed them to be agents for the Confederacy. Just the same, nobody was willing to extend the welcome mat. Had they not ate their fill from the food they carried, they would have gone hungry that night.

They could sense that among these throngs of Southern regular army, regular militia, and rag tag groups, all was not as it should be. The tension was real. Residents barely said a word to each other as they went about their business. If a battle was looming then nobody showed obvious trepidation. Yet, a battle was in the offing. At the time, Chattanooga was the site of the largest arsenal that either side held in the war. For the North to be able to control the war, it would have to take the arsenal. The problem was that it lay at the top of a steep mountainside. There were only two things that the North could do to take Chattanooga. The first was to move enough men directly into the area from the North, West and South, to reconnoiter at the foot of the mountain just North of the fortifications and roads leading to the arsenal. The second was to secure enough men behind enemy lines to attack from the rear of the fort and arsenal. There had to be enough men who, knowing that they would be killed, must hold on long enough to engage the enemy so that Union troops could advance up the mountain. The only way the plan could succeed, they believed was for the Union to dispatch additional troops to the East and West. Again, the reasoning dictated, the Rebel forces needed to be too few to guard all fronts. The rebels had advised Esau already that the Confederacy would deploy thousands more troops if necessary.

Till then, the Confederacy was winning the war. To lose Chattanooga would have signaled a turning point in the war. They could not afford to let it turn.

The trio sized up the situation and tried to figure whether something could be done to even the odds. Whatever they planned to do had to be done fast. The city, based on its best intelligence was gearing for what promised to rival Gettysburg and Antietam/Sharpsburg as a defining moment in the war. By now troops were being deployed. Some were in battle lines. Others were in defensive maneuvers. Others guarded strategic points. They knew that for the moment, their ability to make an impact in the city was non existent. They also knew that they were free to come and go, so long as they minded their own business, and stayed away from townsfolk. Everybody in town was edgy. Everybody was suspicious. If those soldiers, slave traders, and even regular citizens had not believed the trio to be spies for their side, they would have killed them there. Coincidentally, the Northern spies who were in town under various guises, would have killed them too, due to the same mistaken conclusion. The only reason they did not was that their cover would have been blown too, and they would have been summarily executed.

They discussed the information that the Rebel leader had given them about the prison that held Union soldiers fifteen miles due East of the city. It was on the Post Road, the main travel road connecting East and West Tennessee.

That fort was a scary appearing building, even from a distance. A filthy place, it had served as a State and County prison for thirteen years before the war. When the war broke out, every prisoner was given a full pardon if he pledged to join the Army of the Confederacy. About a third of the band that they had encountered a night earlier had been released from the facility barely weeks prior. Too undisciplined to be regular army, they found happiness, right at home with marauding bands of cutthroats, villains, thieves and rapists. However, their leaders, all commissioned officers in the Confederate Military, had been ordered to, and would have shot them at the first hint of disobedience or cowardly behavior. In fact, a number had lost their lives that very way.

On entering the gate, they were not simply met, but engaged by a soldier dressed in full grays. He could not have been more than fifteen years old, if that. "Just stop right whar you all is standing, damn niggers. Ah got my shot gun at dead aim, and ah can take out all o ye."

Esau was not about to waste time now. Tired, hungry, and still with work to do, he needed to see the officer in charge. "We were directed to this prison by Officer John Richardson. He used to command this very prison. His men advised us to stay here for safe haven. We have a message for the commander. Please get him here."

"Now lissen to how you damn niggers dun learnt how to talk, all citified and airthang. You all just hold yo damn horses now. Ah will git the cap'n."

Soon they were in the captain's quarters. An unassuming man, nonetheless, he had ambition. As a graduate of West Point, Eldridge Hannibal Hackberry dreamed of duty anywhere other than running a makeshift prison. Pursuant to his orders, he had no cause to suspect that Esau, Plumpsie and Absalom were not agents for the Confederacy. He even seemed to prefer discourse with them rather than those assigned to the prison.

Under the rules, Esau, Plumpsie, still masquerading as a man, and Absalom were permitted to share a cell, away from the prisoners. They were provided food and blankets as well. In their cell, they figured just what was what. The Yankee prisoners, just under four hundred in number, were under lock and key in the cell block off to the south end corner. The prison arsenal, which they passed on approach to their cell block, was barely twenty-five feet away. With pins from her hair, Absalom, on signal from Esau, would unlock the arsenal. They hoped to find weapons and ammunition. "Now Absalom, what we need to do is try and release all the Yankees. I have to try and ensure that Officer Hackberry will place all his men in position to defend this fort. If I can do that, then you and Plumpsie can open the arsenal, unlock the gun ridge, and then just turn it over to the Yankees."

I understands. Just one thing, what will be your signal?"

"It will be something very simple. I got it. When you see me take my hat, and wave it across my body, that will mean that you have five minutes to act. Now, I need to get me just about one hour's sleep. Then I will leave. You should get up and look out that window, right there. I will be there at 6:AM sharp. Got that?"

"There is a problem, bro. That window is eight feet high. I cain't even jump that high."

"Mmmmm. Ok. Plumpsie, you will have to look."

"Me, I am shorter than your brother. And neither of us can jump that high. Anymore bright ideas?"

"Yes, that ain't no problem either. You just go have to stand on this boy's shoulders, unless you want him to stand on yours."

One last thing, boy. That sun go cast a shadow right about here, at this here angle at 6, right?

Right, and if there ain't no sun tomorrow, then you just better guess the time and you had better guess right.

Hackberry was easy. All Esau had to do was say that his mission required he leave the fort. Having come to the prison on the Post Road, which was due West from Chattanooga, Esau wanted to get another view. He rode due South and picked up the Lightfoot Mill Road. His plan was to establish a lookout point where he could monitor the traffic. As he saw it, then only travelers using throughways like this would be either military reinforcements or agents for the South. From his vantage point, he espied two riders approaching a mile away from South, Southeast. No doubt about it, these men were on reconnaissance duty. In that area, they could be with no group but the South.

Quickly mounted, Esau moved to intercept the pair. Putting on his best act, he feigned tiredness. However, using the passwords peculiar to Rebel agents, he had these two in his confidence quickly. One man was rather tall, the other was short. Sizing the two up, Esau wondered in which ways he could get the better of each. He knew that would be necessary. He believed he had come upon the only reconnaissance men out at that time. They had to be eliminated. "So. you see. We got us a group of fifteen Yankee spies on this very road. As you gentlemen know, they are on the same kind of job as we. But, they gots to be taken out."

"Ah do unnerstand what you all trying to say, nigger, but whut I cain't unnerstand is why you all have to look at my boots when you all talk to me. You all wanna shine my boots, boy?

"No suh, I just think they some good lookin boots, and all. I would just like to have a pair of boots just like that."

"Well, I don't care whut you all think o' my boots boy. I'm go let you all shine them, rat after we kill some Yankees. Ha, ha, ha."

The shorter fellow said nary a word. All he did was to join in the derisive laughter with his larger, more verbose buddy. Esau could only think of how, somewhere in the South, each of these boys had a mother who loved him. He knew that was difficult to comprehend, but it had to be the truth. He knew he would have the last laugh.

The taller, bigger fellow deployed on the north side of the road. The smaller guy took a position diagonally across, about thirty yards away. They each had a raised view, allowing them to shoot downward from cover. Esau had to work fast. "I'm just go get out the way, gentlemen. When the shooting starts, I like to be away from the danger."

"Yes, nigger. You all git outta the way", answered the taller one. "Like Ah says, you all ain't good fuh nuthin but shinin shoes. That go be whut you all can do with my boots after we kill these Yankees."

As they laughed, Esau crawled on his stomach, circling behind the smaller quieter agent. He didn't waste any time to feel sorry for the man. Without the fellow's even knowing it, Esau was close enough to touch him. And touch him he did. Whoosh! In a flash, almost in one singular motion, he had his left hand around the fellow's mouth, holding tight, stopping all air to his mouth and nostril. Just as quickly and adroitly he rammed his Bowie knife into the middle of the man's nape, beneath his Capitis. Then he stabbed him two times more, each wound equidistant, first between his Rhomboideus major, and finally at the Trapezeus. The aorta, the right auricle, and the esophagus were all severed, from the rear. He could not have been more dead.

Then he stood and walked slowly to the other fellow. He was stunned, clearly unable to understand why Esau approached. Certainly with Union men nearby, he had no desire to put up with any 'foolishness' from Esau. "Why nigger, you all better git yo silly ass outta the way. I don't want to kill yo, boy. But if I have to I will."

Watching the man very closely, Esau took deliberate, short, quick steps. The night held onto the darkness, but the moon illuminated the dell very well. The eyes of each man were very sharp. They had to be at a time like this. Esau removed a gun from his belt. "You see this gun here, you piece of a saltine cracker. Even in the moonlight I can see that you are as white as a cracker, a pale cracker, a pale salted cracker. You see this gun here? This was your partner's gun, just before I killed him. Now I have to send you to join him in hell. He will be waiting for you."

He looked at Esau as if he was crazy. Then he saw. This man was not crazy. He was as sane and as cool as a cold glass of lemonade. "But why, nigger? Why did you all have to kill Carl? He ain't never hurt nobody in his life."

"That didn't matter. He had to go, just like you have to go."

"But why? Why do you want to kill me?"

"Oh it's because of your boots. Let's just say that I like those boots. For a big ole boy, you got a small foot. I want those boots. The only problem, cracker, is that you won't live long enough to shine them for me."

Not another word was passed. Carefully Esau placed the gun onto a boulder just to his right. He was prepared to give this man a better than fair chance. Esau believed he was faster. What a mistake that was. The gun was cocked and fired in a split second. The Rebel was faster than Esau, after all. However, his aim was not so true as Esau's. His first bullet grazed Esau's temple. However, the force of the bullet did not knock him back. Perhaps that is what saved his life. In that fraction of a second that his adversary, whom he had taunted, raised his gun and got off two shots, Esau grabbed his and fired once. The second bullet went through the meaty part of Esau's thigh, causing a burning pain. His aim, though was flawless. Right between the eyes he caught him. Esau had no emotional attachment to these two killings. It was something that had to be done. It was plain and simple. He looked upon everything he had done, to that moment, as something necessary to free his people, to forge tiny steps toward a victory for the Union.

First tending to his wounds, then he moved the bodies away from the road. To hide them, he merely used leaves, drift wood and cattails from the nearby estuary. Hurting, upset that he had been too casual, he needed to return to the fort. He wanted to be there by six, as noted for his meeting with Plumpsie and Absalom. He had two final things to do. He tried on both hats that the Rebels wore. That of the shorter man was a better fit. Then he took the shoes from the bigger fellow. The fit was not perfect, but it was the best pair he had ever worn. With leaf matter here, some grass there, they were fitting well.

Back at the fort, Esau summoned Hackberry. He explained that he had been shot by Union spies. He learned that men were marching to the fort. According to Esau's 'information' Union men would attack the prison at 6:30 AM that morning. They needed to get their men in position to forestall the Union assault. As he made the suggestion, he removed his hat, and waved it across his upper torso.

Hackberry saw this as his great opportunity. Like all Southern officers, he displaced no forestalled motives for greatness. He envisioned himself the victor in a strategic battle. This affair, he decided, would be strategic for him and the South as well. With this victory, due to preparedness, he would write his own ticket, and punch it to leave this dreary place. On the quickstep Hackberry deployed his men. They covered both sides and the front of that prison. The rear was impregnable due to its topography. The rear, was also where the soldiers, officers, and agents from the North were held captive. While the men deployed, Absalom and Plumpsie went to work. Every cell in the tier housing Union military was emptied. From the arsenal in the fort, they removed 300 hand guns with ammunition for at least twenty full reloads; 200 repeating rifles with ammunition for ten full reloads each; 100 shotguns, with ammunition too numerous to count; and enough TNT to blow the place to kingdom come.

As expected, those boys under the command of Officer Hackberry never had a chance. Neither did he. The Union men were not willing to take any prisoners. They did take care of their business. After the carnage that morning, they ate a good breakfast and prepared to follow through with their orders.

Real battles lay ahead. These were actions to ensure that military personnel and their agents would get there. The officer in charge of the Union brigade thanked Plumpsie, Absalom and Esau, of course. He had two purposes after that. The first was to make an impression on the Battle for Chattanooga. The second was to have an impact on the action in the Cumberland. This created choices. After sharing their information with the officer, the three decided to remain together. In addition, they believed their decision would bring them closer to Isaac.

CHAPTER XX - The South: God Is on Our Side

And your sons and your daughters shall prophesy, your old men shall dream dreams, and your young men shall see visions. Joel 2: (ext. 28)

Esau, Absalom and Plumpsie decided to cast their lot with the Union men headed for the Cumberland. They brought up the rear. Their demonstrated bravery and loyalty could be rewarded by having them protect their flank. They would continue to pose as cooks in the employ of the Army while in truth, they could serve a much more meaningful role if necessary.

Often, the measure of men who have killed is tested and weighed against the circumstances under which one is forced to take the life of another. Esau and Absalom had now completed the most unusual of experiences that take place on earth. This was the actual desire to take the life of a human being, and with no remorse or hesitation, carry through with the act. Of course, the cause was to free their people, and themselves. Then too, by now, they had tried to convince themselves that this fight was God's fight. They wanted to believe they were instruments of the Lord. It was during the ride to Chattanooga that the activities of the prior day and night disturbed the workings of their mind. They didn't have to say a word to each other. They knew what the other thought. A veer to the left at Plumpsie and they could read her mind too. However, she didn't see either of them as ruthless killers. She felt they were good soldiers, just doing their jobs. Her approving smile, and nod of her head convinced them that they should feel proud of themselves. She was proud of them, and that showed. Absalom remembered his early childhood as a slave in Kentucky. Esau recalled his youth, misspent on the Brookshire grounds in Mississippi. Then they let their minds wander to their days in Illinois Town, where they worked, played, learned, worshipped, and felt so comfortable to belong to a nurturing family. No, they concluded. They were not killers. Just the same, they had learned how to respond when crossed. These lads and Plumpsie, through slavery, and as a direct result of slavery, always knew how to take care of themselves. Their learning curve escalated to permit them to exercise, to put into action, what they already knew. They would not, and could not be denied, except for and through betrayal.

Though their mounts were rested, the pace remained slow, but steady. Scouts were dispatched ahead. En route they encountered other Union spies who ferreted messages of a major battle raging ahead. From the early reports, thousands were involved on both sides. Heavy casualties had been suffered and yet, even heavier amounts of wounded and dead were anticipated. Doggedly and with fierce determination both sides pressed the attack. Then there would be some retreat. Then there would be advance, to be followed again by retreat. The conflict went on and on. The main factor preventing a victory for either was that neither side could gain a strategic advantage. The South could not get behind its enemy because their flank was too well protected. The North, likewise, could not surround its enemy. Yet, neither side would accept a stalemate. If there were going to be an edge, eventually, then the South, common knowledge attesting, should gain it. The Union Army was slightly undermanned. They also seemed to be outmaneuvered at key points of the fray. And, all in all, the Southern forces seemed to fight with greater zeal. They had the advantage of defending their own soil. They knew the terrain better and they were in an area where the local populace clearly was loyal to the Confederate Army. They provided every assistance to their boys.

Confederate spotters caught sight of the Union Brigade approaching from their rear. However, at a particularly heated battle, they could dispatch only a token force. They would have been, and should have been happy to simply stall the advance rather than to knock it out totally. For the Union, this would be the perfect time for the Rebels to lose their wits. The Union Army, with its own network of spies, took notice. This bit of espionage was exploited to great advantage. The Union men simply dismounted and proceeded on foot. They knew exactly where they would meet their adversaries who expected to surprise them. When they had not reached the spot the rebels expected, they proceeded. They too were cautious for they felt something wasn't quite as it should have been. On learning of their continuing movement, the Union commander deployed his men into sniper, volley, and marksmen formations.

Those rebels didn't have a chance. Everyone of the thirty troops deployed from the Cumberland was cut down. Some were hit multiple times, some only once. Every man was dead. This marked the first big mistake of that battle. Those men didn't have to die. The rebels knew how many soldiers approached their flanks. They had only to wait them out. No strategic advantage could be attained by sending out the men. Along their route, there were a number of posts from which they might have held off the enemy. This mistake could only be attributed to nerves. The South's generals, until then the bulwark of more efficient planning and strategic thinking, were breaking. The strain was more than they, even in their vaunted senses of infallibility, could handle. Now they were showing that they too were human.

The commander let his men rest after that encounter. They cleaned their weapons, relaxed, and napped for two hours. Before departing they received word that the battle was showing definite signs of turning to the favor of the North. While it would continue for another day, at worst, it could be shortened by the rear flank attack. They continued their slow, methodical pace and by late that afternoon were within a mile of the site. With a well planned assault, they could turn the tide. Oh they would all be killed. But the sacrifice would not be in vain. Engaging more resources in man, munitions, and time, could be just the advantage the Union needed.

The commander ordered dismount. In full battle positions, he assigned the infantry, now, reinforced, one hundred forty-five strong, positioned at nine abreast, to approach from their stations - twenty five feet of distance separating each. That gave an appearance of being many more than their actual numbers. Behind them were the fifteen officers. They were equidistant, three men in between each twenty-five foot group. They approached a full ten yards behind the infantry. Again, the allusion of many soldiers was displayed. There followed the commander and two officers on horseback.

As before, due to nerves, the Confederates rose from their ranks to attack the Union men in front, rather than risk the fresh soldiers from the rear. They were like sitting ducks. Some of these men were actually able to engage in hand to hand combat with the Yankees. Weakened, tired, their resolve killed before their minds and their bodies, they hoped to simply die, rather than to be taken prisoner. Soon the Union Army was just completing a mopping-up operation. Examining the large battlefield, they killed Confederate wounded who appeared to have no chance of survival. In truth, even with poor medical care, many of those wounded, who were then killed, would have survived. The Northern men then took over the sick bay tents in the Confederate camp.

Separated from Absalom and Plumpsie in the melee, Esau helped in the return to a normalized post atrocity camp. The Confederate medics were pressed into service to care for the Union wounded. With the Union medics working alongside them, the wounded from the North were receiving proper attention. Esau did what he could to assist the medics. Then he turned to identify the war dead from the Union Army.

Some of the corpses could not be readily identified. Burial for those men would have to be delayed. Their bodies were salted and left to lay in an open field. He then left there, to search for Absalom. Dusk was falling fast. He knew that he would have to work fast if he were to find him. There he was among the dead, the mortally wounded, the workers and other soldiers, ankle deep in blood, guts and worse. A Confederate prisoner told him he had seen a boy meeting Absalom's description down by the hilly ground at the base of the camp. Burials were being conducted there. Since this was the only area he had not looked, he knew he would be there.

By then, every man who was not dead, was dead tired. Unable to perform anymore work they just lay back, some using corpses as pillows. He searched among the wounded and dead, inquiring of the men, who were too tired to understand what he asked. Due to the strain, Esau began to fear the worse. He wondered whether Absalom had deserted. Maybe he was wounded. Approaching hysteria, he feared he might have even died. Absalom lay a scant two feet away. Seriously injured with bullets in his shoulder and back, he had lost a lot of blood. To survive, it was obvious he would require immediate medical attention and it had to be prompt. Tired, afraid, weary, Esau mustered enough strength to lift his brother, positioning him just right on his back. From there, by foot he carried him the full half mile to the medical tent. Neither Esau, nor Absalom could understand how Esau could muster that degree of strength.

Esau's labors proved all for naught. The medics would not give Absalom a second look while needy white soldiers required medical attention. Esau pleaded for compassion. His protestations went unheeded. He even asked to be given medication to suspend bleeding so that he could apply it himself. That was to no avail. From his days on the farm, he knew how to remove bullets. He asked for the use of their equipment so that he could remove the highly leaded pellets. Again he was rebuffed. In a panic, he rushed the supply area, determined to obtain the equipment on his own. He was followed by two guards in close pursuit. The butt of the rifle of the quicker man found his head an easy target. He was rendered unconscious immediately leaving a permanent indentation on his head.

Esau regained consciousness early the next morning. Camp was broken and men were forming ranks. The main contingent was heading back North with their wounded. They believed a large Rebel detachment would be entering the area and they were in no condition to wage another great battle. They would rather use hit and run tactics from then on. He looked up at the retreating Army, wishing he had strength to fight them all. The pain in his head was a quick reminder as he rose too fast to his feet, that he could take on no one. He looked out and saw the cold, lifeless body of his brother. He walked to him, knelt and cradled Absalom in his arms. He couldn't cry anymore. He had no more tears. Esau had wanted to believe that he was fighting to free the slaves. With the refusal of the Army to treat his dying brother after they had risked their lives to ensure victory for the Union, he knew slaves, ex-slaves, and men born 'free' could not be free. He had been treated like the enemy as well. His could not be a purpose, he reasoned, that could well serve either side.

This was a condition of life that even Twiggs, as well meaning and well intentioned as he was, could not alter. He would simply return to Illinois, regain his money, and leave this war to anybody else who wanted to fight it.

Then he remembered Plumpsie. She had been with Absalom the whole while. Now where could she be? He assumed the worse. He walked over to the area where hundreds of Confederate dead lay. She and Absalom, maintaining the dignity of those who had died on both sides, had decided to stay on and complete burial detail. They would rejoin the Union detachment from the prison later. That group had decided to double back to the prison and approach Chattanooga from the West. Such a move would be considered unprecedented and simply put, suicidal. The entire city had to be impregnable.

Before they were to leave, one of the soldiers had stated that he had seen white men and Indians die, at his hands. He wanted to gain a sense of how it would feel to kill a 'nigger'. He had shot Absalom in cold blood. He was heard to remark that unlike when he killed an Indian or a white man, killing a nigger was nothing. It was like shooting a tin can, a bottle or just taking target practice. They didn't leave Plumpsie a horse, or food. They simply left the two of them there, Absalom dying and her to die.

That battle was known as the Battle of Bessemer. It marked the first decisive recorded Union victory over the Confederacy in the war. It proved for the first time that the Union was not simply in this thing to outlast the Confederacy. It also marked a major change in the conduct of the war for the South in the Western theater. They would abandon all hope of moving the fight to the North. It was clear that in Mississippi, Alabama, Western Georgia, Tennessee and Kentucky they could not take the battle to the Yankee. A dig-in and siege mentality was slowly, but most assuredly, settling into the mindset of the average Southern military man. Only a fool would attempt to proceed North, as had been their goal. That might have proven a winning strategy under normal circumstances. However, their ties to Great Britain and France were running thin because the Confederacy could not afford to maintain these alliances. Their pacts with the European powers were borne out of European ideology, their desire to see the defeat of the limited brand of democracy championed by the young nation.

However, the South needed capital to maintain themselves. With the massive war effort, the drive to maintain slavery, and demands for the common man of the South for a voice, the South was strapped. For England and France, Spain once again posed a threat to their holdings in Asia, Africa and South and Middle America. The handwriting on the wall was that Lincoln's resolve, when pitted against these factors, could not be denied. While Lincoln would demand no malice against the Confederacy, he would not be so charitable for Europe. Protective tariffs, charges of economic espionage, and competition for world markets had been not just hinted at, but suggested by Union mercantile authorities.

At that point, common sense dictated that the South capitulate. Confederate generals were now making the kinds of errors in the East that the Northern generals made at the start of atrocities. Longstreet criticized Lee; Jackson blamed Longstreet; Buckwalter blamed Jackson and Mosby. Their mistakes were inevitable because the full, overwhelming power of the North was exploited. Still they fought on, for no other reason than they felt God was on their side. The Almighty, they believed, would make the difference in their favor. For them to give up the fight would be to refuse God's Holy Direction. They rationalized that even if they lost a full generation of fighting men, they would still win this war because in the final analysis, God would deliver the victory. To them, it was not only treason to believe that they could be defeated, it was tantamount to doubting the existence of God.

For if a slave can have a country in this world, it must be any other in preference to that in which he is born to live and labor for another. Indeed I tremble for my country when I reflect that God is just, that his justice cannot sleep forever. The Almighty has no attribute which can take sides with us in such a contest. Thomas Jefferson

CHAPTER XXI - Isaac's Life Is Spared

Thou shall not hate thy brother in thine heart. Leviticus 19:17

The Battle of Bessemer was behind them. They wrapped Absalom's body in sheeting left behind by the Army of the Union. Away from the other dead, Esau dug a grave for his burial. Plumpsie drew a map which displayed all the local markers, and showed the exact location of his grave. Esau took whatever lumber he could find from old buckboards and made a box. Then they took more sheeting to tightly bind the body of Absalom. The map that Plumpsie drew contained exact markings in footage, depth, and degree from the nearest lake. This would serve to mark the exact spot in case trees were excavated, or clearings were extended. Eventually, they hoped to reclaim his remains and return them to Illinois for a more formal burial, with family. Plumpsie prayed over his grave. They stood there for a few minutes, each concluding that his death needn't to have occurred and should not have. They knew that the same end could befall either of them. There was bigotry on both parts, the North and the South. These were new experiences for them both, and as such, they looked upon these as an opportunity to learn. Again Esau's thoughts turned to Twiggs, then to Mathers. He surmised that for each Twiggs, there were forty Mathers. Esau was changing his mind about everything, and foremost was the war. He wanted to control his own life. Neither the war, nor a return to Illinois would afford that purpose. Life could be too short, and for him, to control one day of his own destiny was too important to lose to a war, where on a whim, his life could be snuffed out. He would not return to fight for the North.

Plumpsie felt no different. She had seen the cruelty on both sides. If there were men up North who felt like the soldier who killed Absalom, then she didn't want to be there either. That they could get away with this kind of murder, the wanton destruction of a purposeful human life was too much to bear. She also needed to get out, but where could she go? For now, her cousin provided the best answer. Indeed he was the only answer.

They packed whatever they could. They carried sheeting, ropes, a pot, a pan, spoons and forks, and extra trousers, skivvies, blankets, guns and ammunition, and rope.

Heading due west on foot, they came upon a pack of wild horses. They had heard of such groups. They only wished that they could capture but one. Perhaps, later they could get another. Even so, without a mount of their own, their chances were slim. He took a rope, and left Plumpsie there. He told her if all went well, he would surely return with a horse. He hoped to simply corral one of the younger, less wise members of the band. He fashioned a lariat, then took a detour of a jagged trail. The gamble was that this shortcut would get him to their lair just after they arrived. He needed luck. He needed the element of surprise. Most of all, he needed Divine

Intervention because he knew the odds were prevalent against him.

A beautiful stallion pushed and herded the pack from the rear. These were classic mustangs, wild appaloosas, most mixed with some Arabian, all under the watchful eye of the big glorious stallion. They were tired, and probably spent for the day. Even so, the leader looked at Esau as if to say, 'dream on, human; you are not even a match for our weakest'. A good judge of animals, Esau knew the wild stallion was right. He couldn't even take the weakest member. But, that would not stop him from trying.

The stallion sized up Esau. Somehow, he understood this was a human that had special tenacity. This would be challenging, the kind that would serve to keep the pack fit, in fine mettle to fend for itself. Esau could see that this was the finest animal, wild or tame upon which he had ever laid his eyes. Surely he had matched fighting strength against the best in his domain and he certainly had always emerged the victor. Such was the requirement of his prize, to mate with all the mares in his domain. Surely any among his offspring would prove strong and resourceful, with his inherited qualities. He sensed something in Esau, that from any other single person, without horses, without a team, would have been sheer folly. This man was smart, and though the stallion could, and would win, he had better be careful. In the end, Esau decided, if he should lose, the horses would simply provide company as he and Plumpsie wound their way Westward.

By evening he had gotten nowhere. He returned to Plumpsie, who had thought he had deserted her. He didn't even reply to the remark when she made it. Couldn't she tell? Didn't she know? He could never do that. They continued along their way, following the trail of the wild horses.

On their third day, they came upon the horses in a quarry, bounded by canyons on the two sides, and only a narrow ravine to permit continued movement Westward. Of course, there was open country on all sides of the ravine, but the horses simply hadn't figured that out. This ravine opened to a clear path through Western Kentucky, near the tributaries of Kentucky Lake. They remembered from their journey East to Chattanooga only weeks earlier. Mountains, hills, dales, open country, and trees all formed to make a beautiful scene. They hadn't really taken it all in like this the first time. Now they simply enjoyed the land. This would also be their best time to gain a horse or two.

Then suddenly, like the strike of lightening on a day when none threatened, the authority of the big stallion was challenged by a younger, stronger, but less experienced horse. He was not as tall as the leader, but wider and more thickly muscled at the girth. He was also eager to do battle with the leader, who just three years earlier had fathered him. They met at the rim of the canyon opening, then bolted to the clearing, each signaling the need for more room to fight. By any accounts, this would be an epic battle. At first their gestures were mock, with each parrying, threatening, allowing the other a chance to withdraw. There were certainly more than enough mares for each to service, more than enough young to protect for both. But, that didn't make horse sense. They were programmed to fight at times like this. The one had nothing to lose, the other everything to lose, but nothing to win. But the stakes might have been even larger. Perhaps the life of a magnificent and beautiful animal was on the line. In such a fight, for the onlookers, timing would be of the essence. If he could intervene at just the right moment, Esau could do much more than save a horse's life. He could also gain transportation.

The leader met the challenge ferociously. As if to show off to his audience of Esau and Plumpsie, he was making a grave point. He would kill the younger animal. With powerful thrusts of their hind legs they inflicted severe wounds on each other. These were followed with bites to each others' necks. Though the younger animal got in his kicks and bites, the leader was determined to finish him off for good. Every attempt by the challenger to run was cut off. He simply was determined not to let him escape to live and fight another day. The appaloosa could find no end in sight and no way out. Hovering over the wounded animal, the big horse studied his wounds, preparing to deliver the final, fatal kick. Esau would not have believed this had he not seen it. Even horses permitted the vanquished foe to run away. That was not to happen here. As he reared, the fallen horse rolled over, stood, and delivered a rear kick to the stallion's head. Now they were both down because the stallion caught him with a partial kick as he fell.

The pack leader still had the upper hoof, because he regained his balance while his younger adversary still lay prone on the ground. However, he discovered he now faced another. It was Esau. He stood before the beaten younger horse, and the leader. He held nothing but his rope. This was the first time a human had come so close to either animal. With his rope, Esau could have wrested control of the now spent animal but he hoped the horse could see that he didn't want to do that. He wanted the animal to understand he would only do that if it were necessary to save himself from harm. Esau didn't have to do that. The horse turned slowly, gave a signal to his fallen foe, and turned to rejoin his family of young females, mares in foal, and growing wild horses - young mares and young stallions.

Esau's move was a wise one. The horse displayed the survival trait that had brought him to the leadership position of the most prominent herd of mustangs in the West. He knew when to retreat, and when not to challenge. Esau did wonder, in awe, what might have been had he taken control of that animal in his hour of weakness. He turned to attend the beaten, bleeding vanquished pony. This horse was going to die. Esau fashioned some balls of clay from the soil and nearby stream. With these he covered the horse's wounds. Then he took branches, twigs, and blankets to cover the animal. With the sheeting he covered the animal's back, face, neck and stomach, protecting him from the still hot sun. "You lost the battle, my friend", he whispered to the animal, reassuringly, "but you have regained your life. I hope to give you back your freedom, because you are too magnificent an animal to be owned by any man. I give you back your freedom."

As he and Plumpsie nursed him back to health, they both decried why life had to be fraught with such struggles by man and animal. He had seen it on the battlefield, and now, having broken the peaceful serene life of the herd, he knew he had made the correct decision to leave the war. Though he still traveled with his cousin, he had made no decision as to where he would go. Would it be back to Illinois, or would it be Mississippi.

They remained in the glen with the horse, determined not to continue until he could fend for himself. With bear, cougars and wolf packs, he would not have lived very long. There is something in the nature of horses, even wild ones who endure this kind of convalescence. A bond is formed, and it becomes stronger on the animal's part than on the human's. As the horse was able to roll over and move around, he would lie close to them at night. He seemed to desire more and more close human contact day be day. As he regained the strength to walk, he was more attached to Plumpsie. He was still attached to Esau, but Plumpsie was his favorite. "Why is this horse so much more in your corner, than in mine?" he asked her. "Ain't I the one who saved his life?"

"That's because he is just a little smarter than you are, Esau", she answered, a faint smile showing on her lips. "He has got horse sense, you know."

"Ah shoot. I don't care. I'm smart too. I know things."

"Do you know that I am pregnant?"

Esau just dropped right there, on the very spot. He shook his head, then threw a twig. He smiled. He was as happy as anybody could be on hearing that news. "Oh Miss Plumpsie. We got to keep this horse now. He go take you back to Mississippi."

"Don't you worry none, Esau. That is why he is tolerating us. He knows I need him. We have a friend for life."

"Now I am determined to get ya'll back. Mississippi here we come. Too bad my brother had to die back there. He would be right proud of his baby and his baby's momma. I should a known, the way you and that boy used to look at each other. Yes ma'am, I should a known. But maybe I talk to quick. Miss Plumpsie, are you sure you want to go back to Mississippi? Do you want to think about living with Absalom's momma and papa up in Illinois? I know they be right glad to see after you and the baby."

"Well, cousin, the thought did enter my mind. But you and I, we both got unfinished business back in Mississippi. Let's tend to that first. Then we think about Illinois. Till then, you just go have to take care of me and the baby."

"Now, I go take care o ya'll. Ya'll ain't got to worry about one blessed thing, Miss Plumpsie."

They walked, they trotted. They were on an all out gallop. They stayed close to the trail, near the border of Kentucky and Tennessee as they went. That horse seemed to understand that they needed to keep away from people and he always found the path less taken. Plumpsie took the travel better than ever. A physically strong young lady, she was driven by her quest to finish things back home. She was also interested in new places. Her natural bent was to maintain communication with people in Mississippi. But she also wanted to explore as much of the country as she could. For her, Illinois would be the first step. She would wait to make her decision final.

They were into their seventh day of travel when they heard the thunder and volley of cannon. Climbing high up a tall tree, Esau surveyed the route before them. Not too far away there was a pitched battle underway. It was between Gray Coats and Blue Coats. If one word could describe this encounter it was ferocious. At some spots, the fighting was by hand, bayonets, sticks, stones and pitchforks. From what he could see, this was a battle reminiscent of the last. Both sides suffered heavy casualties, but the North was winning this battle. Though there were routes for retreat, the South's forces fought valiantly but to no avail. Esau remained perched in the tree until the battle was over. To proceed, he had to go through the battle site. As these things usually turn, he believed he could steal his way up to the battleground, make off with a horse, return to this spot and just wait it out.

Eventually, the rebels were reduced to serving as targets for Union marksmen. As the rebels retreated more away from the battle site, Union men on horseback followed. The gray coats were as easy for the Union men as shooting skeet with low trajectories. They didn't have a tenth of a chance and the North wanted no part of taking anybody alive. Even the men who turned to give themselves up were shot. Some were even made to suffer, with marksmen taking off an ear, then a finger. Others took off legs at the knee with ammunition balls, not bullets. This war reduced soldiers on both sides to the most brutal witnessed in modern warfare. Those men were blood thirsty and Esau was not about to even think of getting in their way. He simply wanted to wait. "Hey you, up in the tree", his cover had been infiltrated by a Union soldier on reconnaissance. He was well behind Confederate lines. "Get it down here now, and be quick about it." It was one of the Union men from the Battle of Bessemer.

"I remembers you", Esau stated, descending the tree. You were back there in Bessemer, up from Chattanooga. I never thought I would see you again."

"Nor I you", the officer replied, lowering his gun. "But I thought you were dead."

"Well, I is sure I ain't dead. At least, I thinks I is alive. I believes you confusing me with my brother."

"Oh, yeh. I remember. He did get it back at Bessemer. That was a shame. The way he got it and all. We had no idea that soldier was a murderer.

I'm glad we got rid of him. He volunteered to go back to Chattanooga. I made sure that his officers moved him to the front lines. I don't believe we will ever see that guy again. I still can't understand why the doctors refused to help your brother, though. Everybody knew what you and he had done to save our hides at the prison. Well, I don't think we got anymore enemy out here. Did you see anyone from your perch?"

"Nah, General. Ain't seen a soul."

"Good! Well, hop on the back here. The least we can do is give you a horse. Our men have been killing rebels with their own bullets. I can't stop them from killing, but they should save their ammunition. The rebels intercepted a large shipment and we need to keep what we have. If not, the rebels can't wait to see that they return it to us, from the barrels of their weapons."

Esau hopped onto the horse, and they proceeded directly back to the battlefield area. Again the officer mentioned that he had seen someone who looked just like him, shot while tending horses for the Confederacy.

Esau was given a horse and food. But, just before he could depart, another officer asked him to help in burying the dead. Esau told them he was on another mission, but they offered him hard currency to help. The offer was good. He couldn't refuse. After all, they gave him a horse, and seemed sincere in condolences for Absalom. They also told him that a stipend would be awarded to the Omer family for the loss of their son. This entire episode was strange. These men were so different from the medics, physicians and guards who treated Esau and Absalom so shabbily back at Bessemer and Chattanooga. Even so, he knew that among these men were white soldiers with the capacity to inflict grave harm upon innocent black men. He knew too well by now that for him, white men had to solidly prove their fidelity before he could trust them. For some, he could trust his ability to assess. For others, based on his gut feeling, he would never find himself with his back to them, or his gun not at the ready. It was not a good way to live. But for black men, it meant survival.

Esau enjoyed a good meal, then reported for burial duty. The officer paid him more than enough, in advance. He also told him that if that were not enough, he could return for more money at the end of that duty. With this new emphasis on regrets, and an acceptance of him as an equal, he decided to wait awhile before his final decision to leave the Army. With his newly developed sense of independence, distrust of white men, greater trust in blacks who shared his struggles, he could really go either way. No matter how he decided, he would return Plumpsie to Mississippi. If that didn't go too well, he knew that she would be warmly accepted at the Omer home in East St. Louis, Illinois.

They had asked him to report to the area where Confederate dead lay decomposing on a knoll. It was almost dusk when he started. He worked until well past sundown before he took a break. Most of the enlisted men were already relaxing under the warm, moonlit night. He only rested for a scant five or six minutes. Work took his mind away from the rotting smell of decaying human flesh. He had seen many animals die. If not gutted, and dressed properly, the smell was always offensive. Of all the species whose deaths he had had to be near, the human body created the most horrible stench. When he was done digging out a wide trench, the other men dropped in three rebel bodies. They all worked quickly to cover this multiple grave and placed three markers into the soft soil. They directed Esau to another area where rebel soldiers were deposited. It was further away from the battleground. These were men whose internal organs distended from their torsos. These created the greatest, foulest odor. Already, turkey vultures, buzzards, ravens, crows, skunks, opossums, feral cats, wild boars, and rats were attracted to the site. They had to be shooed away as best they could because the men had orders not to use live ammunition on scavengers. To deal with this, the men tossed large and small pieces of flesh yards away. They poured lime dust and rubbing alcohol over the dead and hoped the animals would stay away until their work was done. They would have been happy if that had worked with the striped critters most of all. It did. The skunks had no fear of man, whatsoever, nor of the other animals.

As Esau passed the dig area, he heard mumblings among the bodies. The words, those phrases, even the voice had a familiarity. He could not remember from where, but something clicked in the recesses of his mind. He knew he heard the same noises before. He actually walked, then crawled among the corpses, protruding brains, bowels in his wake, blood, organs such as spleens, kidneys, livers, lungs, even hearts and scrotums, and loose flesh all around. The noise, from where did it emanate? He knew those sounds. They took him back, way back. He closed his eyes, focusing solely on the noises. They were growing more faint but he kept going. Among the finest warriors of the Confederacies' fallen men, valiant souls who had given their all, lay a dying support worker. There in all that mass of a mess of brave humanity lay the apparition of what the captain on patrol had seen.

There, left for dead lay his wounded twin brother. It was Isaac, delirious, beyond pain, wounded but not mortally. Isaac continued mumbling and Esau could only hope and pray that the soldiers on burial detail could not hear him. It all came into perfect focus. His twin had taken on the same role for the South as he had for the North. Plumpsie had not lied to save his life. She had told the truth to save his life. He was the spy, the master craftsman who had been known as the shoeshine boy responsible for the deaths of so many Union soldiers. He also was key to Southern battlefield successes. The thought of killing him, as he swore to do when he enlisted was gone. He would use whatever was in his power to save him. There was little time to lose. Obviously the Blue Coats were not aware of his discovery. Isaac continued his delirium, totally unaware of what he was saying, or where he was. He had taken total leave of his mental faculties.

When the men came over, Isaac was no longer mumbling. They helped Esau finish the pit and told him to drag three bodies over. He was to push them down, but not cover them. They would, finish in the morning. They left and told him not to tarry too long. With a canteen, he emptied the contents over the face of his brother, still illuminated by lanterns. The idle chattering and mumbles continued. Esau finally put an identity to it. It was the strange language of communication that he and Isaac had developed as infants, toddlers, just youngsters. Esau saw him as a pathetic creature. Perhaps his life should not be salvaged, given his zeal for their oppressor. He promised himself to deal with that as they returned to Mississippi. If he couldn't modify the attitude, then he vowed to kill his brother himself.

Isaac had bullet wounds to his shoulder and his stomach. He was lucky to have been hit with lead encased pellets rather than steel ball. Like Absalom, he had a chance. If his internal bleeding were not halted through the removal of the bullets, Isaac would be doomed. It was a risky chance but by now, Esau was ready to dare any risk, especially if it meant saving the life of someone he loved.

Isaac came to, as Esau dabbed his forehead. Illuminated by the pale moonlight and the bright lanterns burning strong in the light breeze, he looked into Esau's face. Now fully conscious he wondered where he was. When he tried to move, his pain gave way to fear. For a second he wondered whether he had died and ascended to heaven. This was his brother whom he had feared had died. Then, he concluded, they must be in heaven. As he was about to say something, Esau covered his mouth. "Don't say anything, Isaac", he instructed. Isaac tried to laugh at his strange accent. "You is hurt mighty bad. And we have to git yo to a doctor."

He loosed the hand over his mouth, but Isaac had to say something. He grabbed Esau and held him tightly. He hugged him with all the pent up emotion he had been saving for an occasion such as this. "You doesn't unnerstands, Esau. This be the Army. It don't matter none if you bees wit the Confederacy or wit the Blues. They caint use up no doctoring on me. I is go die. I is just so glad that I got to lay my eyes on you fo I leaves this world."

"I knows all bout they rules and procedures. Now I ain't go tell yo no mo. Keep yo damn mouth shut. Listen to me. Now you and me, we go git up here and go to the medic's tent. Now fo us to pull this off, yo gots to walk like you ain't got no injuries, and no pain. Now here, git to gittin."

He helped Isaac up. The boy did understand. All his life he had been told that his brother had run away because he hated his family. Isaac had believed it too. Now, Esau risked his own life to save Isaac. The master was a great liar. Finally it sunk in. Isaac understood his gullibility and his stupidity. In the face of his brother's determination, Isaac had no alternative but to go. He walked that two hundred yard path, climbing a steep incline, and strode confidently into the medical bivouac. The guards recognized Esau, and Isaac kept his head low. "I gots some things to get from Ole Doc,", Esau explained.

"He be waiting fo us."

Isaac was shocked at the ease with which his brother could tell an obvious lie. Since his dad was tortured and killed by Master Brookshire, he hadn't ever seen a black man attempt such. He was even more surprised that the soldiers accepted it so quickly. Isaac still didn't know exactly what his brother had in mind. By entering the medic's tent, he knew though that it had something to do with saving his life. He still couldn't understand how. The surgeon and the medic had just finished what was their last operation of the day. They had tried to save a Union officer but he expired on the table. The nurse asked Esau to help take him out back. He obliged and the nurse continued to his quarters. When Esau returned, Isaac had fainted. The surgeon was attending him. "This fellow is hurt bad", the surgeon explained to Esau. "My assistants are gone. You have got to help me save him. Let's get moving."

Esau was in shock, a different shock than the medical shock afflicting his brother. He didn't have to force treatment onto his brother by a reluctant surgeon. He didn't even want to ask the surgeon to operate. Esau had believed that was out of the question. If he had just been able to use the equipment, and obtain some antibiotics, basic germ killers, he would have been happy, and appreciative. With those items, Esau would have operated himself.

The physician was ordering him to help. Isaac was bleeding from the mouth. The plasma gushed in starts and spurts. As he worked, Esau seemed to know exactly what he was doing. He looked at the equipment, and gave the surgeon the right tools even before he asked. He even wiped the sweat from the specialist's brow, and fanned him when he was pressing a wound. The doctor just kept on working. He had done many of these bullet removals and stoppages of internal bleeding. He gave each bullet to Esau as they were removed. He didn't care that his erstwhile assistant placed each into his pocket. Working quickly, he stitched Isaac. He removed whisky from a drawer, gathered all the surgical tools, and washed them with the whiskey. Then he took another bottle from the drawer, opened it and took a hearty swallow. Following that, he offered Esau one too. "You know, Doc, I done cut open and gutted a lot of animals in my day, but I ain't never seen nothing like that."

"Well now you know. It isn't all that different, now is it?"

Esau was puzzled. Through his father, Reverend Omer, he had learned the name of every organ on an animal, from horse, cow, pig, hen, turkey, deer, bull, bear, stag, even snake to fish. He could identify the innards of the little critters too. To him, the only real difference was that human beings created a nastier odor than all the others. "I do guess yo makes a good point, Doc" he answered. He knew this conversation was going somewhere but he didn't know where exactly.

"Yes sir, young man, the similarity is so striking that it's almost sinful. You know what, young man, it's about time for you, and your twin here (Oh yes, I knew he was your twin, the minute I saw him.) set your sights on something to do when this war is over. Your people will need good surgeons and physicians. Both of you can stay here and learn from me. I can teach you everything you need to know. When this is all over, I will see to it that both of you are certified."

At the time the only thing Esau wanted to look forward to was leaving the camp with his brother. He had to navigate the same route that they came in. He was going to chance it because it was the only thing he had left to do. "Well, Doc, I does preciate yo saving my brother's life. Yo is a real angel sent down from heaven. But now, we got to be going."

The surgeon sensed Esau's fear. He knew that with the condition Isaac was in that they could not get very far. Esau became visibly worried, scared as he went to move his brother. "Don't worry about quitting camp, young man", the physician calmed him down, easing his worries about the next move. "I can help you out of this."

Esau already felt he had done more than enough. The last person he wanted to place into harm's way was this good doctor. "I is open to suggestions."

"This is no suggestion. It is an offer and a bargain with you. I want you to promise me that when this stupid war is all over, you will give serious consideration to becoming a medical doctor, just like me. I know you can do it. A fine young man like you will be an asset to his people. I am from Massachusetts. Here is my name, and business address. Call on me."

After giving his business card to Esau, the doctor went for two horses. He draped one dead man over one, and Isaac over the other. "Now you make sure you bury both those boys deep", he yelled, as Esau led them through the middle of the encampment. "Those two men had a dreadful disease and I don't anyone getting too close."

The soldiers gave Esau a wide berth. They heard what the surgeon had said. No doubt, by morning, they wouldn't want any part of Esau's company either. The Officer of the Day was still on alert. He felt sorry for Esau. He must have worked all day and night, still on the job. He gave him another two day's pay, and suggested that he not work anymore the next few days. Then he suggested that he best return to his duties involving observation.

CHAPTER XXII - Ya'll Be Ready!

Go home to thy friends and family and tell them how great things the Lord hath done for thee, and hath had great compassion on thee.
St. Mark 5: 19

The boys and Plumpsie remained at their secluded campsite until Isaac's strength permitted modest travel by horseback. Esau removed his saddle and placed it onto Plumpsie's horse. He rode bareback. Plumpsie and Isaac filled him in on just how dreadful matters were back on the plantation and in town.

The more he learned, the more incensed he grew. Even in light of all this, he was not quick to understand or champion the thievery of money by the likes of Mathers and his henchmen up North. For now, Esau decided he had some debts due him back on that plantation. He decided that he would not quit the South until he had been repaid. Well, he said, we go take about as much as we can get from the white people at Brookshire anyway. He insisted that they leave nothing out. Even the stupid duplicity of his twin had to be confessed.

For his part, Isaac finally seemed to want to make a confession. "Esau, I has been so foolish. All these years, Massuh and Ole Buck King, they had me thinkin yo runs away cause yo hates yo family. I ain't nevuh thought he wudda sold yo. Even though I knows he wuz go sell me. That man, he lied to me all my life. I wuz so stupid and dumb to believe a man like Massah Brookshire. I gives that man the best I gots."

Isaac was becoming more angry too. He had been a fool, a big fool. No matter how the war ended, he knew that he had to make serious changes in his personal life, no matter what.

Esau bade him to calm down. Isaac could let loose his anger in due time back in Mississippi. "The thing I can't figure out, is why and how you have been permitted to live so long, Isaac. When I first realized that you were the famous black spy, I wanted to kill your carcass, myself. Well, I must admit. You did your job well. When I saw you on the ground down there with those rebels, I couldn't let you die. Oh here, by the way. These are the two bullets the doctor took out of you. You see the size of these bullets? They is little; ain't they? They show how close you was to death."

"Well, brother, man. We hear tell bout yo too. The South, they got a price on yo head."

"Well now, just don't yo be gittin no ideas."

"Ya'll just doesn't know how close I cudda come to it, Esau. I done turned in Ole Amos. He be tryin to kill me, and Ole Julida, she scream cause Ole Fitzpatrick, he be tryin to have sex wit her and everything. They burns that man alive all cause a me. I even gots Ole Will kilt."

"Isaac, that be our daddy!"

"So I learns, later on. So they splain it to me."

At that point, they were nearing a village. They wanted no part of any people in the South. It was too late in the day to make their way around it. They actually back tracked until they returned four miles to a pond. There they would camp for the night. They prepared a light meal, cared for the horses, then simply enjoyed the still night. "Now I want both of you to tell me once again about all that has transpired at the plantation. I don't want any details omitted. I want to know everything about Master Brookshire, his wife and daughters, and his sons. I want to know about all the slaves and all the people from town who work on his land. Isaac, tell me one thing now. Do you know how our mother died?"

If he had any doubts about his brother's sincerity, then the answer would prove or disprove them now. "To tell you the truth, Esau, I don't rightly knows how she die. To tell yo the truth, alls I knows is whut Massah Brookshire say to me. He ain't nevuh permit nobody to talk on it. He say she up and died right after we wuz born. He say she be too weak to carry yo and me both. He say he go git Ole Doc Pritchard, and he come and doctor on her and all. But she bees too weak to live. Now, I don't believe that no mo. To tell yo the truth, I cain't rightly say how she die."

That was proof enough for Esau. The notions of altruism about their master were dispelled. But Esau was not sure that his brother hated the master. That is what he wanted. To move him in that direction, he decided to tell the truth. "She died because she was weak all right. I learned of the truth in Illinois. Everybody know the truth, all over the South. You see, Isaac, everybody honors the gift of our momma. But it was not weakness from bringing you and me into life, into this evil world. She died because of Master Brookshire's butchery. Right after you were born, he made her return to the fields. When she brought forth me from her tiny body, Ole Buck King was beating her with a horsewhip. Our mother was a hardworking slave. She always tried to do her best. Naomi told me that Cassie made a wish when we were born. She said a prayer to God, and made a wish that one day her two boys be free. Well brother, man, I don't know if we go ever be free, but right now, I do believe that that brave woman, that woman who was just a child herself, she is more free now than you or I will ever be."

The revelation was too much for Isaac. The reunion with his brother, the true facts of their mother's death, the true character of his master, the truth about how whites felt about blacks, even the good news on reuniting with Plumpsie were mind bending, sense blowing events. These accounts all the more showed what a fool he had been. However, he was thankful he had finally seen the light. He cried uncontrollably, weeping loudly. It was not out of any sense of what had happened to him. No, it wasn't that at all. It was due to his quiet acceptance of the whole litany of lies and the role he had been inculcated into playing. He had actively worked to preserve the lies, and exploitation. He championed that way of life. It had provided an existence of splendor, wealth and ease for the whites who owned them. The slaves' lot was misery. That misery supported the bankrupt morality that allowed this system to exist and endure.

Esau permitted the self pitying for awhile. But he had too much to do. There was too much to learn, and too much to teach. "I has been such a fool, Esau", Isaac sobbed, uncontrollably between the words. "I jus doesn't knows what to do. What is I go do?"

"The answer is as clear as that big fat nose on yo face, boy. The only man is a fool who cannot learn from his mistakes. You and me both, we have a lot to make up for, Isaac. We will begin at Brookshire Farm. The only man who is truly sorry is he who cannot atone for his sins of the past. Now you know. You can make up for all of them. Now as I said. We are returning home. I want you to tell me all about everything and everybody. I want you to describe every person who is there so that when I see them, I will know who everybody is. Most of all I want you to tell me about Fitzpatrick. I want to know this Julida who refused to sleep with him. She saved your life because she is an honorable woman. Fitzpatrick saved your life. But he got some real dues to pay. And for you, for me, for Plumpsie, and for every slave on Brookshire Plantation, whether they want to or not, they all got a heap of dues to collect.

The trip back would take more than a short while. Avoiding people, settlements and military, they decided to cross the Mississippi and follow the trails West of the states in war. They would enter their home state from the West, in Louisiana, rather than from the East. Each day along their circuitous journey, Plumpsie and Isaac had to relate in narrative everything that went on back in Collinsville. Nothing could be omitted. At times, they would forget a minor detail but Esau served as their reminder. For Esau, every character and every event were important. Esau wanted everything in correct chronological order. He wanted these factors to sink into Isaac's head correctly. His brother had to retain the true significance of the nature of the slave owning class. Almost every other black person did.

Their trek was not without danger. By now they were more adept at handling life's disorders and managing to come out on top. Although they sought to avoid human contact, at times it was unavoidable. Even when it became touch and go near a place known as Hayes' Gulch in Louisiana, they were able to avoid trouble by advising they were scouts for the Confederacy. When they chanced onto a Union band, the story was that they were performing espionage for the Blue Coats. With their familiarity of some of the battles, large and small, they were able to pull it off.

At long last they approached the home that Isaac knew too well. He would have been happy to burn it all down now. The young man seethed with anger.

"Stop, stop right here!" Plumpsie shouted. They were on the ridge, just west of the city, well before they had reached the plantations. This was nearer to the Rogers' home, where she lived. She didn't want to stop, though.

She simply wanted to look upon it. It held no real meaning or import. Somehow, she knew she would see her grandparents before they quit the state. This would be her final goodbye to the place she had known as her home as a slave. Quietly, she longed for the opportunity to burn it down. "Okay, boys, thank you for that. I just wanted to look at it once more. Esau and Isaac, can you boys promise me one thing?"

"Sure, Miss Plumpsie", Isaac actually answered first. "Whatever it is you want. We will do it. In fact, we will be much obliged to do it."

"No matter what happens at Brookshire, I want you boys to bring me back here. I want you to burn down the Rogers' home. I don't want to set the fire. I just want to see it burn, all the way to the ground."

They didn't have to answer. This was something they would have wanted to do regardless. Plumpsie realized simply by their acquiescent smiles that they were on the same wave lengths. No mercy would be showed to them either.

Esau's memories, even on the active descriptions from Plumpsie and Isaac were vague. The people were not. He was drawn to one conclusion. The same types of people are everywhere. No matter where one travels, he can never really get away from where he came. He had them take him to the big barn which held infamous meaning. It was during the construction of that barn that their mother had died. The animals on Brookshire Farm, he remembered, fared much better than slaves. As a symbol of their frustration, and of the frustration that his mother most surely must have felt, he decided that it would be the first structure to burn. He didn't even want to hide out in it. The destruction of that barn would be the first phase of his plan to rain destruction onto the entire estate. He would not be satisfied until Master Brookshire was ruined.

For now, Isaac and Esau made themselves comfortable behind the haystacks near the 'done fudging creek'. It was at the base of the lake. Isaac talked with Plumpsie and Esau about coming to terms with their people. This journey would be the longest and most painful in his life because it was not physical. In every way it was metaphysical. He had never had to admit that he was wrong. It was easy to admit his transgressions before people who had not suffered because of him. On the other hand, standing face to face with his blood kin who had been harmed would be a different matter. He thought of Peter having denied Christ, from the sermon given by Ole Fedderson just before he died. Then it hit him. Fedderson was talking to him, about him, and explaining to the slaves assembled that they would have to relive Christ's example with Isaac. Armed with Peter's example, he felt strong enough to face the slaves. He would beg their forgiveness. Now, he could understand why they wanted to kill him. Even after his confession, if they still wanted to kill him, he would have to understand that too. After all, he decided, death could be a welcome friend because he would rather not live with the pain of not being forgiven. Yes, now Isaac loved his people. But unlike the other slaves, he didn't hate his oppressors. Nor did he continue to love them. In his mind, their lot and the lot of blacks like him was to suffer eternal damnation in hell. The most horrific legacy, he concluded, was that this punishment in hell was the future of their race, the whites. Theirs was a tortuous future, from where there was no way out.

The first to be summoned was Thomas. After him was Nathaniel. Plumpsie simply told them that a friend waited for them in the haystacks. One can only imagine the expressions on their faces when they saw the boys together. Both older men were speechless. Their tears of joy did all the talking that was necessary, and more. Hugs, kisses, remembrances in the mind were not enough. Nothing could describe the moment. Isaac began to express himself first. "I is returning to my peoples. I has a lots to say. Can ya'll gather all the slaves and bring them out here. I has mo to say."

The morning was still young. A full assembly was forming. Isaac had made a tremendous beginning. This ritualistic exercise had played itself and repeated itself time after time. Usually Master Brookshire called the slaves to give a short lecture, and pronounce the sentence of death by either burning a slave alive, or beating a slave to death. All they knew for sure was that they had better be quick about meeting when they were told. At that point not one slave could even think of what was in store for them. This would be one session, they would soon discover, in which the pent up fears, apprehensions, dreams and goals of a complete mass of people could be realized in one fell swoop. This would be a day of deliverance, reckoning, salvation, and triumph, all rolled into a glorious, overcoming supplication. Oh What a Happy Day!

Hubert 'Rap' Brown visited St. Louis and East St. Louis during the summer of 1969. Staying at my apartment on West Pine Street, he made a statement to the group of young men crowding into my apartment about power. He read from a book that was written by Martin Luther King, Jr. This book had been a gift from his good friend, Stokely Carmichael. Many people were not aware of this but according to Rap Brown, Stokely and Dr. King had deep discussions about the direction of the struggle for equality. Here is a statement, from which Rap read, which he stated emphasized their shared awareness about power:

When a people are mired in oppression, they realize deliverance when they have accumulated the power to enforce change. The powerless, on the other hand, never experience opportunity - it is always arriving at a later time. Martin Luther King, Jr.

Chapter XXIII - Surprise Attack

Let them be confounded and troubled forever; yea, let them be put to shame and perish. Psalm 83:17

And my eyes have looked down upon my foes, and my ears have heard of the fall of my wicked adversaries. Psalm 92: 12 (The New American Bible)

More and more, month by month, week by week, day by day, the North was moving the war to the South. Activities consisted of skirmishes and well organized raids on farms. The Union had taken to employing local people, the few brave men and women who didn't like what the South was becoming. They had been effective. However, their victories and the damage inflicted had been discounted by the Confederacy. In truth, that obstinacy contributed to the downfall of the South in the war. It was the primary factor that their citizens let themselves be used by the North. Another fact was that the Confederacy found themselves worried about the next hit and run tactic. They were now deploying more troops to address the new menace. How odd this was.

When the war began, the South used the tactic successfully. Now, the Union had turned the tables. If one were to gauge the value of these hit and run maneuvers, the effectiveness overall was astonishing. Of course their targets were small, and their expenses were so small that the guerillas didn't even request reimbursement from the sponsors. Their greatest value was that they never lost a man or woman to this kind of warfare.

Due to their own intelligence gathering program, the Rebel Army had developed a credible network in Mississippi. The most important person in the group was its non-military, civilian leader, Charles Rogers. He controlled a non-uniformed detachment that could be buttressed by gray coats when he needed them. Charles had shared some vital information with Uriah Brookshire about their activities. Since their plans would surely meet with great success, The Master wanted to view the intended slaughter of a Yankee force of intelligence officers and regular army of the Union.

Charles, the Master, and the soldiers assigned to his unit were but miles away from the 'Yankee lair', an underground bunker in the Great Pine Forest on the Louisiana border. It was about one hundred-twenty five to one hundred-fifty miles due East of the Brookshire plantation. The command in Richmond had given orders to kill every single member. As Lee's brain's trust saw it, this would be a devastating blow to the Yankee underground war movement. Their greater hope was that wiping out this crack unit would undermine the Yankee guerilla raiders, and Southerners sympathetic to the North, throughout the territory.

It was the kind of encounter Brookshire and Charles had dreamed about. Master Brookshire had requested permission and it had been granted, to observe the slaughter from the command post. The planning was for the attack to result in not a single Confederate casualty. For attacks like this to succeed, the Confederacy leadership believed in the over assignment of troops, especially marksmen. This, they believed, had marked value in portraying their side as invincible. Their mind games were not to be denied. The entire group, save for a skeleton crew at the camp, departed for the bunker.

They would show no mercy. The war had degenerated into this evil mentality on both sides, save for a few just men who simply could not execute wanton slaughter. No such person, though, was part of Charles' combatants. The fighting had become bloodletting and blood thirsty. Barely seven years earlier, in the 'Indian Wars' had such cruelty been on display. It was odd and ironic because members of both sides fought side-by-side in fulfilling the adage that the only good Indian was a dead Indian. Now for the South, the only good Yankee was a dead Yankee. For the North, the only good Southern Rebel was a dead Southern Rebel. "Apparently, we have orders from President Jefferson Davis, himself, to search out and destroy this enemy", Major Doherty, the military leader, confirmed to Charles Rogers and Brookshire. "This should not take too long. As Ah see it, the sentries will be nullified before our attack, by one of our own boys who has infiltrated. We will have a free road to attack when that takes place."

Brookshire hoped for a quick victory. He wanted them to kill the Union spies so he could return to Collinsville by the morrow. Brookshire's sacrifice was that he would miss two days of management of his plantation. It was only to be overcome by witnessing the destruction of the cause that had cost him losses of millions of dollars of money, tons of cotton, and the ruination of his livestock. If nothing else, this victory for Major Doherty would serve as a moral victory for him and Charles.

In the thickets of the Black Pine Forest, the men rested after a hard day of training. They were completing two weeks of training in guerilla tactics and had laid the groundwork for a massive assault against the enemy, and on enemy soil. They had been thorough, competent and patient. Every man was an expert in his own field. Every man was trained to prove invaluable to their side. At that point, their problem was that not one of the group was aware that their position had been uncovered. At least one, among their party, was a counter spy. Through his successful work, they had been betrayed. The deal to seal their doom had been struck. Against those odds, they didn't have a chance.

The two sentries, posted in the cover of shrubbery, bushes and trees, used binoculars to view a wide expanse of territory. They could see any approach, man or group, large or small. However, if anyone could get past them, the approach to their fellows would be easy. As long as the lookouts were looking out, the men in the bunkers were safe.

Midway through their watch, the guards were brought food. They ate on the job. It went with the duty. They could leave their post for one purpose only. That was to retire behind a bush or tree 'when nature called'. "I cain't hold this any longer", the heavier guard groaned to his workmate. He unbuttoned his fly, and grabbed 'soft paper', hurrying to a bush.

His partner moved his own food to the side, as required. They were well trained. He took a position more in the middle now because he had to look at the entire area. "Make sure you all move far away from me. Last time you all did this, your smell spoiled my appetite."

With the binoculars at his eyes, his workmate, not really having to relieve himself, whirled out his dagger and plunged it into the back of the unsuspecting sentry. Pulling it out, he plunged it deeper, deeper, in and out, in and out. He didn't want to desecrate a corpse, but he had to be sure. He knew that Confederate spies probably could be watching him by now. He had to make his getaway. It might have been a matter of spy, assigned against spy, for all he knew.

The sentry was the traitor. He removed his partner's canteen, using some of the water to clean his knife. He finished his food, then ate what was left of his partner's food. He remained but awhile, to see the beginning of the end of the boys below.

The contingent led by Major Doherty stopped just short of the perimeter of the bunker. Their plans were made well. The first group to approach the bunker was composed of men in civilian dress. They wore men's and women's attire, with their guns shielded from view. Their friend, who had dispatched the second sentry, signaled that they could proceed as planned. Then he quickly disappeared, ostensibly to continue his work to compromise, and take the lives of other men.

On observing the unobstructed approach of his 'civilians', Major Doherty released the second group. When they started out in battle formation, the civilians were coming upon the grizzly scene that lay before them. The slayer wanted to arouse them, to prepare them for the kind of carnage that lay just before them. In a few moments, the bunker was surrounded on all sides. There were rear and side exits. If any man tried to escape from those, he would be cut to rivets.

Everything proceeded like clockwork. There was an eerie calm, and emotionless sense of doom pervading the air. All factors were perfect for an ambush. Maybe they were too perfect. It was so quiet that the Rebels wondered whether anybody was inside at all. Due to his orders, the Major could not wait too long. Dispensing second thoughts, he gave the final signal to begin the assault.

He approached the sentry station with Charles Rogers and Brookshire. He examined the remains of the knifed soldier, only to discover the horrendous, horrible wounds. Obviously the killer wanted everyone who saw the dead soldier to see how his murder had gone beyond the call of duty. The wounds were clearly the work done by one who hated his enemy with a passion. The dead man's body was a mess, and foul smelling too. Buzzards waited in the trees, Ravens walked along the ground.

The major wondered. He had been able to move in too easily. This just didn't sit right. Since the sentry had been killed, why didn't the 'Rebel spy' remain to finish the deal? Why had it been so easy? Why were his orders to kill? Might these men really have information of value to the Confederacy? Could that information have been overlooked by their 'man'? These were questions that would have to be answered after the slaughter about to ensue.

The Confederates rode over the hill to attack. From cover, the spy watched as the carnage began. He could not temp fate any longer. His orders were to leave even before a bullet was fired in anger. The Rebel yell, the Confederate screams, it was on. The only shock of this attack was felt by the rebels. The men in the bunker below were taken totally by surprise. The gunfire and blasting caps were heard by the other man as he rode away.

Small, out numbered, and contained in a killing area, the courageous soldiers, nonetheless, fought as hard as could be expected. Now, down to the last man, their leader, he could not bear to give them the satisfaction of the kill. He ignited his own body, his clothing containing sensitive military papers in his pockets. He was shooting at Rebels as he burned. Realizing that he could hold sensitive military information, the rebels tried to extinguish his burning body. They were too late. Everything was up in smoke. Even his bones smoldered.

Charles Rogers and Brookshire shared the exulting men's joy in their victory. Major Doherty didn't even incur any wounded men among his force. However, his reserve remained, pondering his next move, trying to understand things which were too simple. On the whole, to him, they seemed far too simple. The men had tasted their first blood. They wanted more. Their euphoria was so great that the only thing that could affect it was defeat. They felt invincible.

They searched the bodies of the fallen. There was no identification on the men. If ever there was truth to the common adage that dead men told no tales, it was now. This created an even greater puzzle for Doherty. The more he dwelled on this and the more he considered the other factors, the more convinced he grew that there was more, much more, involved in this battle than met the eye. He longed for the return of the moment when he gave the order to kill every man inside the bunker.

The sentry had left the bunker heading due South. There, fifty miles away, he alerted his regiment, fellow soldiers, officers and other spies, all Union forces, that the largest, strongest contingent of Southern military in Mississippi was at work killing their own men. The Union plan was to infiltrate the select Confederate spying team. With their most effective agent, the plan had succeeded. The South had attacked its senior cadre of intelligence officers, knocking out their own chance of sabotaging key installations in the North. Their work was crucial if the Confederacy had even a small chance of turning the tide against the Yankees. There was one important reason for the astounding success of the Union effort. The master spy who planned it all was none other than Rex Cotton. So sure was he of the victory, that he volunteered to infiltrate the Confederate group. It was Rex who killed the sentry. It was Rex who succeeded once more in this cause to free all men from slavery in the Americas.

If they moved fast, the back door was left open for the Union forces to proceed Eastward. They had in mind the destruction of a key installation to the state's ability to hold its own. Their sites were set on the Brookshire Plantation. Their orders had one goal - total destruction. Civilians were not to be harmed. However, if they interfered, all due and necessary measures were to be used to insure success. Even if Major Doherty had figured it out, he could not have done anything about it. Neither his men, nor their horses could return in time. Master Brookshire was about to learn the great lesson of modern warfare. When atrocities exact extensive use of resources of a land, the invaders have more options. Losing the use of the resources of the land, or losing the land meant that the war would be lost too. Unfortunately, as they continued to assess the carnage, the Rebel force had no awareness of their loss. At least they could save some time before returning Eastward. The bunker was perfect as a final burial place for fallen men. They just needed to cover the points of egress.

But now, after that ye have known God, or rather are known of God, how turn ye again to the weak and beggarly elements, whereunto ye desire again to be in bondage?
Ye observe days, and months, and times and years.
I am afraid of you, lest I have bestowed upon you labour in vain.
Galatians 4: 8 - 10

In the past, when you did not acknowledge God, you served as slaves to gods who are not really divine. Now that you have come to know God, - or rather, have become known by Him - how can you return to those powerless, worthless, natural elements to which you seem willing to enslave yourselves once more? You even go so far as to keep the ceremonial observance of days and months, seasons and years! I fear for you; all my efforts with you may have been wasted. Galatians 4: 8 - 11 The New American Bible

Chapter XXIV - Yes, We Are Ready

For the LORD is good, His mercy is everlasting; and His truth endureth to all generations. Psalm 100: 5

When they were all gathered, Plumpsie came from behind the haystacks first. Then came Isaac. Quite naturally his appearance brought hisses. Then came Esau. Everyone knew who he was. There was just silence. Dead Silence. Then everyone began to smile. There was jubilation, though subdued, at the sight of their long lost brother. "As ya'll knows, this here be my long lost brother, Esau. He and Plumpsie done nursed me back to health, after I is left for dead by my own Rebel forces. I has been such a fool. I wuz responsible fo the death o' Ole Uncle Amos, and my daddy, Will too. I is responsible fo so much bad stuff. Now I is come to my senses. I is not afraid no mo. I knows I has been a Judas."

"Lies, lies, lies, lies and mo lies. That nigger lyin thru his teefes", snarled Jesse, a middle aged slave, a younger brother of Amos. "My brother ain't had no right to try and kill yo sorry lil ass like that no way. He be crazy at the time. But we ain't go be caught by yo lies no mo, Isaac Brookshire. I just welst to kill yo soory, skinny, runt o a ass myslef, but I knows massah, he and Ole Buck King, they kills my ass right off. Yo ain't worth gettin us kilt. We doesn't want yo round here no mo. We doesn't want to hear yo lies. I sho nuff doesn't."

Isaac looked about the area. The same sentiments were written on the faces of each slave. They all felt the same. The lesson was painful. Esau understood his suffering. He also understood the suffering of the other slaves. Now Isaac wanted to address the crowd more, but before he could speak, Esau moved up another step. Often words can be meaningless. Action, on the other hand, can speak volumes. Esau wanted the slaves to understand one thing. He commanded center stage. "My brother was engaged in the same kind of work, for the Confederacy, as I was for the Union. We met barely two months ago on the battlefield. God only knows why Isaac, our cousin Fredericka, (I ain't never liked the nickname Plumpsie) and I were meant to meet up there. Now, He done brought us back here, safe and sound together."

"I knows Esau, he be tryin to straighten thangs out. But that ain't his job. Whut I knows in my heart is that I wuz a fool. Massah, he and his henchmen, they done got in my brain, and cost me to thinkin wrong", Isaac interrupted. He was really truthful about standing for something of worth. "Well, I can unnerstands if ya'll don't believes me. In my mind, knowin how evil and crazy I wuz, I wouldn't believes me neither."

But for the lead in words by Esau, they might have set upon Isaac there. From his life in the North, his role with the military, his coming of age, he had become a man. He had the wisdom of a philosopher and his presence was a strong one. Clearly he was the leader among the men at that plantation.

"If yo brother is repented, then let him go up to the big house and kill the Master", came a shout from the rear of the crowd. "Let him kill em all!"

It was one thing for Isaac to admit the error of his ways, being truthful about it to the slaves. To vengefully persecute those who had duped him would be to place the blame on them, rather than on himself. He surely perceived that it was due to his own weakness, not solely the logic and depraved deviousness of Uriah Brookshire that had controlled his behavior.

"That be just like a nigger", came another declaration from the crowd. "All the time tryin to git another nigger to do his work that he ain't got the guts to do his own self."

Like the staccato crackling of corn fritters frying in a pan of lard and tallow suet in a heavy iron pot, the admonition pierced the heavy early fear laden morning, fog filled air of the field. The words were cruel, biting, and would have been true but for the wrong context. They fell hard upon a crowd that in other circumstances might have been hovering on the brink of a lynching, shattering their life's purpose, instilling in them a greater crazed fear that they had less control over their own lives, their purpose to exist. They wanted to believe in the message of the statement. They wanted to believe that each and every slave was an innocent victim. Most assuredly, they had been wronged to a person by men like the master. That was easy to believe. It was the truth.

Nervous energy abounded. Restlessness messed with the minds of all. The slaves were crazed with discontent, and the need to act out in a manner they had never felt before. Esau simply raised a hand, and all attention turned to him. Again there was silence. He held the fore. It was as if, for the time being, time had been suspended in space. If anybody had as much as breathed, everyone would have heard it. Everyone would have felt it too. They were stunned, speechless, willing, but unwilling to believe that this mere boy seemed to have them under his spell, controlling their thought, behavior and their collective will. It was as if the spirit of his mother had possessed the boy.

Some actually saw the same ring of light about him as they said was with Cassie that morning she had died, scarcely one hundred yards from the very spot on which he stood. The boy was touched, they believed, by the Spirit. As such, they dared not go against his will. En masse, they felt that Spirit fall upon them. Its effect could not be denied. Not a soul could move. It wasn't fear. It was refreshing. They felt content, replenished and wonderfully at ease with Isaac, each other, and the world. And Isaac, that boy felt a contentment with himself that seemed to predict the peace of mind that had eluded him since his reunion with Esau and Fredericka. "Now you all can believe", Isaac enjoined the crowd, half asking, half pleading. "Ya'll sees the same way my brother had a affect on me. Just like whut he doin to ya'll. My brother, he done been sent from the Lord!"

It all seemed logical. The slaves had believed they would never see him again. How happy, yet fearful they were, to understand. They would not have believed that their worlds would be brought so strangely close together, that one who had been gone for so long, not seen in so many years could be here. His presence had a more compelling effect than any one of them would have anticipated. It was good news, and briefly, they believed he had come to save the slaves, to free them from their bondage and lead them to a land of plenty, an Eden where they would be free, live free, and enjoy justice.

One by one, they walked up to embrace Fredericka, Esau, and even Isaac. Plumpsie decided her real name would be used from now on. However, she dumped the Rogers name, and displaced it with Absalom's last name. In the spelling, however, she made one slight difference. Where there had been an 'e', she displaced it with an 'a'. She told Esau that The Reverend had misread the true spelling of his aadopted name from the Book of Genesis.

Now obviously with child, she explained that she had married Esau's brother on their mission. From now on, she was to be addressed as Fredericka Reed-Omar. Each slave felt that he was in touch with history. They hugged their new heroes, determined to follow their lead in completing the task of their revolt. The day of the word was at hand. Ole Fedderson, they fondly remembered, had preached about it. Like a bolt from heaven, they recalled, deliverance would come when they least expected it. His only advice before he departed this life: Ya'll Be Ready!

The Benefits of Brotherly Concord

Behold how good and how pleasant it is for brethren to dwell together in unity!

It is the precious ointment upon the head, that ran down upon the beard, even Aaron's beard; that went down to the skirts of his garments;

As the dew of Hermon, and as the dew that descended upon the mountains of Zion: for there the LORD commanded the blessing, even life forever more.

Psalm 133

CHAPTER XXV - We Don't Want Vengeance; We Want Justice!

Envy Thou Not the Oppressor, and choose none of his ways.
Proverbs 3: 31

Fitzpatrick was married to the master's younger sister. At times such as this, when Brookshire had to be away, his brother in law and sister had stayed over, to look after things. The slaves had sealed off all doors and windows to the mansion's first floor and held the entire building under their control. Thomas, the house slave who often attended Master Brookshire, was charged with rousing Fitzpatrick. As had become his custom, he knocked once, waited about sixty seconds, knocked lightly again, waited again, then entered the room. He was the only person among the plantation with that privilege. Neither the master, nor Fitzpatrick could be so bold.

Due to his affliction, Fitzpatrick had not maintained any sexual activity with his wife for several years. Thomas, like almost everyone else, believed this was the reason that he had grown to prefer black women, black men, and black boys and girls. He could have his way with slaves with impunity. Isaac had first seen his actions in his preference when Fitzpatrick accompanied the master and his group to New Orleans for the grand horse races. Esau had it figured out when Isaac told him about Fitzpatrick's preferences on their journey from the war. It had been enough to make him puke, a pleasure he would save for Fitzpatrick. As usual, Fitzpatrick was not with his wife at the time. Thomas told her that a matter of grave importance was at hand. The master, he lied, was returning early from the West. He wanted to seal a business deal and needed Fitzpatrick immediately. Carlotta, his wife, had no qualms about the urgency. She also knew exactly where her husband was. She wrote the note, then gave it to Thomas. Carlotta would never have imagined what lay in store for her. This could be the most tumultuous morning of her life.

Jesse accepted the responsibility to run and fetch Fitzpatrick. Like the others, he didn't have to be told where he could find him. Jesse handed him the note from his wife, even as he was engaged with a young black slave. Nothing else, except maybe the presence of Brookshire himself, would have made him stop.

The white employees at the manse paid no attention to the strange goings on. To them, everything was under control. As soon as Jesse returned, he went directly there, to report. He told them he had delivered the message and that Fitzpatrick was on his way. At that point, Thomas returned to Carlotta's bedroom to advise that her husband was on his way home. He also told her that a few others were to meet him in her bedroom. They were Fredericka, Isaac, Esau, Jesse, Aunt Thessalonia, the new zovan, and Calvin, who had taken to delivering the Sunday morning sermons, offering prayers when needed, and performing the marriage rites. Calvin was a big, gruff sort, who was also very intelligent.

He was a man who liked a good brawl as much as anyone else. On one occasion when Master Brookshire had pitted him to fight an oversized slave from a plantation in Alabama, Calvin admonished the man for being led into such a battle. He had told the fellow that he was 'go give him a good old time Christian butt kicking'. Just to be on the safe side, against the large man, he told him that the Lord wanted him to win and that only a fool would mess with the Lord. That man actually refused to strike a blow at Calvin. When he was done, Calvin stood, then knelt over the fallen foe and prayed. That is the kind of man Calvin was.

Carlotta, a whimpering sort, surprisingly showed no fear. She believed that if the black men and woman there meant her any real harm, they would have killed her by now. Then too, to scream and bawl would do no good anyway.

Having now arrived at the mansion, Fitzpatrick paid no attention that every thing was out of kilter. The slaves were not reporting to duty. Empty milk containers lay next to filled ones. The normal exchange had not been completed. There were even slaves surrounding the house. They knew they should have known better. Their work stations were in the fields, barns, and smoke house. He didn't even notice that the slaves who were in the house were not assigned there either. He paid no attention to the guns they carried in plain view. Jesse theorized that it was the simple behavior of a man deprived of completing the sex act when he wanted nothing more to do. Though Fitzpatrick looked somewhat older, he was still a young man. Balding with a comb over, and a beard that needed trimming, he was prematurely gray too. His custom was to knock at his wife's bedroom door before opening too. This time, due to the urgent message from her, regarding his brother in law, he dispensed with the usual manners and burst in. "Do you all know how to knock, first, Mr. Fitzpatrick?" his wife asked him, ashamed that he had lost his manners as had the other young men in her room. "Ah am so sick of you all. Truly Ah am. Ah really am."

He was about to apologize when he realized that she was more than angry. She was irate and it was not at the people who had infiltrated her bedroom. It was at him. Had her brother been there, she would have wanted to lash out at him too. He was away fighting a war battle when he should have been home, taking care of his loved ones. Then he saw that his wife was looking beyond him. Turning, he saw what she was looking at. He didn't like what he saw. What was worse, is that neither did they. He thought he could do something about what he saw. They knew they could do something about what they saw. That was the difference in a nutshell. He realized the important fact of the moment. He had been duped by Jesse. To add insult to injury, Jesse had returned long before he, and he didn't even use a horse.

Fitzpatrick focused on Isaac, then Fredericka; next he scowled at Thomas and Jesse. Worse yet, he actually sneered at Esau because he knew who he was. The man displayed his stupidity, which was only exceeded by his impulsive behavior, borne from his compulsive personality. "What is the meaning of this? Ah demand to know", he raged, still not aware that he was in no position to make demands. The man had snapped and he would have to pay dearly. "What do you all niggers mean, coming up here like this? You all tricked me into my wife's room, the purpose of which Ah do not rightly know. Git the hell out now before you all git me steaming mad!"

He pointed to the door as he raged. They said nothing. Again he looked at Carlotta. Now she sat at the side of the bed, still wearing her sheer gown but no covering robe. She sensed that whatever they had planned for her husband would most certainly involve her. It was obvious. They had the central players in this drama all behind closed doors and in her bedroom. They had a lesson for her too, and she knew it. She simply hoped it was not a painful one.

Fitzpatrick made a move for Esau. He was the culprit. They were under his influence. The troubles just began on his return. The young man was too quick. At the last second, he artfully dodged out of harm's way. Regaining his balance, Fitzpatrick tried again, attaining the same result as before. After this attempt he fell to the floor. Imagine his embarrassment when Esau helped him up, straightening his shirt and jacket. Of course Fitzpatrick felt utter disdain. He clenched his fist and swung mightily at him this time. It was as if Esau knew he would try that because he never looked at him as he eluded the blow. Once more the angry man attempted to hit him. This time the blow landed firmly into Esau's open palm, which he clenched around the man's fist, and squeezed as if in a vice. Fitzpatrick fell to his knees, wincing in pain. His whole hand from the wrist to the fingers was as white as snow. He couldn't even straighten his hand, even after Esau released his grip. As Fitzpatrick regained his footing, again with Esau's help, they briefly made eye contact. A black man had never done such a thing to him. The final physical assault was a shove, a hard shove, forcing him all the way back, some twenty feet, to his wife's bed. "What is the meaning of this? What are you all trying to accomplish here?" he asked again.

"Tell him, tell him the answer Ah beg. Why must we endure this living hell from you all?" Carlotta asked, just as her husband had, only more softly and less threatening than he had done. Like him, she was even more insulted by this behavior. No matter how difficult her relationship with her husband had become, she could never accept the interference of black people into their private lives. This, after all was her bedroom, one she had enjoyed since her birth. It should have been off limits to them, and they should have known and respected that.

"We are here to help restore your marriage to this piece of swine as it should be, Mrs. Carlotta", Esau explained, now moving closer as he talked. "Everybody knows that you, and Mr. Fitzpatrick don't sleep together like husband and wife anymore. So we come to help ya'll out."

"We don't need help from the likes of you all", she answered. "We are able to take care of any problems that exist, thank you all very much."

The pomp, the swagger, the manner of an aristocrat so infuriated Fitzpatrick that he tried again to strike Esau. Just as adroitly, he ducked and dodged to avoid the thrusting attempts. "Listen you dumb ox. You couldn't hit me unless I wanted you too. You are so stupid, you would probably miss then too. If you try that again, so help me I shall break your nose. Now sit down and do as you are told."

"You have no right to talk to him like that, or to treat us this way. My pappy owns you, and you and you and you too." Surely Carlotta felt these were terms with which they all could relate. Her deceased father was the original owner of the slaves.

"We can talk with you any way we please Carlotta. Now don't play games with us. There is a war going on. These times are too serious for playing games. Now you must realize that we want to set things back right with your family. We want you and your husband to act like normal married people."

"All right, Esau, you made your point. Then me and my wife will live like normal married people do."

"Now listen, Fitzpatrick. You are trying my patience, and I don't like young men to try my patience. Now we won't ask you again. We are here to see you behave like a normal married man with his wife. Now the time has come for you to do as you have been told."

He turned to look at Jesse, Isaac, Fredericka, and Thomas. "Your brother is a mad man. Can't you all talk some sense into his head? Surely you all can see that your cousin is behaving like a fool."

There was no reply from anyone. They would not even think of countermanding Esau. Yet, they didn't know what to make of his orders.

"You have exactly one minute to treat your wife like she is married to you." This warning was cold. Esau was set to enforce his demand. If the consequence was one that forced Fitzpatrick to protect his wife, then Fitzpatrick would have to endure that.

"You all don't have to give me a minute, nigger. Ah know what to do with my own wife. Ah don't need you all to tell me. Do your worse, nigger." Sternly, stubbornly, Fitzpatrick called Esau's bluff. He would endure the ultimate indignity, death from the hands of one's own slave, rather than accept a single order from the slave.

It seemed that Esau had guessed wrong. He realized that a white gentleman considered the welfare of his wife greater than all else. With the threat of death no longer an option, he turned to the second tact. "Do you know why your weasel of a husband will not sleep with you as his wife, Carlotta?"

"Sure Ah knows why", she answered quite confidently as if she knew and she approved of his choices. "He has found favor with the black wenches, bitches, whores, broads and heifers. It's something that all white men do. Even my dear old pappy did it, as you all no doubt are aware. Why, some of you darkies are my own brothers and sisters. Mr. Fitzpatrick will come back to me when he is good and ready. And Ah shall be waiting for him."

"Listen you dumb ninny. It's not that at all. Your husband has an issue." Angered at her choice of words, obvious insults to black women, Esau blurted it out. He really wanted her to figure it out herself. But she never would have. The husbands of proper Southern aristocratic ladies don't catch clap and worse. She would not have guessed it anyhow.

She would have accepted him before she heard that. Now, she didn't want him to touch her. Fitzpatrick still thought he had won the mind game with Esau, even though his wife now knew the awful truth. Now he could protect his wife from contracting his diseases. Esau played his final trump, one he knew would be a good one. "You leave me no choice Fitzpatrick. You come around our women and our young men. You put your mouth and your filthy tongue on the most private parts of their bodies. You do this in the slave houses, or should I say slave pits. You perform the sex act, and other filthy acts of perversion with slaves for all to see. And you have the unmitigated gall to say that you can't demonstrate the same thing even with your own wife. Yet you can do so to my people. I really didn't want to do this, but I think you have forgotten how. I think what you need is a demonstration on your own wife, like you have been doing to slaves."

Not only did Fitzpatrick and Carlotta not expect this, but neither did the slaves. They were absolutely astonished, even when they saw Esau move to unbutton his fly. "What do you all mean to do?" asked a stunned Fitzpatrick, as if he didn't know.

"Like I say, you and your wife need a demonstration. I will use her, to so demonstrate, just like you have been doing with the slaves" was his answer, the words coming out slowly, clearly and audibly. "After I give her a reminder, then every male slave in this room will follow me. After this day, I think your wife will have a good recollection of just how good the sex act can be."

That was Esau's final trump. He knew that the ultimate fear of the white man was that their women would be sexually exploited by black men. At least, that was what white men articulated. In truth, blacks knew that white women enjoyed the sex act with black men.

Though still very young, Esau believed he had it figured out, that this greater fear haunted men like Fitzpatrick. No matter what the reasons - Fitzpatrick's or Esau's - no white man, no matter what his true fears, could refrain from doing whatever was necessary to prevent what Esau threatened. There was one way out for Fitzpatrick. It was a solution that could only be exercised by an honorable man. He had a clear path to the balcony on the North side of the bed room. Though the window was locked, if he had any honor left, if he had any substance as a man, that outlet offered the opportunity for saving his honor. Though the likelihood of death was that option, no one was surprised when he was too weak to take it. No one, that is, except his wife. This man was spineless. No matter what, he could not see himself taking that means to prove that in the end, he could be a real man.

Even if this meant inflicting her with his venereal diseases he had to do it. Sweating profusely, afraid that he may not be able to perform, sorry for himself, but not for his wife, he sat on the bed, turned to her, and began to fondle her. When they had been enjoying the pleasure of each other, she used to be as active as he. Now she could not enjoy the giving of pleasure. Passively she allowed him to explore her erotic zones. Soon his passions were aroused and he was ready to perform sexually with his wife. Briefly, as with slaves, he enjoyed the audience. The slaves remained there until he had completed what he had to do. It was not so difficult after all. Few slaves, young or old, appreciated this man. He was loathed. He had become accustomed to passive partners. Carlotta was no different. When he was done, they didn't even permit him to wash, nor her. After all, they reasoned, he never permitted slaves to wash after his nasty deeds.

They left the room after he was done. As they descended the stairwell Thomas asked Esau whether he was serious about carrying through the threat he had made in the bedroom. Esau never answered. He just ignored the question. No one ever asked him again after that. The truth is, he never understood what the question was. He simply thought Thomas was commenting about the weather.

* * *

With Master Brookshire with the Confederate Army, the only person who might have been able to strike fear into the slaves was Buck King. It was essential that he was kept away from the mansion. He fitted into their plans after the display in Carlotta's bedroom. During the while, he had been kept busy back behind the kitchen. The man liked the way Nellie Mae, the Brookshire's cook, fixed greens, pork chops, grits, okra and Indian pudding. When prepared just right, he couldn't resist them. Neither could he leave such a meal until he was finished with more than two helpings of everything. That meal, so early in the morning, caused him to retire to the barn, find a soft spot of hay in the loft, and fall asleep. He had only lay there a few minutes, barely shut his eyes, when he received the shock of his life. There standing above him were Thomas, whose back he had beaten at least one hundred times; Jesse, who though young, had suffered humiliating beatings from the man; Esau, who had never forgotten what he had been told the man had done to his mother; and Isaac, who only recently came to hate the man. "Got damned niggers, what in the name o hell ya'll doin here. Cain't a man get a minute o sleep in peace? What in the name o hell......why Ah don't believe what my eyes is seeing...." First Buck complained. Then he just smiled, and smiled. Then he smiled some more. Then he laughed.

The smiles were not returned. The laughter was ignored by the black men. They saw nothing funny. Buck began to understand. Esau's return was not cause for a happy reunion. At least, for him it wasn't. That they did not jump away, that they let their eyes become a direct study of his, he found intolerable. This could only mean one thing, that they wanted to subject themselves to another beating and he would oblige them. He still didn't quite get the whole picture. "Looking for this, Mr. Buck?" Thomas asked derisively, waving Buck's favorite instrument of brutality in front of him. "If yo looking for this, then we is go give it to yo... just like yo done always gave it to us."

Confused, dazed, he fathomed he was dreaming, perhaps having a nightmare. That had to be what it was, what with Isaac and his long lost brother, Esau, together, it had to be a bad dream. He rubbed his eyes, blinked, then rubbed them again. He swallowed hard, gulped, and swallowed hard again. His throat had become so dry that they could hear the saliva pass his larynx and go down his esophagus. "Now you boys knows this is Ole Buck, Ole Buck King. Now you all ain't suppose to act like this. Now you all just give that there bull whip back to Ole Buck and he promise to forgit just how stupid ya'll been acting." Buck grinned, gritted his teeth as he bargained that the men would accept his offer, with the obvious lie of forgiveness.

They were just about to beat him there when there was a commotion outside. It was the regiment of intelligence officers who had turned the tables on the Confederate troops at the Black Pine Forest. These men had caused Major Doherty to attack and kill his own crack intelligence officers. Peeping through the door in the loft, Esau sent Thomas and Jesse out to assess the situation. He and Isaac remained with their 'prisoner'.

Though many in this group wore the blue uniform of the Union, the slaves were not quick to trust them. Thomas would be the spokesperson for the group. When he did realize that the men were truly officers from the Union, Thomas began to cooperate, answering questions, and giving information; he understood exactly what he was doing and was proud of it. He told them about the hospital at the base of the plantation, explaining that rebel wounded obtained the most competent medical care in the South. He confirmed that the plantation served as a training site for enlisted men. Then he gave the most important information that the Union men wanted: confirmation that Master Brookshire provided cotton, livestock, horses, and food to the Confederacy, free of charge. Then came the most startling news, that slaves had been ordered to participate for the Confederacy.

At that bit of news Buck King seized the opportunity to escape when no one was watching, as his captors trained their eyes on Thomas. He bolted past Esau, leaping from the double doors at the top of the loft. He landed easily onto four double stacks of hay and scurried to the Union troop. "He is lying fo sho....that nigger is lying", he yelled, running to the men, not even realizing that they were Union. All he focused on was their race. Certainly as white men, they would not believe Thomas when a white man had a different view on the matter. "Them got damned niggers done took over the whole dang plantation. Hell, tain't no telling what these niggers done did to Baron Fitzpatrick and Miss Carlotta. We all is so glad you boys done showed up. Now we kin catch us all these sabotaging, backsliding gull darned niggers an whup us some asses."

"Hold on, hold on, sir. Just calm down for a minute", the leader of the contingent asked, getting down off his horse. "I am glad we are here too. We have been looking for this place. You say this is the plantation of Uriah Agrippa Brookshire?"

"Yes sir ee. It sho enough is that."

"And you say that the brother-in-law is about. Where is he? And where is the master?"

"Oh. him and his boys, they went up to the Black Pine Forest to watch our boys kill some Yankee spies. Hear tell them Union boys had them a whole mess a Yankee spies up there. Master Brookshire, he go be back tonight." Buck volunteered a ton of information. He continued to make no connection between the blue uniforms and the men wearing them. All he could see was that they were white men. His perception was that they were his rescuers.

"Please go get the son-in-law. He is to tell us what must be done to these men who would take such actions here."

Buck ordered one of the field hands to go for Fitzpatrick. While waiting he continued to explain how his employer had come to assume the leading role for the cause of the Confederacy. He used his products from his farm, his wealth and influence to help defeat the Union. When the men returned with Fitzpatrick, he was greeted with a broad smile and a friendly handshake from Buck. Fitzpatrick looked horrible, as if he had had not one minute of sleep throughout the night and morning. "Look at this damn man. Cain't you all see those niggers done put him through a living hell?" Buck continued his tirade, now enjoining the men to empathize with Fitzpatrick.

As Buck went on, Esau joined the group. He said nothing, content for Thomas to continue as the spokesman. While Buck ranted, the leader recognized Esau. He was the very same officer whom Esau, Absalom and Fredericka had rescued from the prison in West Chattanooga, Tennessee. They made eye contact for a brief second, then continued to listen to Buck. Fitzpatrick made the same error as the foreman. He identified the men as white too. He looked well past the blue coats, hats and trousers. When Buck paused to catch his breath, the leader seized the second, just quickly enough to ask a question. "What would you wish to be done with these Negroes?" he asked. "You may have your say now; do you want it?"

"Why yes, sir. We wanna beat they assess. Beat em good. Hell, a beating is too good for all of em." Buck made no secret of what would give his heart the greatest pleasure.

"And what say you, brother-in-law? Do you want to beat them too?"

turning to Fitzpatrick, he would give him a chance to speak. "What did they do to you?"

"These niggers humiliated me", he answered, still unaware that these were Northern military men. "Right in front of my wife, they made fools of both of us. If I had my way, I would have a picnic right here and right now. I would pick these five niggers right here and that girl. She ain't no good either."

"What do you mean? Did they rape your wife and make you look on?" he asked Fitzpatrick to be more explicit. "If they did that, then I shall join you in stringing them up, but we will not celebrate over a grand serving of food."

"Oh no, they did not do anything such as that", Fitzpatrick answered. He was passive now. There was no emotion in his voice. The only time he showed passion was when he spoke of lynching the slaves. Yet, he felt reassured that the white men were on his side. "What they did is far worse than a rape. These niggers made me have sex with my wife. They know I have been sleeping with black men and women, sir. They know that black men and women, even black children, boys and girls have become my preferences. Why now, should I go to my wife?"

"So, you sir are telling me that these boys made you do something with your wife that a man is supposed to do with his wife?"

"Yes, that is correct, all those niggers. They made me take her. They know no God fearing gentleman will risk giving a disease to his wife, when black slaves are everywhere." He talked more coherently now, assured that the guilt of the slaves would be punished by their execution. Fitzpatrick scanned the area for ropes. Trees abounded.

"I see. They made you do it, but why you, and why that way?"

Now, suddenly, Fitzpatrick was afraid to answer. He had already said too much. His personal affairs were in open discussion with strangers, slaves, plantation employees and members of his and the master's families looking on.

Esau had been taking it all in too. He was really tired of the charade. He wanted to move on and he knew the captain was wasting time. Certainly he had work to do. "We had to teach that man a lesson", he raised his voice, not simply for the military people to hear, but the entire throng assembled. "This man has been raping black women, even children. You now what, to him, our women are not good women. They are fit to be used for his deviant pleasures. He also uses our children, and our men. Our women are beautiful. Our children are good, wholesome and innocent. Well if he can force his diseases upon my family, then he can give his disease to his own."

The officer took it all in. He and everybody else knew that Esau spoke the truth. "You sure talk different for a black man. I find it hard to believe that you're from around here. Where are you from anyway?"

"Why Captain, sir, I am from the North just like you. Judging by your dialect, I'd say you are from somewhere up North, North East to be exact."

That's when the import of the man and the others hit Fitzpatrick, Buck King and the others like a ton of bricks. Now they knew they were doomed. Forlorn, depressed, psychologically drained, Fitzpatrick had nothing else to say. He thought the worse had come. Buck King, however, pleaded for his hide. He dropped to his knees and begged the leader. He crawled to Esau, to Thomas, to Fredericka, to Jesse, and then to Isaac. These were the very people that he asked to string up barely ten minutes earlier.

For the moment they did nothing to Fitzpatrick. Buck King didn't fare so well. His was the punishment that he had feared the most. He had always found extra energy to horsewhip or bullwhip a slave, male or female. He had also used the measure against whites who ran afoul of him or the master. The Captain supplied the rope. They tied him to a stake, the very same stake that they had used on Will. Before they began, they looked around. There were others, juniors to Buck, his assistants, his foremen, and his various flunkies who simply hung around for the chance to see black folk beaten. They didn't even bother to run. They were smart enough to know that they could not outrun even the older, slower slaves. They simply walked up and permitted themselves to be tied down next to Buck. "You pronounced your own sentence, Mr. Overseer, the Captain announced. You said that you wanted to beat the slaves. I have sentenced you to serve that very punishment."

The punishment didn't begin immediately. The troop was on a timetable. The men were left tied. The backs of their shirts were torn open. The bright morning Mississippi sun shone down on their bare backs. This would serve a fitting prelude, all agreed, to what they had brought down upon themselves.

The Union men ate a marvelous breakfast, as well as the one prepared for Buck King first thing that morning. The leaders had further discussion with Thomas, Esau, Jesse, Isaac and a few other older slaves about the topography, area entrenchments, arsenals and the hospital. They would hit the training quarters first. Then they would clear the hospital and use dynamite. Next to go would be the armory at Meridian. The slaves gave them their promise to keep quiet, thanking the men for serving the purpose of justice. Esau promised to return to duty when the business there was completed. They wanted him to do one more service before he left. He was asked to torch the plantation, especially the fields of cotton. Nothing, not even slaves quarters was to be spared.

All the slaves watched the punishment to Buck and his men. The Union troops could hear their screams even as they moved on the training field and hospital. There were two differences between what Buck endured now, and what occurred when he was on the other end. For one, the beater gained no pleasure. The second was that the present victims cried out and wailed. Slaves never, or rarely cried out in pain no matter how severe the beating.

Slaves truly derived no pleasure from beating these men. It was something that simply had to be done. To that extent, it was like the impressions on Plumpsie, Absalom and Esau when they were in battle. Their intent was to ensure that these men would be beaten so badly that they would never want to take a whip to the back side of a black person again. Their mission was accomplished. They seared Buck King's flesh to the bone. Flies alit on open wounds on backs, necks, scalps, buttocks and the backs of legs. They let the other men remain unconscious, but Buck King did not enjoy even that. Whenever he lost consciousness they moved to his face and threw water. They slapped his face only slightly. He had to endure it all. These men and women had never beaten anybody. It was strange because they always knew exactly when a man was about to faint under the strain or die from the pain. They were careful not to kill anyone, and most certainly, not to kill Buck King. "Please, Esau, don't ya'll hit me no more." He begged, and pleaded. He almost passed out just from asking. "Old Buck is powerful sorry. Uncle Thomas, you know Old Buck ain't meant nothing. Please don't you all beat Old Buck no more."

"Don't you think he done had enough?" Thomas asked Esau.

"Has he had as much as you have received over your life time, Uncle Thomas?" came Esau's answer, in the form of a question. "Has he had as much as Will, my daddy; or as Cassie, my mamma; or as Amos, your own brother; or as Old Fedderson; or as our cousin, Amos; or as Nathaniel; or as Taymer; or as William; or as Joshua; or as Elijah; or as Johnny; or as Charles; or as Raymond: or as Luther; or as Martin; or as Marvin? That man has beaten too many slaves in his day. Tell me did he beat your mother, Louise enough?

They sent a lookout to climb the highest tree on the grounds. Esau wanted to know whether Master Brookshire was returning. There was no sight of him, but the lookout summoned them to the tall Magnolia tree, the tallest on Brookshire property, off the main entrance, headed to the road. From a branch hang the remains of Fitzpatrick. He knew what would be in store for him. This time, he wouldn't let the slaves lay claim to his last deed on earth. He did it himself.

Buzzards flew over Buck King. He and his workers were finally cut asunder. However, they were not dead. For the final insult, Esau and the others took the ball peen hammers and let loose the most powerful blow to each hand of each man. Their purpose was that these men would never be able to grasp a bull whip, a gun, or any instrument that could bring harm to another human being. They would never even be able to ever ball up their fists again. Then the men were ushered to the edge of the plantation and left there. Strength permitting, they would have to find their own way back to town. Buck King was left in the same spot from which he had been released. However, he had much less strength than the others. The buzzards, flying overhead would be denied. The men wanted Buck to live. Thomas came out to him, aimed his rifle at Buck, then raised it overhead. Without even looking he fired one shot. The bullet pierced the heart of the largest buzzard in the bunch. He fell two feet from Buck King. Buck had to lie there in his own blood, urine, vomit, sweat and feces. All he could do was watch, watch as the other birds swooped down, devouring the carcass of their relative. Buck saw firsthand what would happen to himself if he couldn't get away. He didn't move one inch until the other birds had cleaned the spot where the big bird lay. That was when they sniffed at Buck.

All in all, on the Brookshire Plantation there lived 537 slaves on that day. Of that number, 210 chose to depart with groups, headed in different directions. A total of 48 others chose to cast their lot with Esau, Isaac, Fredericka and Jesse. Then, another group of 74 rugged individuals, men and women simply struck out on their own. They told no one of their plans. The remainder remained at Brookshire.

CHAPTER XXVI - Fiery Flames of Freedom

But for torching the place, any work of and by any slave at the Brookshire plantation was done. Certainly Esau, Isaac, Fredericka, Thomas, Jesse, Naomi, and a few others had to leave the area. The twins wanted everyone ready to leave to accompany them and Fredericka. However, some had plans of their own. Thomas, for instance, had sisters, brothers, aunts, uncles, and three children whom the master had traded to plantations in Alabama and Georgia. He was forty-eight years old now. More than anything else, he wanted to see his closest relatives.

Naomi had longed to see the ocean. She said she remembered her mother's stories about how their forbears in Africa enjoyed the sand, the breezes, and endless nights on the beaches. She was heading due South to return to the place that best reminded her of the beauty of her forebear's Southwest Africa. Jesse wanted to ultimately go West. He wanted to get as far away from Mississippi and the memory of slavery as possible. He would stick with Esau and Isaac until a point. He would know when he would have to leave them for good.

And so it continued. Not even young mothers with babies were content to remain. They didn't have a clue as to what the future would bring. As long as it was away from the Brookshire Plantation, that was good enough for them. Many of the Brookshire slaves wanted to connect with others who had been sold or traded away also. Although the master had arranged a number of marriages among his slaves, many had soft spots in their hearts for others. Like so many of this group, Jesse had some romantic feelings too. He asked whether anybody had ever heard of what had become of Louella. Fredericka was the only one who remembered. As her reward for delivering the message to Barabbas, Louella had also been shuttled to the North by the Underground Railroad. Fredericka had visited her in her work for the 'Confederacy'. She lived just outside Memphis in a community of free blacks. It had been odd, Fredericka thought, because she had asked about Jesse too. Though she had had a number of men, she was now alone. Jesse was told where he could likely find her in Memphis. Those slaves took everything of functional value, such as food, clothing, blankets, sheets, knives, forks, guns, bullets and the like, that they could find. They took every horse on the plantation with them. Some claimed sheep, cattle, wagons, coaches and equipment to repair wheels and axles when they would break down.

Everything went well on that last recorded day of history on the Brookshire Plantation. The only hitch came from Reverend Rogers and his wife. Having heard of problems at the estate, they came over as fast as they could. Their reward for the trip was that they were relieved of their coach, the four horse team, and their money. Their driver, a slave, even opted to cast his lot with Fredericka and the twins. He had stopped just under Fitzpatrick's body. As the group drove past him, Reverend Rogers pulled his Bible and opened it to the Ten Commandments. He began to recite them from the top, with special emphasis on the verses referencing to kill and steal. "Stop, the wagon. Hold the horses!" Fredericka yelled, having taken a plush seat inside the coach that her grandparents had owned. She jumped out and ran to her grandparents because Mrs. Rogers had just come to the side of her husband. Looking up at her grandfather, Reverend Rogers, she yanked the Good Book from his hands. She opened the Book, and found the passage that she wanted. It was the 17th Verse of the 25th Chapter from the Book of Ezekiel:

And I will execute great vengeance upon them with furious rebukes; and they shall know that I am The Lord, when I lay my vengeance upon them.

Reverend and Mrs. Rogers learned more from Fredericka by that scripture reading than they wanted to know. Each lesson was painful. The little slave girl was a little girl no more. She hadn't been for years. She was able to read, and worst yet, understand scripture. At once they knew then that it was she who had betrayed their son and started things in motion to save Esau from slavery. The particular passage that she read had a numbing effect. When she dropped The Book, Reverend Rogers turned to the Chapter and verse to see whether she had quoted it accurately. She had. "My God, My God", he screamed, looking to the heavens as if he wasn't standing under the hanging body of Fitzpatrick. Their most important lesson was yet to be seen. Of course they would return to nothing but embers not just at their home. Fredericka herself would later torch the church too.

Kerplunk!!! Down it came, a headless body right on top of the couple. The head, at the neck, still dangled above. It was an awful sight. They must have remained there for hours, too frightened, and too stupefied to move. As had become their wont, they waited for someone to come and clean them, to remove the body for burial. No one from the exact number of two hundred slaves who remained on the grounds of the plantation would think of helping them.

One curious note about the Brookshire Plantation was that when the Master inherited it, there were exactly 200 slaves that he owned.

It all would have ended there but for one simple reason. Esau had a fortune of his money hidden behind a quicksand ridge in East St. Louis. He would lay claim to his half, and give the other half to Fredericka. It belonged rightfully to her baby and her. She would meet Absalom's family, and have the choice of either staying there, connecting with his blood relatives in Georgia and Alabama, or proceeding on Westward with the twins and their party. Esau also would withdraw all his savings from the bank. That he would do legally.

The last plan he had was to make the officers of that bank pay for their treachery with Mathers. He had already exacted from Mathers what he wanted and more. As he saw it, the bank would be even easier. Considering all that he had done to that date, who would have doubted that he could accomplish that too?

How would the slaves, friends, relatives and anybody else who was interested know about it? He promised to write a book about it. If and when they would ever read it, then they would know.

Imagine that boy. His last suggestion was that they learn to read. Now with freedom at hand, that was the most important task for them to do. If they really wanted to keep abreast of his life and work, that is all they had to do. He also promised to write. Hidden meaning: Esau was advising the slaves that the best way to prepare themselves for freedom was to learn to read. At that time, nothing else was more important.

* * *

The newspapers recorded a robbery of the bank in 1867. Since the men were masked and well disguised, there were no accurate descriptions. However, a number of eyewitnesses swore that they detected black, and dark skin at the bottom of sleeves, and the nape of two of the robbers. As a black man was the first to lead the South at Fort Sumter, so too was a black group the first to participate in and lead a bank robbery in this country, the first after the war for the abolition of slavery.

MORE ABOUT WILLIAM J. MOORE

No matter what reference people gave to my grandfather, it was always with affection and respect. Everyday of my life, I heard my mother, my aunts and my uncles make mention of the effect that 'Papa' had on their lives. It was always positive. Likewise, everyday of my life I heard my brothers or sisters, and my many cousins bring up the name 'Big Daddy'. Likewise, these references were not simply positive, but almost reverential. In his day, black men named William were known as Willie. I recall many a time at church outings, weddings, and funerals, many people wanted an audience with 'Willie Moore'. It was as if no one could have felt their day was complete without a kind word with, or from Willie Moore. I remember an understanding of his value to people in social activities. His credo was characterized by the three Ls, an expression I first heard from A. Phillip Randolph. He always <u>looked</u>. More often that that, he <u>listened</u>. And, more than anything else, he <u>learned</u>. I also saw these qualities in his children - my mother, my aunts, and my uncles. 'Brother Moore' was, of course, his most recognized title. This was due to his devotion to the lessons from the Bible, and his staunch participation in and dedication to the church. Most church going folk used the titles Brother and Sister only on Sunday. Again, out of respect, so many people in East St. Louis and the surrounding area believed that one had to use something more significant than Mr., or Sir, with him. It was never 'yes sir' or 'no sir'. It was either Yes, Brother Moore, or No, Brother Moore, at the grocers, at the service station, even on his job.

He had a number of brothers and sisters. Some of these had children. Therefore, I heard 'Uncle Willie' used many times. Yet, when my many cousins used the term, it was used not as a simple title, nor to simply denote a relative per se. People who used this term seemed so proud of the association.

When he moved on (he shall never die) as he would have wanted it, his funeral attracted people from all walks of life. I met people for the first time who had a story about Brother Moore.

- He took my wife to the hospital, saving her life.
- He bought food for my family, when we had none.
- He put gasoline in my car, so I could go see my new baby.
- Brother Moore came by my house to ask me to go with him to visit my dying daddy. I had no way to get there myself. I was so happy that I was with my Daddy when he went to be with the Lord. Brother Moore made it happen.
- I was walking home from the grocery store, both arms loaded down with food. I prayed for an angel. I had no cab fare or bus fare. Out of nowhere Brother Moore stopped his car. My prayer was answered, praise God.

The sanctuary literally gushed with accounts like these. I don't believe that even he remembered all the favors he had done. Though he had no desire for personal recognition, or to be singled out for respect for all these good deeds, he was proud of three singular aspects of his life. The first was that he had been a good father, a good provider to his children. The second was that he was a good man, a good human being, a good friend. The third was that he was a good, faithful believer in the Word, having committed his life to Christ.

When he moved on, he was alone. Flora and I had been visiting at my mother's house that night. We had every intention of stopping at his house, just to visit, to chat, to spend quality time. But the hour grew late, and I thought it was too late to drop in that night. I remember very vividly saying, he is probably asleep. Yes. He was just sleeping.

About The Publisher

The publisher has expressed interest in additional narrations that my grandfather gave us. The first is about the Race Riot of 1917 in East St. Louis. On an intensive collegiate research project in 1962, I gathered significant information on the circumstances leading up to the riot. Some data were culled for a book on the subject, written by a college professor who assigned the project. I plan to use my notes from that period, and comments from my grandfather to recreate those times.

The second narrative involves the honkey tonk, blues and jazz wars in East St. Louis. This will recreate the heyday of the city when music ruled, and musicians were kings.

Many of you who read this book, no doubt, have stories and narrations also worth telling. My publisher is also interested in these. She would be delighted to hear about your project. Please write her at:

Aria Publications
PO Box 1237
Centreville, VA 20122.

Her name is Aria M. Antyc-Arolf.